THE WILL TO FLY

THEWILLTOFLY

BY LYDIA LASSILA
MOTHER & OLYMPIC CHAMPION

WITH THE ASSISTANCE OF
ANDREW CLARKE & DAN EDDY

Text Copyright © Lydia Lassila. 2016
Design Copyright © The Slattery Media Group Pty Ltd, 2016

First published 2010, *Jump: The Lydia Lassila Story: An Olympic Dream*
written by Lydia Lassila and Andrew Clarke.

This edition, revised and updated, written by Lydia Lassila with Dan Eddy.
All rights pertaining to *Jump: The Lydia Lassila Story: An Olympic Dream*
reverted by Andrew Clarke to Lydia Lassila.

All rights reserved. No part of this publication may be reproduced, stored in a retrieval system or transmitted in any form by any means without the prior permission of the copyright owner. Inquiries should be made to the publisher.

The book "The Will To Fly" is an autobiography written by and about Lydia Lassila.
The book and the book's publisher are not associated with, nor sponsored or endorsed by,
Binding Films Pty Ltd, the producer of the feature documentary film entitled "The Will To Fly",
or anyone else associated with the production and distribution of the film.

Cover artwork © 2016 Binding Film Pty Ltd, reproduced with permission.
Images courtesy of Lydia Lassila otherwise indicated.
Gold Medal Stamp © Australian Postal Corporation 2010.
This material has been reproduced with permission of the Australian Postal Corporation.
All images produced with permission.
Photos by Getty Images or AAP unless otherwise marked.
Every effort has been made to verify the source of each photograph.
Inquiries should be made to the publisher.

National Library of Australia
Creator: Lassila, Lydia S., 1982- author.
Title: The will to fly / Lydia Lassila.
ISBN: 9780980597332 (paperback)
Subjects: Lassila, Lydia S., 1982-
          Women skiers--Australia--Biography.
          Freestyle skiing--Australia.
          Women Olympic athletes--Australia--Biography.
Dewey Number: 796.937092

Group Publisher: Geoff Slattery
Project Manager: Courtney Nicholls
Editor: Bronwyn Wilkie
Design: Chris Downey and Franky Demaria

Printed in Australia by McPherson's Printing Group Pty Ltd

The Slattery Media Group
1 Albert Street, Richmond, Victoria, Australia 3121
www.slatterymedia.com

CONTENTS

	FOREWORD by Steven Bradbury, OAM	7
1	THE JUMP	11
2	THE SEED IS PLANTED	13
3	GYMNASTICS, MY FIRST LOVE	20
4	LEARNING TO LOVE AGAIN	31
5	ONE BATTERED ROOKIE	63
6	SALT LAKE 2002	77
7	RIGHT-SIDE-ITIS	88
8	IN THE SHADOWS	104
9	TORINO AND THE BIG BLOW	117
10	RETURNING TO TURMOIL	135
11	THE A-TEAM AND THE SILENT PARTNER	155
12	GAME ON	181
13	IN THE MOMENT	194
14	FAMILY AND FRUSTRATION	203
15	PATH TO SOCHI	213
16	LEAVING MY MARK	241
17	WHAT NEXT?	259
	MY SIX STEPS TO GOAL-SETTING	261
	THANKS	264

'Our greatest glory is not in never falling, but in rising every time we fall.'

Confucius, Chinese philosopher, 6th Century BC

ONE IN A MILLION

BY STEVEN BRADBURY, OAM
AUSTRALIA'S FIRST
WINTER OLYMPIC GOLD MEDALIST

Australia's Winter Olympians were once referred to as feel good oddities like Eddie the Eagle and the Jamaican bobsled team. In the '70s our Winter Olympics medal chance was speed skater Colin Coates; in the '80s downhill skier Steven Lee and speed skater Danny Kah were given a shot. In '92 at Albertville and '94 at Lillehammer aerial skier Kirstie Marshall was favourite for gold, but still no winter medal....

Kirstie inspired a generation of aerialists, but our first medal was not in the air, it was in the 5000m short track speed skating relay; I was proud to team up with Kieran Hansen, Andrew Murtha and Richard Nizielski to bring home a bronze.

Since then the floodgates have opened. Would you believe that Australia has now won 12 Winter Medals, five of them gold.

Eddie who? Jamaican what? We're no joke: that's history.

That Australia has become a force at the Winter Games can partly be attributed to the Olympic Winter Institute, from its beginning in 1997 with great ambitions, including the audacious idea of taking high level gymnasts and turning them into aerial skiers. Due to injury Lydia Ierodiaconou missed out on competing as a gymnast in the summer Games. Gymnasts have a short lifespan, with many retiring in their teens. Lydia was one of the first to make the big and brave jump to aerials.

I'm so glad Lydia has told her amazing story, and it's a real honour to have been asked to write the foreword. As a fellow winter Olympian I know what it's like to toil away at your craft in complete anonymity—Brisbane is as much the centre of the speed skating universe as Mt Buller is the Mecca of the world of aerial skiing!! Lydia's story is one of Aussie guts and determination; a prime example that if you chase your dream with passion and hunger it doesn't matter what sport you pursue, or where you're from.

Once every four years Australia sits up and takes notice of our winter sports daredevil superstars—people like Alex 'Chumpy' Pullin, David Morris, Torah Bright and Lydia Lassila. In this 21st century the winter sports are faster, more dangerous and more exciting than ever before.

This book will take you on a rollercoaster ride of triumph and tragedy—a classic journey into the mind of a champion. In her first year as an aerial skier Lydia dreams about doing a quad twisting triple somersault—a Full-Double Full-Full as the aerialists call it. At that time only a handful of men could do it.

Unless you happen to be a curler you've got to be tough to make it in a Winter Olympics sport and the aerial skiers are the toughest. Landing jumps from four stories above snow that may or may not be yielding, while flying along at about 65 kmph, all day, every day it's inevitable you're going to get hurt.

To describe Lydia Lassila as tough is an understatement. Nothing can stop her when she sets her mind to a challenge.

Growing up with three older brothers she had to be tough, but she's taken it to a new level—she's a machine. Not in a macho Robocop kind of way, I mean in a focused, *I dare you to try to stop me* kind of way.

To date nobody has managed to stop our Lydia. Not leeches

at Lilydale, not a smashed shoulder and not the piercing screams that echoed through TV sets across the world when Lydia ruptured the cruciate ligament in her knee during the 2006 Torino Winter Olympics.

After that injury, she left no stone unturned in her preparation for the Vancouver 2010 Olympics. With her A-Team at her side—including champion mogul skier and Finnish Olympian 'Late' Lassila, Lydia gets the gold.

In 2011 Lydia starts a family with Late, giving birth to Kai. You'd reckon it's time to move on to greener pastures: she has it all, great husband, new baby, Olympic gold in the kit bag, body still in one piece…but not Lydia. That bloody Full-Double Full-Full is like an itch in the brain, an itch that when you finally figure out where to scratch it just itches more. Lydia has been thinking about that jump since the first time she saw a man do it in 1999. No woman has even thought about doing it, it's crazy; or she's crazy.

Now it's 2012 and Lydia is back into her beloved sport. She has that one big box to tick—she is coming back to do the Full-Double Full-Full in Sochi, 2014.

Can you even imagine what Lydia took on? Think about the thousands of hours training, the time away from family and friends competing around the world, then throw in a new-born baby boy while running her own growing business.

I competed at four Olympics and now have three kids of my own—if I was doing both of those things together I'd be suicidal. But there's more—Lydia's master plan includes creating a documentary as well. Lydia is not only aiming to attempt the Full-Double Full-Full but to leave a legacy that will last a generation. I can read her mind—there needs to be evidence. Filming began in 2011. What incredible planning and foresight.

From 2012 to Sochi 2014, Lydia takes it to extremes. Many months are spent training in Ruka, Finland. Ruka is so far north you might bump into Santa at the local store. There's daylight for just four hours a day, the temperature never gets above zero, and she has a two-year-old in tow!

There is an upside: there's snow 10 months of the year, critical time she can spend on the snow.

Australia had the best women's aerials team in the world for many years—from Kirstie Marshall to Jacqui Cooper to Alisa Camplin to Lydia Lassila. More recently China has taken over. These amazing girls forged a path, built a legacy for Australia in a winter sport.

To get back on top we need to build a water jump facility in Australia—*no* snow for 10 months a year down under! It's been a long-term project that Lydia has pursued doggedly. If it's built, Lydia hasn't ruled out another Olympic Campaign in 2018.

Top athletes in every sport are role models even if they don't want to be. For some having others looking up to them and maybe emulating them is a burden. Not all sporting heroes are built to become role models.

Among terrorist attacks, sporting scandals and negative media today's world is short on true heroes and short on real role models. Lydia Lassila is the one in a million—true blue Aussie hero, superior role model.

Knowing Lydia makes me feel proud to be Australian. Her story is a must read. Maybe her story will help create more heroes.

Oh I almost forgot…that Full-Double Full-Full.

I had the credentials to access the media section at the jump site through the finals at Sochi. Lydia slowly skied past me after every jump. I didn't say hi, she didn't acknowledge me. I wasn't there in a media capacity, I was there to show support to a friend. Lydia knew I was there but she was in the zone, communication was not necessary. Rumblings about Lydia unleashing 'the jump' had been building for days. Before her final jump I couldn't stand still, the tension was unbearable. Nobody spoke for what felt like an hour. Finally it appeared on the competition scoreboard:

Next Competitor: Lydia Lassila, Australia.

Jump: Full-Double Full-Full.

The crowd gasped, nobody spoke.

No bullshit, it was one of the best nights of my life.

STEVEN BRADBURY, OAM

CHAPTER 1

THE JUMP

My eyes scan down the in-run and I stare at the jump. I don't see or focus on anything else—it's just me and the jump. My breathing is slow and calm. I hear the crowd, but they don't come into my thinking. I know what I have to do. All my focus is on this jump, one final jump. The rest is irrelevant.

I can feel my nervous energy and my heart is pounding, but I am calm. I am ready. I am committed. I believe. I'm not nervous, but I'm not confident. I'm in another place—a different zone. One more jump for glory, or oblivion—either way, I am not leaving anything on the table tonight. I will not hold back. *'Breathe, Lyd. Breathe.'*

The take-off is all I think about: *'Just hit your take-off.'* Everything else will fall into place. I force away all other thoughts. To do this, I have a phrase that I say to myself: *'water under a bridge'*. With these words I expel all thoughts that are irrelevant to this instant, to my jump. The judges are ready and my coaches clear me to go. I clap my hands twice—I'm not sure why—and turn my skis down the in-run. *'Make it happen.'*

My speed picks up as I cut through the fog. The jump is before me. An icy, big, white wall four metres tall that will throw me into the air as high as a four-storey building. I'm not scared of it and I squeeze my body tight and hold my position up and off the jump. *'Yes, that felt good.'* I am airborne and on autopilot, flipping and twisting into the air through the night sky.

The jump feels just as I had visualised it at the top of the in-run. It is just as I had seen it the night before and the thousands of other times I had rehearsed it over and over in my head—Lay-Full-Full. I can see the landing through the entire jump, like an eagle honing in on its prey. Everything seems to happen in slow motion. I hear my coach Mich's voice directing me through the air. But my body knows what to do: *'Eyes down the hill. Chest forward.'* I land effortlessly, so light and with such ease that it feels like I have been floating. This time, it's not a dream. It's not imagined, it's real.

I scream with excitement as I ski to the finish area, my arms pumped to the sky. I feel instant relief that it is all over, relief that I have done what I came to do. My score comes up and I am ranked number one. All the sacrifice and pain has been worth it for that one moment. My plan has worked perfectly. I wait for the final competitor to jump. She's in the air, but it's going wrong. She crashes. I've won.

I had two jumps to perform at Cypress Mountain that night of 24 February 2010. No more, no less, and both counted. Each aerial skiing jump takes about three seconds, so that's six seconds in total. *Six seconds* does not leave a lot of room for error. There are no second chances. Olympic Games competitions create extraordinary pressure. Not only are they the most important events of an athlete's career, they also come around just once every four years. The Games are the biggest stage in the world of aerial skiing, and I wasn't looking for a podium that night in Vancouver.

I was jumping to win.

CHAPTER 2

THE SEED IS PLANTED

In many ways I was destined to do something like aerial skiing. As a young girl, all I wanted to do was jump, somersault and twirl. I was fearless and I was a show-off. I liked impressing people with my skills, liked getting the reaction of, 'Oh my God, what are you doing?'

I was forever climbing and hanging off anything I could and when we had friends over for dinner, Mum would get me to put on a show. From a very young age, I was an entertainer. One of my best tricks, when I was about two years old, was to lift myself up and do a flip when I was walking along the street holding two peoples' hands. Whoever was holding my hands at the time would freak out because this tiny girl had just hoisted herself up and flipped over. I was just happy that I'd entertained them. I loved shocking people more than anything else. I loved the reaction I got—it was addictive. I'm still doing it, I suppose, although there's no one holding my hands anymore.

I was born on 17 January 1982, and named Lydia Sara-Marie Ierodiaconou. I was the youngest of four children and the only girl. George, my eldest brother, was born in 1976, so he's got six years on me; Daniel is four years older than me and we share a birthday. Every birthday he reminds me that he'd wanted a train set that year, but instead all he got was a baby sister. The next one down is Peppi (his name is really

Joseph, but we've always called him Peppi), who is two years older than me. Peppi has always been a natural athlete with loads of talent, but he never wanted to take sport seriously, he just enjoyed playing it.

I don't remember childcare or structured programs being available before kindergarten age when I was growing up, or at least they weren't as common as they are today. Today, there are all kinds of play centres and kinder gyms and I probably would have loved that as a kid. However, I don't remember being bored growing up. We used our imaginations and played—we were forever building cubby houses, playing in the park and kicking the footy or hitting the cricket ball in the back yard. We also had a big rumpus room downstairs where we used to roller skate or skateboard, and play tennis and table tennis.

An uncle whom I loved dearly passed away when I was five. His name was Uncle Peter and he was a real stirrer. My family grew up in Sunshine, a working class suburb in Melbourne's west that became home to many migrants who settled in Australia after World War II. From when I was a two-year-old, Uncle Peter would stir and joke with me, saying, 'Lydia, even in Sunshine you need to speak posh.' So every time he came around during his regular lunchtime run he would say, 'Hello, Lydia,' and I'd stand at the top of the stairs, pout my lips, hold my hand out limply and say with my best posh accent, 'Hellooo, Uncle Peterrr'. It was all part of an act. I wanted to impress people, and for him, that meant trying to speak posh, or at least that's what I thought.

Mum and Dad, although active, didn't come from a structured sporting background and never competed seriously. So I guess they didn't realise that I had talent and was destined to be an athlete of some sort. Dad wasn't into organised sport; his passion was the ocean. To this day, he is a keen diver and fisherman, and in his youth he was an excellent swimmer with an incredible lung capacity who could easily swim the length of a 50-metre pool without taking a breath. Mum wasn't a swimmer, but was an excellent all-round athlete in her school days. She liked competition and still plays in ladies' weekly tennis tournaments. Nevertheless, they both believed that their children should learn to swim at a young age, especially because we spent all our summers at the beach in Lorne, a coastal town along the Great Ocean Road in Victoria.

THE SEED IS PLANTED

Even at the age of three my interest in acrobatics was obvious, so every Wednesday Mum took me to the local church hall in Sunshine for calisthenics, which involved flips, twirling batons and rods. Before long, Mum and I became tired of the make-up and the shows. I can remember Mum sewing the sequins on my costumes until all hours of the night, and she hates sewing. Dressing up four-year-old kids in sequins and packing on the make-up was a little too much for us, and although I was progressing really fast I wasn't allowed to move into a higher group because I was too young, so I got bored and we stopped going. Ultimately, calisthenics wasn't going to last—it just wasn't me.

> *Mum: 'When I took Lydia to calisthenics for the first time she was the child who didn't come running to mummy every five seconds. She was at the front, eyes glued to the instructor, trying to copy her every move perfectly.'*

OK . . . so I was a little intense then.

As a child I was also a bit of a parrot. By the age of two, I knew my street address, my phone number, who discovered Australia and who was our Prime Minister. My brothers would tell me to, 'Say this!' and I would; 'Do that!' and I did. At times they used that to their advantage and I'd fall prey to a lot of their tricks, a classic one being, 'Lydia, I'll time you to see how fast you can run and get me a snack from the fridge'. I'd run off as fast as I could, eager to know how fast I was.

Before I could read, I could recite my favourite books word for word. As Mum read, I'd follow along the words with my finger and pretend I was reading the book. *The Very Hungry Caterpillar* was my favourite. I amazed quite a lot of people with that, most thinking I could actually read.

I was a very 'monkey see, monkey do' kind of a kid—a very visual learner—and I think that has helped me throughout my career. If I see something I can replicate it, and maybe that's why I'm a quick learner. I think one of my best attributes as an athlete is being open to feedback and then making immediate changes to improve.

I grew up in a male-dominated family but I wasn't a tomboy. I loved pink and wore dresses. After calisthenics, I told Mum I wanted to be a ballerina so she enrolled me in ballet classes. But instead of classical ballet it turned out to be jazz ballet, which was not what I had in mind. At the age of four I knew what I wanted, and jazz ballet wasn't it. After a few lessons I was told off for doing cartwheels and my phase of wanting to be a ballerina was over. It just wasn't stimulating or challenging enough.

Mum had four children by the age of 30. Times have changed, I know, but looking back it was wonderful growing up in a big family. There was always someone to play with and we always had excitement of some sort in the house. My extended Greek Cypriot/Italian family was huge. On Mum's side, the Italian side, we had three first cousins, but on Dad's side, the Cypriot side, we had 14. My fondest childhood memories were the summers we spent at Lorne with all my cousins, aunties and uncles and my grandparents, Yaya and Papou, on my dad's side of the family. I never met my nonno (Mum's dad), as he passed away before I was born, but I have fond memories of my nonna and her garden, chickens and Chihuahuas.

Mum was amazing in how she could cope with pressure. Unexpected nappy changes, screaming kids or people dropping over for dinner were all handled without complaint or any sign that she was under stress. We would often have unexpected guests at the dinner table and Mum was able to put on an amazing spread in a matter of minutes. It is perhaps the most important skill I learned from her—the ability to deal with pressure and cope with the unexpected. She thrives on it and she is amazing.

Our family spent summer holidays in Lorne and we all used to bunk in our grandparents' house, a white weatherboard. Eventually, as the family continued to grow, all my aunties and uncles bought their own lots of land in the same street and built houses. We all still spend our summers there and I'm sure we will for many generations to come. I've travelled to a lot of different parts of the world, but Lorne is still my favourite place. I have so many great memories from there and I love the sound of the ocean, the smell of the bush and the feeling of salt water on my skin. Lorne offered an abundance of activities for everyone—we went fishing, diving, surfing, swimming and played beach cricket and soccer; we bathed in the sun, collected seashells and enjoyed fish and chips on the beach; we explored the bush and built elaborate cubby houses with Dad's building materials and the tools from Papou's shed. At night there was more fishing on the pier and board games till all hours of the night. Competition among the cousins was rife. Who could build the best cubby house? Who would catch the most fish? Who was the best at Monopoly? All I wanted to do was measure up to the boys and beat them in whatever I could, but being one of the youngest cousins, winning against them was rare.

Bouncing on the trampolines on the Lorne foreshore was my favourite activity and I never got tired of it. Mum had to peel me off or bribe me with an icy-pole to get me to leave. Carl, the manager, could do spectacular tricks and he was the first person to teach me how to flip and that really fired my desire for acrobatics. He didn't mind me bouncing all day and even encouraged it because I often drew a crowd, which was good for business. Flips and acrobatics on the trampolines were the only things my brothers or cousins couldn't match me in. That was my special talent and mine alone.

When I was six, we went on a summer holiday around Europe for three months. Other than it being an amazing, adventurous trip, it coincided with the 1988 Seoul Olympics and it was my first recollection of an Olympic Games. I watched the swimming, the athletics and all sorts of other sports, and I remember following it all and thinking, 'Wow, there's something special about the Olympics.' I didn't know what sport I wanted to do because it all looked awesome, but I knew from that time I wanted to be an Olympic athlete. I, too, wanted a shiny gold medal around my neck.

I was good at most things I tried, but with three older brothers there was no chance I was ever going to get a big head, and it's the same today. If ever I started to get too big for my boots, they'd give me a reality check.

All of my brothers enjoyed playing sport, but none of them took it as seriously as I did. I was always tiny, but I had biceps when I was three and was a really strong little kid. I was also very feisty and the boys used to really push my buttons. They used to rev me up, first making me angry and then getting me into a rage as all three of them plus Dad poked fun at me. Being a girl as well, they were always tormenting me about what I could and couldn't do. That was like a red rag to a bull.

Their favourite torment when I was young was playing the Michael Jackson song *Thriller*. I had seen the film clip by mistake on the TV and was absolutely petrified by it. Just hearing the tune would send me into a wild panic and I would beg them to stop playing it. They thought it was funny. Another thing that used to send me right off was the story about where I came from. My brothers and my dad used to say that I wasn't really from their family—that they were driving along one day and they saw a little pink pig (me) on the side of the road at Old MacDonald's farm. Apparently Old MacDonald didn't want me, so they picked me up and brought me home. I used to get so worked up, screaming, 'I'm not a pig, I'm not a pig!' but they just laughed. Even Mum couldn't contain herself. To this day my nickname is 'Little Miss Piggy', 'Piggy' or just 'Pig'.

Dad is a concreter by trade and the boys occasionally went to help him at work while I was left behind—'No, you can't come, you're a girl,' they would say. But sometimes I'd get to go and Dad could see I wanted to work and that I wasn't afraid of getting my hands dirty. I really wanted to do the same things as the boys and I wanted them to see me as an equal but they never did—or if they did, they didn't want to accept it and would certainly never admit it.

Without realising it, I learned a lot about internal strength from Dad at that time. He taught me that nothing in this world was free, that you had to work hard if you wanted to be successful. That mentality was instilled in me and I applied it to everything I did. I wanted success, but knew that it would involve hard work and no half measures.

Being small didn't worry me too much because I was winning running and swimming races. I was a great athlete throughout school—I could sprint, run long distances and jump. At every school athletics day I'd put my hand up for everything except the throwing events. Swimming was the same. At one stage I really wanted to do Little Athletics, but Mum wouldn't let me because she didn't like all the 'pushy' parents involved—mine were the exact opposite. I suppose I was hunting for a sport that would satisfy my urge for competition. I tried swimming, but while I enjoyed the training, it wasn't stimulating enough for me. I also wasn't the best, so it took a back seat for me.

When I look at little kids today, I can spot the potential athlete in them straight away. A family friend named Liam is into cycling and obsessed with all aspects of the sport. Liam wants to be the best, he is winning races and I can see in his eyes the same intensity I had when I was young. I remember looking at other kids when I was little and recognising that they weren't the same as me. They just wanted to play, they lacked focus or they gave up too easily. They just wanted to have fun. In that regard I was definitely the odd one out in my family. I took sport seriously, I loved competition and I loved to win. Sure, I had fun doing it all, but I didn't do anything half-heartedly. I did it with intensity.

Mum also put me into Young Talent Time, a singing and dancing school. My brother George did it because he loved Michael Jackson and was always trying to mimic his moves. The only problem was that he's tone deaf and lacks rhythm, which is why he didn't last long. Mum said, 'Lydia likes to dance and show off, so she should also try Young Talent Time.' However, we quickly realised I couldn't sing or dance very well either and wasn't very talented in that area. I got bored and I don't remember ever looking forward to going, so Young Talent Time didn't last.

It was a bit of trial and error for Mum. She could see that I was a bit of a performer and that I was showy—I wasn't a shy kid and I was pretty confident—and so she finally put two and two together and enrolled me into gymnastics. I was eight when I started, and finally we'd found something that was perfect for me. It was challenging in so many ways. I had to work hard but I enjoyed the outcome, I enjoyed the results. I could run, jump and flip, and best of all I could compete.

So after years of torment from my brothers and struggling with Mum to find something I really wanted to do, here it was. I was a gymnast at heart.

CHAPTER 3

GYMNASTICS, MY FIRST LOVE

Mum took me to Footscray City Gymnastics Club, partly because George had gone there when he was younger. George had been a really scrawny kid who looked like his arms and wrists would break, so she had taken him to gymnastics to try to get him a little bit stronger.

When I first started, the coaches put me through a series of tests to assess my level of strength and aptitude so they could work out which squad they should put me in. I remember there was a huge rope hanging from the roof that was about 20 metres long—though it seemed like 50 metres to eight-year-old me—and one of the tests was to see how far you could climb up that rope. Mum had left to do some errands, but walked back into the gym just as I reached the top of the rope. I saw her and immediately started waving frantically to get her attention, holding the rope with one hand, 'Hello, Mummy, look at me!' Poor Mum nearly had a heart attack, and I was lucky she let me return the next week. Little did she know it wouldn't be the last time I was going to scare her.

The coaches who assessed me put me straight into Level 4 with my first coach, Samantha. From there I progressed quickly and gymnastics became my new obsession. I loved everything about it. I loved the smell of the gymnasium and the chalk on my hands.

I loved training and pushing my body hard. I loved competing, not only in competitions but also against my teammates and for the coach's attention. I loved my teammates and the friends I made. I loved the discipline. But mostly, I got a real kick out of improving. I always wanted to be better and that remains my motivation today.

I really pushed Mum to get me to gymnastics, unlike some of the other kids who were being pushed by their parents. I just loved it and I really wanted to be there. I remember sitting at the front window of our house after school, watching the street and waiting for Mum to get home so that she could take me there. If she was even a minute late I would start to get really anxious—I hated being late because I felt like I was missing out on training. Unfortunately for me, I was always late. It is understandable now, given the running around Mum had to do—after school she also had to drop my brothers off at music, soccer or tennis. I was so paranoid about being late that I would sit in the middle of the back seat and stare at the clock on the front console of our car. I would say, 'Mum! We're now five minutes late. Don't you know what I can do in that time?' Every minute at gymnastics counted for me, even more so because my parents had restricted the amount of training I was allowed to do. I wasn't allowed to train on weekends or holidays because that was family time when we would go to Lorne or other destinations. I tried to bargain with my parents and so did my coaches. They would say, 'Come on, she's really good—and she'd be even better if she could do Saturday training.' But my parents wouldn't budge. They had strong values and they stuck to them—they always put family first and I didn't get any special consideration. If I didn't like it, they would pull me out of gymnastics altogether, so I didn't have a choice. This made me focus harder on training. I didn't waste a minute and I never cheated on an exercise. I really wanted to make the most out of every single training session and always gave 100 per cent. My parents and brothers didn't understand, and even today I don't think they do. They knew I loved gymnastics and that I was good at it, but they didn't know it consumed my every thought. They didn't know I went to sleep every night visualising my routines over and over in my head.

Missing training and knowing I could be better ate away at me.

My coaches prepared a special program for me to do during the holidays when I was away from the gym, a training program with exercises I could do every day, and then I'd add a few more of my own. When we were at Lorne I'd lock myself in my room for hours and do the exercises, then I'd go for runs up the hills and through the bush. I'd practise my flips on the beach and trampolines. I pretended the floorboards were a balance beam and I'd practise my beam routine over and over—I was nuts! But by the time I returned to gym after each holiday I was so strong and fit that I was raring to go. I didn't really lose any fitness and I was often in better shape than all the others who had trained throughout the holidays.

At the time, gymnastics was all I wanted to do and nothing made me happier, but of course I did have other interests—I loved being at the beach in Lorne with my family, I enjoyed playing music and I swam in a squad, but that was all on the side. What I really looked forward to was going to every single gymnastics session—there wasn't one that I didn't want to do.

I also loved the structure gymnastics gave me. I would arrive home from school, make myself a snack—my favourite was two-minute noodles with a couple of eggs mixed in—and then head off to gym for four hours. That was my routine and I loved it.

By the age of 10 I had progressed to Level 6 and into a higher squad with a new coach, Nikki. I remember our gym hosting a competition and some elite gymnastics scouts coming along to search for talent. I wasn't competing, but I knew the elite coaches were there so I started showing off with one of my friends. One of the coaches spotted me and spoke with Nikki. They asked if I would like to join the elite program, which is the squad you need to be part of if you ever want to make it to the Olympics. It was a no brainer for me—of course I wanted to go. Normally, parents jump at the opportunity to have their child coached by the country's best coaches, but not mine.

Back in those days, there were two options—an elite program in Cheltenham (a south-eastern suburb of Melbourne) or the Australian Institute of Sport in Canberra. Some children moved away from home and boarded with other families, either in Cheltenham or Canberra, and a lot of parents relocated their entire family so that their child could have the opportunity to train for the Olympics. Often parents changed jobs and other siblings were just dragged along, all in the hope that their child was going to make it. We still lived in the western suburbs of Melbourne, so the daily commute to Cheltenham plus the schedule of my three brothers was going to be difficult. My training would need to increase to two sessions a day, before and after school. I would train on weekends as well as school holidays, and I would need to change schools. I didn't mind, I understood that was the sacrifice I needed to make and I was prepared to move away from home to Cheltenham or Canberra and give it a shot. But there was no way I was allowed to go. My parents were not prepared to sacrifice my whole family and they didn't want me being raised by anyone else. I can understand it now, but at the time I was completely shattered. I tried to reason with them, explaining that it was my only chance to make it as an Olympic gymnast—in fact other gymnasts started elite gymnastics when they were a lot younger than I was at the time. But Mum and Dad were firm in their decision. I cried and I cried. 'You don't understand what this means!' I told them. But it didn't help. They wouldn't change their minds.

In many ways I was jealous of the kids whose parents pushed them to do gymnastics. Those parents would have jumped at the opportunity for their child to join the elite program. Mine were the complete opposite and at the time it seemed like they were doing everything to hold me back. I was 10, I wanted to go to the Olympics, and that was all that mattered. I knew there were gymnasts not much older than me competing at the Olympics. It didn't seem fair.

Nikki, my coach, was from Romania. She had trained at the same gym as Nadia Comăneci, and while she was older than Nadia, she had stories of their times training together. I was so fascinated with her stories and the conditions they trained in that Nikki lent me videos of Romanian gymnasts, which I watched over and over. I knew all the gymnasts' names and the tricks they performed—I was obsessed. I also watched all the Olympics, World Championships and any other international competition footage I could find. My bedroom was plastered with posters of my favourite gymnasts. I knew all the top competitors by name and their routines—I even knew what their training regimens were like. So the fact that I wasn't even going to get the chance to be like my idols was really disappointing.

These days, the only remnant of my gymnastics past is a framed quote by Nadia Comăneci.

> 'I work on a certain move constantly then finally the move doesn't seem so risky to me. The move stays dangerous to my foes, but not to me. Hard work has made it easy. That is my secret. That is why I win.'

I can't count the number of times I've recited that quote to myself—to this day, it's with me whenever I am afraid or a task seems impossible or out of my reach.

Nadia was the best of her time. She achieved the ultimate—perfect 10s—at the 1976 Montreal Olympics and changed the face of her sport forever. What she did was out of date when I was a gymnast, but it was the image of her that overawed me, along with the concept that perfection exists and can be attained if you work hard enough. I suppose I'm still trying to live up to Nadia's standards. I'm trying to be the best of my time, and essentially I'm trying to break the mould and push the boundaries of women's aerial skiing.

Gymnastics is an intense sport, but like many sports it's one that can empower an individual with a skill set they can apply to the rest of their lives. Among other skills, it teaches discipline, time management, planning and goal setting, and it instils a work ethic. The elite program was not an option for me so I had to settle for continuing gymnastics through the national stream program. As a Level 7 gymnast, I made my first Victorian state team when I was 12 years old.

I then made the switch to Niddrie Gymnastics Club, which had a really strong team at the time. I had outgrown Footscray City, and Nikki had taken me as far as she could—I needed to be around stronger gymnasts who would push me a little harder.

Tracy Hortin was the coach at Niddrie and I liked her. She had a strong squad of girls a little older than me and in a higher level so it was good for me to be around them and be challenged more. Under Tracy I developed quite quickly and I won every overall Victorian Championship from Level 7 through to Level 10, the highest level in the national stream. Beyond Victoria, I was Level 8 and Level 10 overall National Champion and runner-up for the overall in Levels 7 and 9, not to mention all the individual apparatus victories I had. In simple terms, I couldn't have had better results in the national stream and it was all on 14 hours a week, the maximum time I was allowed to train. I made the most of those training sessions and was very productive in them. Other girls were training twice as many hours, but they weren't training at the same quality—they were often tired and stale, whereas I was always fresh and raring to go.

As I progressed through the national stream, the elite program remained out of the picture for me, a distant dream. The national stream is in a different ballpark to elite gymnastics—compared to my 14 hours, elite gymnasts train from 35 to 40 hours a week. They trained on holidays. I was at Lorne on the beach during holidays. It was serious business and I would have loved a taste of it. Although I was a very good national stream gymnast, I always had a feeling that I wasn't becoming the best I could be—I always felt like I was champing at the bit and being held back. I had all the elements of being a great gymnast: I had plenty of heart and passion, I was tough and I worked hard. The only bit missing was the time required for training, and there was nothing I could do about that, so I just did the best with what I had.

Beyond winning Level 10 National Championships, there was nowhere for me to go, other than to repeat Level 10. Then something very rare happened. At age 15, after I had won Level 10 nationals, I was approached by Michelle De Highden and asked to join the elite gymnastics program that had been set up at Methodist Ladies College (MLC) in Kew, one of Melbourne's top girls' schools, where she was a coach. After all these years, a second chance! My parents knew what it meant to me, and this time, after years of me trying to make them feel guilty, they didn't object.

We had moved to a farm in Diggers Rest in north-west Melbourne when I was 12, and the drive from there to Kew was quite daunting. At the time, I was going to Westbourne Grammar School in Werribee, a private co-ed school. My brothers also went there, and I had great friends and I was an A-grade student, but with the increase in training load it made sense to transfer to MLC, where I would be training twice a day. Schooling wasn't a part of the scholarship, but it certainly made it easier to get into the school and for the school to understand the requirements of my training. Not only would I be switching schools, but I would also be leaving my friends and teammates at Niddrie gymnastics.

I knew it was going to be a tough challenge because I had a lot of catching up to do, but I would never have forgiven myself if I didn't at least give it a try. My training went from 14 hours a week to 35—I was doing two sessions a day and in the beginning I was absolutely exhausted, but with time my body adjusted and adapted, and the training sessions became easier. In addition to Michelle, I had a Chinese coach named Derui Qu. He was a phenomenal coach and although he worked me hard, he was kind at heart and funny.

My daily routine was completely different now. I was out of bed at 5.30am and on the road to MLC by 6am for training by 7am. The morning session went until 10.30am, when I'd shower and start school at morning recess after a snack. I had class until 3.30pm, and then it was back to the gym until 7.30pm, when Mum would pick me up. I'd go home and do my homework, eat dinner, have a shower and go to bed. Then I'd do it all again the next day.

Mum went out of her way to support me. She was my personal taxi service as well as a super mum who still had time for the rest of the family. I suppose that as a kid you don't realise the financial burden you often place on your parents. Mum and Dad had four children in private school all at once, plus all our extracurricular activities. We all played musical instruments and we all did sport after school. Mum was a stay-at-home mother—she made our lunches every day from primary school through to high school, was our personal chauffeur, kept an immaculate household and delivered lunch to Dad at his work every day, and never once did she complain.

My dad worked hard. As kids, we never felt like we were deprived of anything but we were not spoilt. Instead of Nintendos, we played Scrabble and Monopoly or Trivial Pursuit. We always went on holidays and picnics, we had a good education and were allowed to play sport and music and follow our own individual interests.

My parents' decision to not allow me to go to elite gymnastics was not for financial reasons, but moral reasons. They didn't want me to give up my childhood, they didn't want me to miss out on school and they wanted me to stay part of the family. I can understand that now.

The first thing to suffer after I started elite gymnastics was indeed my schooling. I've never taken my academic education as seriously as my sport, but I was an A-grade student throughout high school and no dummy. But by missing classes, I inevitably fell behind. I had to drop subjects such as Japanese, which I loved, and also music, because I couldn't keep up. I had to simplify my curriculum going into VCE so I wouldn't fall behind.

I also struggled socially. I was in Year 11 when I started at MLC, and I went from having loads of friends and knowing everyone at Westbourne Grammar to not knowing anybody, not a single soul. I had come from a year level of 300 girls in the western suburbs and now I didn't know where I belonged—other than in the gym—or who to hang out with during lunchtimes. It was really hard to fit in at first and I missed my friends. With time, I met some lovely girls and developed good friendships but it was definitely difficult in the beginning. My whole life had been about the gym. My best mates were from Footscray and Niddrie gyms, but I wasn't there any more. I was in an elite program with girls at least four years younger than me, most obsessed with the Spice Girls, and at a school on the other side of the city, so I often felt alone and it was pretty hard emotionally at times. But I kept reminding myself I was there for the gym.

In terms of gymnastics, things were going really well. I adapted to the workload and I was a strong, ripped unit, a powerful gymnast who was picking up new techniques fast. My goal was set on making the 1998 Commonwealth Games team and, if all went well, the Sydney 2000 Olympics—no easy task by any means, but with the way I was improving I was in with a chance.

Other gymnasts my age had already competed at the Olympics, but they had been in elite programs since they were six and I had a lot of catching up to do. So every day I gave it my all, gave myself the best chance I could to improve. It was a different routine to the one I was used to, not just for me but for my whole family, especially Mum. There was no more Lorne on weekends or holidays. I was tired and working as hard as I could, but in a way I felt special—special to have been given the opportunity to try. I used to look at my younger teammates and wish I was their age, wish I could turn back time. Some of them had what it took to be great gymnasts, but some didn't. I'm not sure those in the latter category even wanted to be there—maybe they were pushed, I don't know, but I wanted to shake them and say, 'Don't you realise the opportunity you've been given? Stop mucking around!'

The first setback occurred when I injured my ankle in a fall off the uneven bars. I slipped off the bars and my foot landed in a crack in the mats. Normally we had another mat covering the crack, but for some reason it wasn't there that day. I sprained the ligaments in my ankle quite badly and it took a good six weeks for me to be able to resume full training again. It was terrible timing as the Commonwealth Games trials were fast approaching and I couldn't afford to lose any time. While I was recovering I was really limited in what I could do in the gym—all I could do were strength exercises and uneven bars and keep off my ankle. I was strongest on vault, floor and beam, so my best skills were out of play, but on the plus side it gave me a chance to work on my weakest discipline, the bars. Missing any training time in gymnastics is catastrophic. Coaches freak out if you miss even one session, so you can imagine the impact of an injury like that. I still showed up to training every day and did what I could, and my body became very chiselled and strong, but I wasn't doing what needed to be done. I was losing time.

I was so frustrated that a silly little mistake could have such severe consequences. My window for making the squad was already slim, and it was probably the first time I doubted whether I was going to make it in gymnastics. I rehabilitated through the injury and competed in one of the Commonwealth Games trials, but I wasn't ready and I scrambled up my routines. The night before the trials one of my cousins had tragically lost her life, which was obviously a huge shock for our entire family. I wasn't ready for the trials in any case, but that was the final straw in a poor lead-up. I didn't compete very well and missed out on a place in the team.

After I got through the ankle injury, my wrist was the next part of my body to break down—I had overloaded the joint with all the bar work and additional strength exercises. It got to a point where I couldn't swing on it or even open doors. I had cortisone injections, but they didn't help and the joint continued to deteriorate. There was never any temptation to take banned substances to help me recover from injury—it was bad enough dealing with the ancient remedies of a Chinese coach, like wrapping your ankle in cabbage to reduce swelling or using teabags for rips in your hands. Even contemplating steroids or anything similar was just not going to happen. Importantly, no one ever suggested such a path to me.

I did an about-face with my life at that point and just packed it in. Quitting gymnastics 18 months after joining the elite program was the hardest decision I had made in my life to that point and I was extremely gutted, but I was realistic enough to know that it just wasn't going to happen. It was a hard decision, but deep down I knew it was the right decision for everyone. I couldn't imagine life without gymnastics, it had been my passion for so long and life was immediately different. I could eat anything, I could sleep in and I had time to do other things. I could live a normal life. I could even concentrate a bit more on school. Inside, though, I felt a little empty and lost. I felt like a failure, but I knew I had really given it my all—that there wasn't any more I could have done.

But what was I going to do now?

I decided to stay on at MLC to finish my schooling rather than change schools again, and I had a whole summer at Lorne that year, which I really enjoyed. When I went back to start Year 12, I began coaching some of the juniors with Michelle. It was good to be involved with the younger gymnasts and I think I had a fairly positive mindset. I wasn't bitter like some gymnasts when they finish, I wasn't jaded, I loved the sport and I still do. I'd had a great experience and I think I did the best I could, given the circumstances.

It was a bit of a struggle to get my studies back on course after being behind in Years 10 and 11. I didn't go into Year 12 expecting top marks, but I ended up doing okay and getting back on track. It took about six months for my wrist injury to settle and for me to be able to turn a doorknob properly. I felt all right mentally, and I had put gymnastics behind me, but I missed being an athlete. I missed the routine of it, the training and the competition and was soon searching for the next sport that could fulfil my urge—at one stage I thought of taking up kayaking; I also wanted to be an iron woman and was interested in surf lifesaving and triathlons.

Cirque de Soleil rang me up, too. At the time, Cirque wasn't as big as it is now. These days, ex-gymnasts can have a great career and earn a living in a circus like Cirque, but at the time it didn't really interest me. Deep down, I didn't know what I wanted to do. I even tried Miss Fitness and aerobics. I liked the physical training because I've always enjoyed working my body hard and building strength and definition in my muscles, and I liked the aerobics routines, but somehow I didn't enjoy it as much as I did gymnastics.

I wasn't sure if I'd ever love a sport the same way.

CHAPTER 4

LEARNING TO LOVE AGAIN

About halfway through Year 12 I got a phone call out of the blue from a lady named Rachel Johnson. She was a coach at Jets Gymnastics in Eltham and she was also a ski instructor. She was working closely with the Olympic Winter Institute (OWI), the organisation that ran all of Australia's elite winter sports programs. The OWI was looking to establish an aerial skiing development program, one that no one else in the world had explored. It involved recruiting ex-gymnasts to see if they could make the transition into aerial skiers, and Rachel was ringing to see if I'd be interested. Aerial what? Rachel also mentioned that one of my good mates who competed for Jets, Liz Gardner, had expressed some interest. I gave Liz a call and we had a chat about it. Neither of us had skied, but we both wanted to know more. Being a gymnastics coach as well as a ski instructor, Rachel was the perfect link between the two sports.

We were invited to a meeting at the OWI offices in Melbourne, where Rachel and the Institute's CEO, Geoff Lipshut, gave us a basic explanation of aerial skiing. They had prepared a sales pitch, which included a video showing everything from great jumps to horrible crashes and all the different places around the world that aerial skiers go to train and compete. I was blown away by the flipping and twisting that was going on, and instantly imagined myself doing it. It really seemed like an exciting sport, and one that had all the elements that appealed to me. It involved acrobatics, it had elements of danger and risk, and we would be able to travel the world. When you eventually got good enough, you'd be able to compete on the World Cup tour with the Australian team. Geoff and Rachel also told us that we could actually earn money from the sport if we were successful, as there were different levels of scholarships and prize money to be won. If you became good enough, you wouldn't even have to pay for airfares, accommodation or coaching fees! Jacqui Cooper was number one in the world at the time and she managed to make a living off prize money and sponsorship. Comparing it to gymnastics, we thought, 'Wow, what a bonus! We could actually make money in this sport.' In gymnastics it had been quite the opposite—you paid for everything and got nothing in return, at least financially.

Aerial skiing sounded fantastic. I don't know whether I was just glassy-eyed and looking for something new or whether the sales pitch was really that good, but the sport seemed well suited to me. When Geoff then mentioned a chance of going to the Olympics, my ears pricked up and I was sold. A second chance to fulfil my childhood dream and become an Olympian? I felt as if I had been born again.

That said, I really knew nothing about the sport. I knew nothing about the snow. All I knew was that I was halfway through Year 12 and an opportunity was being presented to me. I figured at least I could learn how to ski and I had nothing to lose. The sport was appealing to me and I was ready for a new challenge. I needed it. Not that I wanted to get out of school, but, let's face it, this was an opportunity to be an athlete again and I couldn't pass it up.

> *Geoff: 'I thought Lydia a very determined and bright individual from day one. What I did not know was whether she would walk the walk and not just talk the talk.'*

Rachel understood the culture we'd come from in terms of our discipline, training regimen and dedication, so her job would be to teach us to ski and chaperone us into a new life.

After the meeting, the OWI sent us more information in the mail and invited Liz and me to a ski camp at Mt Buller, where we would learn how to ski and see aerial skiing live during the Mt Buller World Cup. This was 1999 and I was 17. I don't remember there being much of a thought process other than talking with my parents. They had as little idea about it all as I did, but they were supportive. They knew I'd first have to learn how to ski before jumping, and that made it easier for them, I suppose. I remember my own sales pitch: 'It's a progressive sport, you don't go off jumps straight away, you have to know how to ski first and if I don't like it, I won't do it.' So they thought, 'Well, what harm is there in learning to ski?' We weren't a skiing family and the sport is expensive in Australia, so learning how to ski for free was a good deal and an excellent opportunity. Mum and Dad were on board and away I went.

The program was a real experiment. The traditional approach to aerial skiing was to take a strong skier and teach them acrobatics, and, before us, that was how aerialists were made. They'd already experimented with Jacqui and, although she had a fascination with acrobatics as a kid and occasionally bounced on trampolines, she had no structured training in acrobatics and she couldn't ski. She had started at 17 as well and had become a success. Kirstie Marshall, a pioneer of aerial skiing, had a background in gymnastics but also grew up skiing. Perhaps this is where the idea originated. Both Jacqui and Kirstie were very successful—they had both won numerous World Cup events and World Championships, and had been ranked number one in the world at some stage during their respective careers, so Australia already had a pretty good track record in women's aerials. (Interestingly though, while both Kirstie and Jacqui had been number one, neither had managed to secure an Olympic medal.) Alisa Camplin also had a background in gymnastics, although she was still on the rise when I started rather than at her peak.

The difference this time was that the OWI was hunting out high level gymnasts to make the transition rather than waiting for them to come to the sport, and Liz and I were the first guinea pigs. While there were aerial skiers who had already come from a gymnastics background, no other country was specifically recruiting gymnasts to teach them to become aerial skiers. I guess the program was really exploring whether we could transfer the skills we had learned in the gym to aerials—skills like balance, co-ordination and general control of our bodies while in the air, which we had learned over time.

I'd only been up to the snow once before being asked whether I wanted to join the aerial skiing program. My dad had never been to the snow, but one of his mates finally persuaded him to go for a boys' weekend. I was still doing gymnastics at the time so I couldn't go, but my brothers did. They loved it. Dad had seen some vacant land at the base of Mt Buller at a place called Sawmill Settlement and, being a builder, decided to buy a lot and build an A-frame cottage. I had started to go with Dad to help him build the house, but, as I was still doing gymnastics at the time, I never tried to ski because I couldn't risk being injured. After retiring from gymnastics, however, I went up one weekend to try it for the first time. Dad and my brothers had been on snow several times by then and—in their minds at least—were already experts, so they decided to show me how it was done. None of them had had any lessons, but they looked like they knew what they were doing. It was a strange sensation at first, to have the ground slipping away from you and not be in control, but it didn't take long for me to get the hang of it.

When Liz and I went to Mt Buller in 1999, I quickly discovered Rachel's one-on-one coaching tips were a lot better than my brothers' and Dad's. There wasn't much of a ski season that year and the resort was rather bare. Liz and I had no equipment of our own, so Rachel took us to get fitted out in the hire shop. It was weird being a beginner again after being highly skilled in gymnastics. Going from being highly skilled in one sport to elementary level in another was the most difficult part for me in transitioning to aerial skiing. Even though I was having a great time, being a beginner again was a strange and annoying feeling. Small kids would whiz by me while I was trying to grasp the basics, and I remember wanting to get over that beginner's hump quickly so that I didn't feel embarrassed skiing down the slopes—I've always been impatient like that. But Rachel told me that I had a pretty natural feel for my skis and the edges straight away, and I progressed rapidly. I was like a sponge, absorbing every word of feedback, trying to make changes on every turn, trying to copy the techniques of other good skiers as they skied down the slope. I wasn't embarrassed by small kids for too long.

In aerials, the skiing element is more critical than you might think. If you don't have a good feel for your skis you're less likely to land your jumps. The stronger skiers are able to land more jumps, whereas weaker skiers tend to be more inconsistent on their landings and have a tendency to be a little more unbalanced when they hit the snow.

I spent a whole year learning how to ski before doing my first flips. I still love free skiing today and often go to ski camps, but I don't consider myself the best technical skier and I am always looking for ways to improve. These days are spent more on jumping than actual skiing, but I try to go for a burn as often as I can.

We spent weekends and holidays of the 1999 winter skiing at Mt Buller from July to when the snow melted, which was around mid-August that year. Being beginners, Liz and I were none the wiser that it was a horrible snow season. I can remember us skiing on strips of snow three or four metres wide on the Summit run, but we didn't care, we loved it. We were like pigs in mud and skied from first lift till last without taking time for a lunch break. We just couldn't get enough.

The Mt Buller World Cup was held at the end of August after most of the snow had disappeared. I vividly remember the image of the jump site for the World Cup. There was not one patch of snow on the whole mountain except for on the jump site because the work crews had somehow managed to collect all of it to build the site. Seeing aerial skiing live was amazing—all we'd seen up to that point was the video clip that Rachel and Geoff had shown us. Watching it live was a totally different experience, and I think it confirmed for both of us that this was what we wanted to do. We were so hooked at that stage nothing was going to stop us.

Although we were miles away from taking our first jumps, we got to help build the jump site and prepare it for the World Cup. We chopped the landing for the athletes—a process that involves aerating the snow with shovels so that the landing zone is soft—and learned everything about preparing the hill for jumping, like making sure the transitions into the jumps were smooth and bump-free. It was hard work, but we were eager to know the ins and outs of the sport.

It is only live and in person that you start to grasp the height and the speed and the enormity of what the aerialists do, especially the men, who inspired me right from the beginning. From that first day, a seed was planted in my head that one day I was going to be like them. The women were good but the men were mind-blowing.

In addition to Rachel, another coach came on board to work with us. He was Christoph Jehle, a former German aerial skier who was married to an Australian and employed by the Australian team. He was the development coach and assigned to us, and as well as coaching us in skiing, he would be the one to teach us our first flips. I liked Christoph from the start. He was a funny guy who was particularly pedantic about his looks and we were always laughing at his German accent, which was starting to develop an Australian twang. At the World Cup he was constantly feeding us important information, explaining to us all the variables we needed to consider—the effects of the wind, for instance, which in gymnastics had never been a factor, or the importance of having the right speed coming into the jump and having the right take-off position on the jump. We understood the need to be good skiers so that you could land jumps. There was so much precision involved, not just from the athletes but also from the coaches, who shaped the jumps and called instructions to the athletes while they were in the air. Without this knowledge and precision, a jump could go horribly wrong, and when that happened it could hurt. A lot. We realised very quickly that it wasn't as easy as they made it look. No dramas, though—I was up for the challenge and I'm pretty sure Liz was the same.

> Liz: 'Right from day one Lydia was on a mission. She had already decided she was going to be a champion aerial skier and it was obvious in her gung-ho approach to every aspect of her training. I always admired her for her ability to clearly see her pathway and know what she had

> *to do to get to the top, something that more than once inspired me to keep pushing.'*

Speaking of challenges, as well as taking on a new sport I was also juggling Year 12 at the same time. I managed to keep up with my schoolwork because we just skied on weekends and holidays. Like before, I was used to managing my time wisely and always got my work done on schedule. I must admit, however, that I was a little distracted and my schooling once again became secondary.

After I had graduated from school, Liz and I headed to Whistler in Canada, where our national team was based at the time, for the northern hemisphere ski season from November to February. Having only ever skied at Mt Buller, I was completely shocked when I saw how huge the mountains were and how much snow they had on them. There seemed to be an endless number of runs to choose from and they went for miles, making every day different and exciting. It was just heaven for us and we skied all day from 9am to 5pm, rarely even stopping for lunch, we were that keen.

As we became more competent and confident during that season, we started goofing around in the terrain park and the half pipe, practising taking air with our skis and doing spins. The only thing we didn't do was flip—not intentionally, anyway. We had some fantastic coaches who took us skiing at that point: Steve Desovich, who was the national team mogul skiing coach, Manuela Berchtold, who was a mogul skier on the national team, and Helmut Spiegl, who had coached Zali Steggall to bronze in alpine skiing at the Nagano Winter Olympics in 1998 and to the World Championship title in 1999.

We skied around with as many different people as possible, including some of the good local skiers we got to know. Both of us knew that the better we were at skiing, the easier we would find the jumping—and let's face it, we loved skiing but we were itching to start jumping and start flying.

My body had changed since quitting gymnastics. I had grown and filled out a bit, but was still as strong as an ox and had the same discipline and work ethic. I was used to working hard and that made learning to ski relatively easy. I thrived on information, soaking up all the advice and then putting it into action. I think our desire was a bit of a shock to some of the coaches—they were used to dealing with normal kids and then Cyclone Lyd and Cyclone Liz arrived. We were ready to listen and learn, and I think they really enjoyed coaching us because of our attitudes, even if we were beginners.

The reason the Australian national aerials team was based out of Whistler was because it had a Canadian coach, Peter Judge, and we often went along and watched their training. Although we weren't ready to do any flips yet, we were allowed to ski down the landing hill and get familiar with an aerial site. The landing area was quite steep, about a 38-degree angle, which is another thing you don't pick up from watching aerials on television. We starting doing little jumps to practise landing on the landing hill—just straight jumps, no flips—learning how to absorb the impact and ski down.

But the main focus of that season was to improve our skiing. We skied through fresh powder, through moguls, off cliffs, and through the trees. We had a ball. We'd catch the first lift up in the morning and if it had snowed the night before we'd have fresh trails to ski on. We even went cross-country skiing and snowboarding just for a change.

We really tried to become multi-faceted skiers, which is what Rachel was instructed to make us before they could let us jump. She was a great chaperone and really opened our eyes to the world of skiing. Christoph also joined us for a bit in Whistler, and Rachel and he both had sport science degrees so they also educated us in the gym. That was a bit foreign to us because, while we'd trained on gymnastics equipment, we'd never worked out in a proper gym with weights and other equipment.

The training was all fun. I turned 18 while we were away and Liz was already 18, so we were having a good time going out and socialising, which was so different to gymnastics. We were working hard and training our butts off, but we were able to let our hair down and relax on days off. It was a good balance and as much fun as they promised in the sales pitch. Geoff and Rachel totally understood that it was an important transition period for us, coming from a strict gymnastics background and becoming adults at the same time. They wanted us to have fun as long as we worked hard, and the four of us—Liz, Rachel, Christoph and me—had an absolute ball.

****

In February 2000 when Liz and I were back in Melbourne for a spell, we started a human movement course at RMIT University. It was a fitting course for both of us and it really complemented what we were doing with aerials because it helped us become more knowledgeable in biomechanics, physiology, anatomy and the science of sport in general. But for me, sport was still my number one priority. It was an excellent course for me to do, but I knew it was going to be difficult to study and train with the kind of schedule I was starting to keep. Thankfully, the lecturers at RMIT understood what we were trying to achieve and worked with both Liz and me to make it work. Human movement wasn't a correspondence course, but our lecturers allowed us to do it that way when we were on camps overseas. We still did all the assignments and exams, but we needed some flexibility on attending lectures and often the staff went out of their way to provide us with lecture notes. Obviously it wasn't ideal to be missing lectures, but they accommodated us as best they could. They understood that we were doing a sport that required us to be away and that was one of the sacrifices we had to make. In all the years I attended RMIT University, I never once enrolled myself. Enrolment was in January and I was just never at home during that time of the year, so Mum had to go along and do it for me.

In my family, we valued a university education as being important, and I wanted a degree. If I hadn't been an athlete I probably would have been a physiotherapist or something in the medical field, as I've always had a fascination with the human body. But if I was doing a sport, that was always going to get 100 per cent of my effort and attention, which would make it difficult to do anything else properly.

During that time back in Australia we also did a lot of trampoline training and started using a bungee system that allowed us to get much higher in the air. This is where we started to learn the techniques of twisting and flipping in the air for aerial skiing. Christoph came from a trampolining background so he showed us how the aerials technique was different from gymnastics and what we needed to change. I'd been playing on trampolines since those early days at Lorne and throughout my gymnastics career, so this was a great way for me to transition. It was a pretty natural link for me, even if the techniques were different, and I picked it up quickly.

By June 2000 we were back in Whistler for our first water ramp training. It was something of a whirlwind at the time, travelling here and there for training and chasing snow or water ramps. Most people don't realise that aerial skiers spend more time jumping into a swimming pool than we do on snow. Water ramp training normally begins at the end of May and finishes in October, and it's through this that we learn new tricks—repeating them enough times so they are consistent and we are ready to try them on snow. Landing into water is a safer way to train because the water acts as a safety net and is much more forgiving than snow.

We didn't have (and at the time of writing still don't have) a water ramp facility we could use in Australia, other than an old, dilapidated one outside Melbourne in Lilydale, which had you landing in a muddy, leech-infested pond instead of a purpose-built pool. Lilydale has been somewhat modified in recent years so that beginners can use it, but it's still a far cry from a world-class facility, so the team still needs to travel overseas for water ramp training six months out of the year.

The water ramps aim to mimic our snow ramps and there are different-sized jumps, just like there are on snow—the only differences are that the surface we ski down isn't snow but an artificial surface we call 'meanies', which has the appearance of hard plastic bristles. Also, instead of landing on a 38-degree pitch, we land into flat water which is aerated with a bubble system to reduce the impact. We then need to swim out of the pool, click off our skis on a platform and walk back up the stairs with the skis over our shoulders. And then we do it all again.

So we embarked on our first day of water ramping in Whistler. Christoph's instructions were: 'You've got to start sideways and then jump-turn 90 degrees down the in-run and just point your skis straight.

Don't try to turn, just try to ski straight until you've gone off the jump.'

We were reasonably competent skiers by that stage—not great skiers, but good enough to slide down a water ramp. I remember practising my first jump-turn and thinking, 'This doesn't feel too bad—I've got the hang of this!' It didn't feel the same as snow, not as smooth and a bit scratchy under the skis, but I was still sliding just fine. Then I took a bit more speed and did a jump. The first jump we had to try wasn't a flip, it was just a straight jump, but once we got the hang of skiing down the new surface, we started mucking around doing flips and other tricks. It was so much fun just playing around.

I still remember the first flip I tried on the water ramp. I didn't quite make it around, stalling in the air then landing on my face. I came out laughing my head off with a blood nose. The next time I got it around and was fine. I learned fairly quickly that the ramp should do most of the work for you. That's what it's designed to do. It's meant to flip you—what you have to do is put your body into a position that *allows* it to flip you. As beginners, we were instructed not to do anything outside our capabilities—we were just getting a feel for the water ramp and its surface, and for landing into the pool and swimming out with the skis still attached.

The jump we started on wasn't designed for flips; it was a mini-jump, really, designed for mogul skiers to practise upright jumps. Once we were confident on that, we moved onto a bigger jump called a single, designed for single flips. It was all very progressive. Each ramp is different depending on the sort of jump you are planning to do. They have different heights and angles to throw you into the air differently.

Some jump explanations are needed at this point: a Single is a single flip, or one rotation; a Double is a double flip, or two rotations; a Tuck or Back-Tuck is a flip in a tucked position; a Lay is a flip in a straight body position. We then combine the flips, or somersaults, with twists. A Full is a flip with a 360-degree twist and a Double-Full is a flip with a double twist (720 degrees). A Double Full-Full is a triple-twisting double or three twists and two flips.

We started with the front flip once we had 'graduated' to the singles ramp, and then we started Back-Tucks and Back-Lays. Next we started twisting, doing Back-Full, adding the 360-degree twist in one flip. I was progressing fast with my jumps and, given I had adapted to skiing quite quickly, I already had certain expectations, and set myself goals every day to improve. Even though Liz and I were beginner aerialists, we weren't regular people; we were trained athletes, trained acrobats. Flipping and jumping was what we did.

On the water ramps, it was important to practise the landing even though we were hitting flat water. Ideally you want to pretend you're landing on snow, with your chest and arms reaching forward as if you're landing down the steep landing hill—you need to do that on snow because if you are too upright you fall backwards, which is why it's good to get into a habit of doing it properly into the water.

We did that initial water ramp camp for six weeks with the aim of learning a single Back-Lay and having it ready for the snow season in Australia. We repeated Back-Lay after Back-Lay, one after the other. Our target was 50 a day and the aim was to get it as straight as possible. We worked on getting the flip rotation just right so that we were not flipping too fast or slow. We practised and practised. It was monotonous.

I progressed well with the intensity of our training. Soon my Back-Lay was ready for snow, and by the end of the camp I was allowed to have a crack at some doubles. I remember when I did that first double on the water ramp, Jacqui came up to the top of the ramp to make sure I knew what I was doing. We often do that if someone's doing a new trick for the first time or if they're a bit nervous. Essentially it's just a handholding or camaraderie exercise and, being experienced, Jacqui came with me.

I wasn't nervous, really, but I just stared down at the jump as if I was boss and said aloud, 'Right! Jump!' and down I went. Jacqui just laughed. Most people are very nervous and quiet before they do a new trick, but I was fairly aggressive and fearless as a youngster. But even now, whenever I do a new trick, I pretty much say the same thing to the ramp.

I did about 10 doubles that day and it was great to do something new—scary, but exhilarating going off a bigger jump, hoping I would do two flips but not knowing for sure. However, I handled those first ones really well and without drama.

At the end of the camp we came back home and went up to Mt Buller in August to do our first flips on snow, the simple Back-Lay. We were forerunners for the Mt Buller World Cup that year, which was exciting. That meant that we weren't in the actual competition but we opened the event with our jumps and acted like a test run for the judges. The World Cup competitors were doing their bigger tricks and it was a great experience for us to be jumping alongside them.

Doing our first jumps on snow made us feel like we were becoming real aerial skiers, rather than just gymnasts who were learning to ski. We started to feel a part of the group, accepted into the team. We had started as outsiders, as gymnasts, but now we were skiers and the journey had really begun.

I wasn't nervous on those first snow jumps, but there was some trepidation because there was so much that was unknown. I didn't know if the jump would feel the same as on water, or how it felt to land on the steep landing hill as opposed to landing in a swimming pool. It was exciting.

My first jumps went as expected—neither better nor worse. But what I aimed to do was transfer what I had learned on the water to snow. Obviously the landing is completely different to water and that was the main thing I had to adjust for and learn. I didn't land my first one very well, but I stayed on my feet for my second and didn't crash one the whole time at Mt Buller after that. With each jump I got more confident and consistent. Figuring out the landing was the main objective, and I managed that well. It's not just the fact that the slope is on such an angle, but that all the visuals are different too. Rather than seeing the water and the pool, you're seeing the knoll—the flat part under the jump—and then the steep landing hill.

> *Geoff: 'The most impressive single memory I have is that Lydia was able to not only commit to whatever volume was asked of her, but also do the volume at a very high quality. Via Rachel, we were very conscious of every activity*

> *to fast track her with the best possible fundamentals (pre-jumping), but with controlled risk. Rachel and I realised quickly that her progress and performance was a benchmark of the best and fastest possible. This has since been proved correct; no one has progressed faster. Once she started jumping with Peter Judge, the game changed completely and Lydia was making super fast progress to get to the 2002 Olympic Games, but with significant risk as well.'*

I really enjoyed the Mt Buller World Cup that year. Jumping in front of a big crowd was awesome, even if we were just forerunners. It was good to perform again, to feel butterflies. I had missed that since retiring from gymnastics.

It was also becoming clear to me how I felt about gymnastics, my first love, and my concerns about whether I would love another sport as much. I realised that it wasn't just gymnastics I was passionate about—it was being an athlete. It was the training, the competition, the adrenalin. The search for improvement mattered to me and I think that's still the same today. I didn't come from a family that had passion about any sport in particular—it wasn't as if my mum, dad and brothers were all ice hockey players so therefore I would play ice hockey. I loved gymnastics but it wasn't just the sport, it was more about me being an athlete and the challenges I created for myself. That's what really made me tick. That's what I was born to do.

So I fell in love with aerials. It was a challenge that I wanted to conquer. I was quite sure of myself in the early days—borderline cocky—completely convinced that I had what it took to be successful in aerial skiing. Initially I felt intimidated because I knew that I was at a development stage and that I wasn't good yet, but inside I felt that one day I would contend with the best. As I said earlier, when I first saw the men jumping, I was in awe of them and I wanted to jump like that. Throughout my whole career I've compared myself to the men and set high standards for myself— they did triple somersaults so I wanted to do triples. Those were big dreams considering I had only just started doing singles.

****

Aerial skiing, bar the acrobatics, is very different to gymnastics. In gymnastics you don't have as much time in the air. On the vault, floor or bars, some tricks are done in a straight lay position, but most are done in a tuck or a pike position because there is less airtime. In aerials the aim is always to do your flips straight. A basic trick, like a Lay-Tuck, has the first rotation in a straight position and then you pull the second rotation up into a tuck position. But advanced tricks are always done in a straight position for maximum points.

There is also a huge difference in height. When you're doing triple somersaults you're in the air for about three seconds and you fly more than 19 metres above the landing. That is a lot higher than any of the gymnastics moves, which don't exceed three metres, and that is why, in aerials, you are able to do rotations in a straight position. The twisting technique in aerials also differs to gymnastics because of that extra time in the air and also because there are skis attached to your body. The best way to create the twist when you have the additional weight of skis on you is to use your arms as levers. The more efficient you are at creating the twist by moving your arms, the faster you will spin.

All the tricks in aerials are dependent on speed and the take-off. If you don't have the right speed or the right take-off the jump is compromised, which often forces you to break form and bodyline, and the outcome is very different. It can make or break your jump. And being an outdoor sport, there are so many variables to consider that will affect your speed and take-off. That is why we test our speed all the time. We have a speed gun or a speed clock detecting our speed on the in-run before we take any jumps. You ski down from the place on the in-run where you think you're going to start from, the coaches measure your speed in the transition from the in-run to the jump, and after you get past that point, you put the brakes on and slide up the jump or off to the side.

Another important aspect is knowing how to read the snow and weather conditions because they can change even from one jump to the next. You need to pay attention to changing speeds and constantly make slight adjustments. For instance, if there is a headwind just before you are about to jump, it will slow down your speed, so to compensate for that you need to step further up the in-run to gain more speed and cancel out the effects of the headwind.

There was so much to learn in the beginning and so many details to pay attention to, as well as the technical aspects of learning how to ski and jump. I had no idea when I started that it was going to be such a precise sport, and to be honest, I loved the precision. It suited me.

Early on I would do as the coaches instructed, no question. Since I didn't know what I was talking about, I put full faith in them that they knew what I was supposed to do. But as I gained more confidence I started to learn and make my own decisions based on the way things felt and the little changes I could make that impacted what I was doing.

In late November, following the 2000 Mt Buller World Cups, we went to a place called Silver Star in Canada to continue our jump training and improve our skiing skills. We were there until February and by that stage a new group of recruits had joined us and were also learning how to ski. One of them was my good friend Lainie Cole from the Niddrie gymnastics club, and her partner in crime was Bree Munro, also a former elite gymnast. After I started aerials, I tried to get as many of my friends from gym as I could to join the program. Most didn't have the stomach for it, but Lainie did, and I was happy she, like me, saw it as an opportunity too good to pass up.

Liz and I did Back-Lays the whole time we were there—single after single after single—with the idea of getting our basics perfect so that the next year we'd be able to move to doubles and, if they went well, do some World Cups. It was monotonous training but it was productive, and by the time I left I could pretty much do a single with my eyes closed, which was exactly the point, I guess.

We did 20 Back-Lays in the morning, and I remember a lot of days that season we were training in temperatures of minus 20°C. Then we'd ski all afternoon, followed by workouts in the gym. It was a good routine and we just kept refining our skills. We were becoming better skiers every day and our jumping skills were being perfected, so that doing a Back-Lay became automatic and required very little thought. It was the perfect foundations camp.

My jumping was going really well and I didn't crash all season. Christoph came to me one night after training and suggested we do a few doubles on snow. I had only done around 10 doubles on the water ramps, but when Christoph said, 'Hey, I think you're ready!' I thought I was too. My single Back-Lays were perfect, I was landing every one and he wanted me to be challenged. Even though I had only done a few, the doubles I had done on water were fine, completely safe, and I seemed to know what I was doing.

But I wasn't ready. Yes, I was ready for the next progression, but that would have been to continue doubles on water. There was no need at that stage in my career to push me. There was no advantage in doing those doubles on snow at that point, but at the time I didn't know that—I just thought, 'How cool! All right, let's do it!' In hindsight, given my lack of experience doing doubles, it was a stupid risk to take. But I didn't assess risk back then; I wasn't scared and I thought it would be fun. Christoph felt I was going to be fine and I was stupidly confident. Looking back, if I had a talented rookie who was gung-ho as I was back then, I wouldn't take those chances with them, absolutely not.

I don't know why Christoph wanted me to do doubles. Maybe he was getting bored too. Obviously he had faith that I could do it and that it wouldn't be a problem for me, but that was definitely outside the instructions from the director of the OWI. Geoff would have been completely against it, so we decided to go out and do it in secrecy.

Liz was also at the secret session because she was going for a ski, but no one was really supposed to know. So it was just me, Christoph, Liz and Lauri Lassila. Lauri, a Finnish skier who I met at the beginning of the training camp in Silver Star, was coaching some athletes on the mogul course, which was right next to the jumps, and would often join us for a ski. We had no speed gun and it had snowed the night before so there was about a foot of snow on the in-run and transition part of the jump. We cleared a small path wide enough for me to ski down and I did one or two speed checks with Christoph eyeballing my speed. He said, 'Yeah, that looks OK. Ya-ya, let's go.' These days, I would never jump without a speed gun, but who was I to know?

My first double was too slow and I landed on the knoll,

the flat part under the jumps, but I was fine because the fresh snow was soft and fluffy. For the next ones, I stepped up through the powder snow to try to get more speed. I only did about four and they were all fine, and I even skied a couple out. It was exhilarating going off a big jump, and even though I tried to pretend I wasn't nervous, I definitely was. The adrenalin was pumping that day, knowing I was going to do two flips but not knowing what was going to happen. The fact that I was doing it in secrecy and I wasn't supposed to be doing it gave me even more of a buzz. If anything, that day I proved that I was fearless and possibly a bit nuts, but nevertheless, well suited to the sport. I felt 'macho' and I was happy with myself. Luckily, I survived the experiment completely unscathed.

Christoph was so happy he couldn't help but tell Geoff what we'd done. 'Oh and by the way, I know you were against it, but Lydia did doubles today and she did great.' Geoff went off at him for disobeying orders and gave him a real earful. Clearly he was more interested in the big picture and not destroying any rookies.

> *Geoff: 'To be honest, I was just so surprised. Not a big deal because there was no bad outcome—Christoph got a rap on the knuckles because it is the classic scenario of not much to gain but a lot to lose. We were trying to make smart choices and really control risk till Lydia had developed best possible base skills. Everything up to that point had been about controllable risk. Little did I know that it was just an indication of the next 12 months ahead in the lead-up to the Olympic Winter Games in 2002!'*

****

When I met Lauri Lassila, or 'Late' (pronounced 'latte', like the coffee), as he is more commonly known, I had no idea the role he would go on to play in my life. Late was a top mogul skier at the time, but he had blown his knee the previous season and was taking the current season to recover from his surgery and rehabilitate the injury. He had coached some development mogul skiers from Australia in the past, so since he was having the season off, the Australian development team asked if he would like to help out at the training camp. He was just getting back into skiing anyway so he agreed, and by chance that team was at Silver Star at the same time as us.

I was 18 at the time and one of my friends, Nicole, a mogul skier, kept talking Late up, saying what a good skier he was and how great it was to have him come and coach. She had worked with him before and was already good friends with him. 'By the way, Lyd, you guys are really similar, you'd really like him,' she kept telling me. But I honestly wasn't interested. 'No, I don't want a boyfriend right now,' I told her. 'I'm one year into my aerials and just want to concentrate on that. I'm not interested.'

I didn't think much of him at the start. He seemed really aloof because he was this champion mogul skier and like he thought he was obviously too good for the rest of us rookies. He didn't talk much, which I now realise is just the Finnish way—in fact he wasn't really snobby at all, it's just the way he is until he gets comfortable around people. But I already had my shield up. I wasn't interested and tried to shift the attention to Lainie and my other teammates to get them keen on him.

Even though he wasn't working with us directly, Late occasionally coached us for some skiing, and so we got to know each other. He was a phenomenal skier, light years away from us development athletes, and I must admit I was impressed. And with his Scandinavian good looks, I also thought he was pretty hot.

We really got to know each other in the gym. Liz, myself and all the other athletes were always in the gym working out and took it fairly seriously. As Late got to know us and feel more comfortable, he started to come out a bit and show his personality, and that's when I couldn't help but like him!

Before Late, I had never had a serious boyfriend and I suppose I had always put my sport first. I didn't have time for a boyfriend and I didn't want to change that.

It really was a time of transitions—from gymnastics to aerials, and high school to university. I was becoming an adult and was in a sport where coaches no longer controlled your every move or treated you like a robot. You had to be responsible and I was experiencing a lot of new things at the same time. We would go out to the pubs in the local ski resorts and have a good time on our days off, and since we weren't at the stage where we had to prepare for events yet, we jumped, skied and just had plain, old fun. It was a really wonderful time, and with the new recruits it was a great team—very much a family away from home.

We did have curfew, but one night Late and I snuck out to have a drink and chat. No big deal. We were just friends after all, and I think we both enjoyed each other's company. He came from a completely different culture to me but we found out quite quickly that we shared a lot of similar interests. That made conversation easy and we wanted to hang out with each other more and more. We liked each other straight away—once I had let the barriers down.

I let him know straight away about my aspirations and focus, and he felt the same way about his career and his comeback. We knew that we'd be off at different places during certain times of the year and I didn't want to be the person who was missing her boyfriend. That just wasn't me. So we made the mutual decision to take it easy. We knew that we'd rendezvous in certain spots, and left it as a 'see you then' kind of thing. I certainly had an interest in him but I wasn't willing to sacrifice my sport for him.

When the Silver Star camp ended in February 2001, Late and I went our separate ways, not knowing what the future would bring but both agreeing that we liked each other's company and we'd try to keep in contact. We weren't 'boyfriend and girlfriend' at that stage, and we both did as we pleased. I just wasn't ready at that point in my life to enter into any commitment until I was certain I wanted to be with him, although it didn't take long for us to work that out—I just didn't know if I wanted to be with him for the rest of my life. I'd never been in love and I'd never even had a serious boyfriend, so I was fairly cautious about jumping into a major relationship. He was a distraction that I both wanted and didn't want, but in the end I was able to keep the focus on my skiing.

So I flew home to Melbourne to resume my university studies and Late flew back to Finland. We spoke a few times over the phone but neither of us was ready to commit to a long distance relationship. I did find that I thought about him a lot and missed him in those periods when we weren't together. I wanted to be around him, of course, but I just couldn't at that time.

The next time our paths would cross would be in June and July at Whistler, where I would be training on the water ramps and he would be coaching and training on snow high up on the glaciers.

****

In May 2001, in between university commitments, we scheduled in a water ramp camp at Lilydale, where we continued working on our single flips and I progressed through to a Double-Full—a single flip with a double twist. We also had an intensive trampoline camp and practised double somersaults with various twisting combinations in a bungee harness, in preparation for our June trip to Whistler, where we would spend the northern hemisphere summer training on the water ramps. I had no idea at the time that this was going to be the biggest summer of my life in terms of volume and progression.

By that time I had also started working with Pete, our national team coach, while Christoph stayed focused on the new recruits coming up through the ranks. Christoph had a lot of faith in me, especially after our secret session in Silver Star, and he had planted a seed in my head that if I worked hard I could have a shot at qualifying for the 2002 Winter Olympics in Salt Lake City, which were just eight months away. 'You've got the ability and if you get some more difficult tricks up your sleeve you can make the team,' he told me.

> Pete: 'I remember very well my first meeting with Lydia, I was very impressed with how strong both she and Liz were as skiers and how well they managed the landing hill. Skiing straight down a 39-degree, 30m-long landing hill is a very scary thing, even for experienced skiers,

> but they were fearless—it certainly caught my attention. I knew that something was different. What struck me more than anything, though, was a willingness to have a go. Lydia was not one to let anything get the better of her and, as I came to learn, the bigger the challenge, the more determination and commitment she showed. That, to me, was and truly is extraordinary. I had come by many other athletes in my career with talent, but to find one with talent and a relentless work ethic was a coach's dream.'

At the time, the World Cup team consisted of Jacqui Cooper, Alisa Camplin and another athlete, Shannon Leotta, who trained with her own coach, Frank Bare. Australia could take four aerial skiers to the Olympics and there was one spot up for grabs if I was up to the challenge. But I needed to work my butt off and get some bigger jumps under my belt if I was going to have a chance to qualify. In my mind I had no doubt I could do it. I wasn't afraid of hard work, I loved a big challenge and I was on a mission.

I did almost 2700 jumps that summer, more than anyone else in the world, and I progressed quickly. On average I did 25 to 30 jumps per four-hour session, and two sessions per day. By the end of two months, I had done six new tricks: Double-Full, Lay-Tuck, Full-Tuck, Lay-Full, Full-Full and Double-Full-Tuck. It was a bit crazy, but my coach Pete was as ambitious as I was. Every day and every jump I was eager for improvement. I had an unbelievable motor and an ability to keep my concentration—indeed often my best jumps were at the end of the session. Every day I was the first to start and the last to finish, and I was training at an incredible work rate and intensity.

> Pete: 'I knew the only way we were going to have a chance to get Lydia to the Olympics in 2002 was to go hard on the volume, and because of her great work ethic she didn't whinge when I put the spurs in. She did nearly 2700 jumps that summer, with more than 950 from June to mid-July alone! As I saw it, my job was to move Lydia and

the other girls along as quickly and prudently as possible, and this was met with lots of second-guessing from the armchair pundits. I knew we had to strike a balance for Lydia between perfection and practical application, and that is what we worked towards. She needed challenges in order to rise to the occasion and, most amazingly, the bigger the challenge the more the resolve and the higher the achievement. This is not to say that the approach and path we took was flippant—it was very calculated and based on her innate ability to grasp concepts very quickly, mixed with her commitment to do the heavy mileage to consolidate those concepts. One without the other would have been a formula for disaster, which many people seemed to expect. For me though, meeting our targets was a certainty.'

While water ramping is very physical—you spend most of the day hiking up hundreds of steps, soaked to the bone, with your skis over your shoulders—it is also hard work mentally. There is so much repetition and it requires a lot of mental energy to maintain focus throughout a whole session. But my ability to motor on and remain focused was extraordinary—there is no way I could manage that kind of workload these days. Sure, I was overtraining, but I didn't know it, I just jumped till I had enough and I understood only one kind of pace: 100 per cent effort.

Because of how much jumping I was doing and the fact that we didn't have a full-time physiotherapist with us, I didn't know how to maintain my body properly or read the signs it was sending me. So I started getting injured. First, I developed a cyst on my foot, which was like a bubble where my boot was rubbing on my ankle. At first I ignored it, but it finally got so painful that I went to see a physio in Whistler who had worked a lot with our team, a fellow Aussie named Bianca Matheson. She's a fantastic practitioner and she took one look at me and said, 'Lyd, you should have come to see me sooner, this is really inflamed and your tendon could snap if you keep pushing it.' So I started seeing her regularly and my foot eventually settled down.

But because I wasn't good at monitoring my body, I let niggles turn into injuries, thinking they would get better on their own. I didn't care too much about pain because I was improving so fast with my jumping, and I wanted to get my tricks in the bag so that I'd have the chance to qualify for the Olympics. In one incident, I landed too far forward with my chest into the water, basically on my face, and I felt a crunch in my neck. I didn't really think much of it at the time as it wasn't a particularly bad crash, but I got an instant headache and every time I bent over to do up my boots I'd get a really sharp pain running through my head. I told Pete, who realised that the fact I had actually complained meant I was really hurting, and he said, 'Pack it up for today, kiddo. Go home and get some rest and we'll see how you feel tomorrow.'

I went home and sat in front of the TV for the rest of the afternoon with a headache and sore neck, and then went to bed early. About 10pm that night, I woke up feeling nauseous from the pain in my head and started vomiting. I continued to vomit every half hour throughout the night. My head would feel like it was exploding, then I'd feel extreme nausea and I'd vomit, which gave me a little relief in my head before the cycle started again. I didn't know what was going on. Lying in the foetal position in my bed, I didn't think I was going to make it through the night, but I didn't want to call anyone or wake Liz, who was sleeping in another room and didn't hear a thing. But by the morning someone phoned—it was Pete or Jacqui, I can't remember—and I didn't sound very good.

'What the hell's going on? You sound horrible,' they asked.

'I don't know, something's wrong, I've been throwing up all night'.

They both rushed over and drove me to hospital. I was still vomiting at the hospital, but there was nothing left in my stomach. All that was coming up was bile, which had turned from green to black. It was pretty gross and I was not in good shape. They took x-rays, which found that a couple of vertebrae were displaced in my neck. The doctors said I was suffering from a traumatic migraine so they decided to put me on a drip, but I was so dehydrated from the vomiting that the nurse struggled hard to find a vein. I stayed on the drip all day until my headache started to ease, the vomiting stopped and I eventually fell asleep.

The doctors were concerned that I had bleeding in my brain, so they kept me under observation, saying that the minute my headache had gone I could leave, but otherwise I'd have to go to Vancouver for more tests. After a sleep I still had a headache but lied and said I felt better. I just wanted to get out of there. Luckily, I didn't have any bleeding, which would have been a very dangerous situation. Bianca adjusted the vertebrae in my neck back to their correct positions, but I still had pain for quite some time after that whenever I tried to bend down and it took a couple of weeks before I felt better again and could cautiously start to jump. To this day, it is the worst night I've ever endured and a classic case of how recklessly stupid I was as a rookie. I was just desperate to get back out and jump. Unfortunately, it took more beatings to learn my lesson.

****

Late and I were reunited during that northern summer in Whistler, which was great. He was coaching a mogul camp up on the glacier where a lot of mogul teams trained during the summer, so it worked out perfectly. I was working pretty hard, but we spent a lot of time together after training and on our free days.

Whistler is one of my favourite places in the world and, even in summer, it's such a great place to be, with its awesome village atmosphere and so many things to do. After a day's skiing on the glacier or mountain biking, everyone heads to the patios outside the restaurants, enjoying the afternoon sun and a beer. We'd go for picnics and barbeques by the lakes, and got to know some great local people. I was also able to meet many of Late's friends. They were such good times. I really enjoyed his company, and in a way he was a good distraction for me. I was so driven to become a good aerial skier that I was perhaps too intense, but he seemed to lighten me up a little, and being an experienced athlete, he always had a wise perspective.

Not long after the migraine incident, I landed awkwardly after attempting a new jump. I was doing a Double Full-Tuck—a double twist in the first rotation and then a basic tuck in the second flip—and I over-rotated and landed on my back in an arched position, winding myself badly. It took at least 20 seconds of wheezing and gasping before

I could breathe some air into my lungs properly, but with my rookie ignorance, I continued jumping. I woke the next morning wincing with pain. Even bouncing on the spot or walking down stairs felt like someone had stuck a knife into my back, and jumping was excruciating.

It was hard to breathe so I made an appointment to see Bianca. After an x-ray, she concluded that I had bruised the discs between my vertebrae. Thankfully nothing was broken, but it had happened just before we were heading back to Mt Buller for the World Cups, which opened the 2001/02 season. This time, Liz and I were actually going to be competing and would be doing our first doubles on snow—my first 'official' ones, anyway. I wasn't going to miss out on that chance, so I flew home to Melbourne and went to see every therapist I could find to help me heal. I was drinking all kinds of herbal concoctions from a Chinese medicine guru, but even he said the injury was going to take some time.

My plan at that stage was to do the Buller World Cups, then go back to Whistler and finish off the water ramp season so I could get my new tricks polished and ready for snow. But the only person who made program decisions like that was the OWI CEO, Geoff Lipshut. Pete, the head coach, who saw me train every day, could only make recommendations and he fought hard for me, but Geoff ultimately called the shots from Melbourne. That was always a huge problem and frustration for anyone who coached our team, but Geoff had built the OWI and aerial skiing was his baby. He had been Kirstie Marshall's coach and manager back in her time, and he was able to develop the OWI around her success, so he has always had control over the aerial program even though we trained and competed overseas, far away from his office in Melbourne.

Geoff gave me a Mt Buller ultimatum: 'Lydia, if you land your new doubles in the World Cups, you can go back to Whistler and train for the Olympics.'

Given that it was my first competition and I was going to be doing my first doubles, that I wasn't on a full scholarship and my parents had to pay for my flights, it was a pretty harsh ultimatum. But I was determined to land those jumps. Maybe it was just one of his tests to see if I could handle a bit of pressure.

I wrapped a bandage around my chest, swallowed a few painkillers and started to train. The pain was still there but I tolerated it and was still able to concentrate on my jumping. I did my first doubles and they were a success. I missed a couple of landings in the course of the training week and the competition, but the rest I landed and skied away, which is a decent effort for a rookie. Landing doubles is a different story to landing singles. You are dropping from almost triple the height and with great speed, so learning to land can take time and involve some painful crashes before you get the hang of it. But I was a natural and made the transition quite easily. I was so excited to be a part of the World Cup and it was then that I truly felt like I was becoming an aerial skier.

The event was to be aired live on TV and my family and friends were all there to see me jump. Even Late was there because he had come to coach moguls at Mt Buller for the season. It was the first chance he'd had to meet my family, and I was a little nervous about that. Before they met him, my brothers had joked about it, saying, 'The Finn's finished!' while punching their fists into their opposite palm. I'd never had a boyfriend before, so I guessed they'd be a little protective. But when it actually got to the stage of meeting Late they were the complete opposite. They were actually nice to him, polite in fact! I gave them a lot of grief afterwards, telling them how soft they were for backing down. Inside, of course, I was glad they didn't do anything embarrassing!

The conditions on the first day of the Buller competition were horrendous—probably the worst weather I've jumped in even to this day. The wind was howling and we got everything from fog to hail, snow and rain. It was all really new for me. I didn't have any experience jumping in that kind of weather, but I managed to make the right decisions and stayed safe.

Because of the weather we had delays all day. Every time we'd go out to jump the weather would get even crazier, so we'd go inside for another weather hold. We spent most of the day inside in our ski boots ready to go and I remember Pete saying, 'Don't turn off, just be ready to get up and go out to jump at any time—when they say it's on, we need to be ready'. In the end we had to go ahead with the competition because of the live TV. It was pretty crazy—it was our safety that was on the line, but if the race director, Joe Fitzgerald, said that the event was on we had to jump, blizzard or no blizzard.

Although the event went ahead, it was cut down to a one-jump contest rather than two because we were running out of light, while the men's competition was cancelled altogether for the opening day.

My first World Cup jump was a Full-Tuck and I landed it with a score of 72.74 points. It wasn't a high score because it's a jump with a low degree of difficulty, but it was a decent result, and I was happy I had survived the weather and landed my jump—a lot of experienced aerialists crashed out that day, spooked by the weather. I ended up finishing fifth in my first ever World Cup event, which was excellent, and most importantly, I had landed—if I could repeat that the next day, I'd be allowed to return to Whistler to continue water ramping. That fifth place was also an Olympic qualifying result, which meant I only needed two more top-12 results to qualify for a spot on the Olympic team.

The next day the weather was a lot better and we were able to run a proper competition. I landed both of my jumps, but so did many athletes with more difficult jumps, and I finished in 13th place.

All in all, I landed my doubles in competition, which was a great debut, and I probably exceeded a lot of people's expectations. I was just happy that I was going to be able to go back to Whistler and that I had passed Geoff's pressure test. I was still a beginner, it was the first time the other competitors had seen me compete and I don't know what they would have thought—I had come from nowhere fast. Given the weather, the pressure and my lack of experience, Pete was impressed with my performance. He was happy with how I handled it and that I did my job. It was also a good lesson and great learning experience for me. That weekend I learned to expect the unexpected and to be on my toes and accept that, in aerial skiing, the conditions are never going to be perfect but you've still got to jump.

> *Pete: 'No one really expected Lydia to make Salt Lake City, particularly those inside OWI circles, but I thought it was possible. I knew that if she could read the landings as*

well as she had on water, the conversion to snow would be rapid. She was so technically strong in execution and in finishing tricks that I knew she would be able to convert far faster than normal, and sure enough she did. I had to push very hard for Lydia to get a start at Buller—originally they wanted her and Liz to forerun. Once there, she was able to complete not only her first doubles on snow, but also her first twisting ones, and a Full-Tuck to boot, which from a technical and psychological standpoint is very difficult. And in the weather on the day, to have finished fifth in her first World Cup! That's when things started to happen.'

Back then, the Mt Buller events were the start of the World Cup season, but there was a long break to the next events as we waited for the snow to fall in the northern hemisphere. So we went back to Whistler to continue water ramp training. I had had a taste of competition and I wanted more—I had proven myself to a lot of people and earned my spot on the World Cup team, but I wanted to make it to the Olympics and knew I still had a lot of work to do on the water ramps to get some bigger jumps ready. The Salt Lake City Games were in February 2002 and I was determined to be there.

****

Heading into the 2001/02 World Cup season, the top spots in the world in women's aerial skiing were occupied by Jacqui Cooper and Alla Tsuper from Belarus. The Chinese and Canadian teams were quite strong too, as was Evelyne Leu from Switzerland, who was always a contender with her triple somersaults.

But aerial skiing has come a long way since those days. That's evolution, I guess. If you look at the progress from that time through to 2010, it's been an amazing development. Each year boundaries are being pushed. Women are jumping much higher and doing much more difficult tricks and the scores reflect that. Back in 2001, no woman had ever scored over 200 points—these days, you need at least 200 points to make the podium. More and more women are doing triples, the competition is tougher, and if you want to be successful you have to be prepared to take risks. You have to force yourself beyond your comfort zone. Each year we are raising the bar, and we have the sport's pioneers like Kirstie Marshall and Jacqui Cooper to thank for that.

Before Salt Lake in 2002, there was only a handful of women doing triples and, compared to the men, they were far from perfect—in fact not even in the same ballpark. Jacqui was the most successful triples jumper at the time because she could land. Her form and technique, however, were quite poor. But if she landed she won, because no one else was throwing tricks that matched her degree of difficulty. Some tried, but it was a case of hit or miss, particularly on landing. Some athletes took heavy falls, which deterred them from getting back up on the jump. Jac was pushing it at that time, competing triples when some women couldn't even imagine themselves launching from a jump that big.

I saw a lot of faults in women's jumping, which is why I chose to draw inspiration from the men. There was a huge gap between men and women and I was determined to change that. But first I had to get the basics right. I didn't doubt I was capable of jumping like a man. There are all shapes and sizes in the men's field—tall guys, short guys, stocky guys, lean guys—so to me it didn't matter that I was on the short side. In terms of the actual tricks, there was no logical reason why women couldn't do high quality triples as well. I didn't feel like there were any barriers. I knew it would be difficult, but not impossible. But as I was still just learning the basics at the time, I kept those thoughts private.

A lot changed in terms of our team dynamics that summer. An Olympic year often does that—everyone gets 'Olympic fever' trying to do everything possible to prepare for the Games and get an edge over their competitors. Liz hadn't progressed though her tricks as quickly as I had and wasn't aiming to make the squad for Salt Lake City. Jacqui was the centre of attention—our program revolved around her and she made sure she got everything she wanted and needed. Alisa was on the rise, and she got fed up being in Jacqui's shadow so she hired her own coach, Todd Ossian. And then there was me. Not even on the 'shadow team' for the Olympics (the group of possible contenders for the team); not even a speck on anyone's radar. But I was determined, and I had dreams of golden things around my neck, even if I was a rookie. I loved working with Pete and I felt I was getting the attention I needed, so I just did my work. Jac, Liz and I worked with Pete while Alisa broke away on her own.

Jac was quite influential on me at that time. She wasn't getting along with Alisa, and I was the next person in rank, so we became pretty good mates. She's a fun, high energy girl and she really taught me the ropes and took me under her wing. She already had 10 years of experience in the sport and, at the time, she was the person to beat. She taught me a lot of the things I needed to know—who were the important people on the World Cup, the places we were going, and what to expect about the World Cup and the Olympics.

Jac and I trained together, roomed together and travelled together. She gave me advice and guidance that only experience can teach and, in turn, I offered her help and support leading into her Olympic campaign. As mentioned, technique at that time was Jacqui's weakness and she was having trouble with her most difficult trick, a Full-Full-Full—a trick with three twists in three flips. I had already developed fairly good basics and could quickly identify her problems, and there was one problem in particular in her take-off, so I helped her try to make it better. We called it 'Operation Full-Full-Full'.

Jac needed someone around who could reassure her that, 'Yes, you're on track, you're going to do it'. It was also good for her to have someone around who wasn't a threat, which was the reality at that stage despite my own desires. And it was good for me to have someone with that kind of experience to provide the many unknown answers. After my results at Mt Buller, Jac lined me up with a ski sponsor, IDone, a Japanese company, which was a huge help, and they provided me with skis and have remained my ski sponsor ever since. I had never had any kind of sponsor before so I was lucky to have Jac put in a good word for me. She was so helpful in that regard and the friendship worked both ways.

When I left Australia after the Mt Buller World Cup I knew there was going to be a chance that I wasn't going to be able to come back home before the season was over. It was going to take every ounce of me to make it to the Olympics, and I figured I might as well take all my winter gear over so that if I needed to stay longer on the water ramps I'd have everything I would need for the snow season—and that's what ended up happening. I went back for more water ramp training in September, and then committed myself to not coming home until after the Olympics in February. I was in for the long haul.

CHAPTER 5

ONE BATTERED ROOKIE

I had already had a huge summer as I worked my way up from a single flip to double-twisting doubles at the Whistler water ramps. Each water ramp season, an athlete might learn one or two new tricks, three at the most. That summer I learned six.

I continued to jump far more than anyone else in the world—60 doubles a day was normal for me, with my record, according to my training diary, being 69, more than some athletes complete in a week. I was really pushing myself hard and I wanted to get better fast. I wanted to improve, and Salt Lake City was a real motivator for me to keep going and push through.

Early in the northern summer, Pete and I had decided that we would aim to qualify one more new jump for snow: a Double Full-Full, or triple-twisting double. Pete had faith I could qualify it in time for the snow season, so we worked hard and started churning out some numbers. I had already done quite a few Double Full-Tucks, so the next progression was adding an extra twist to replace the tuck. I didn't know much about scoring or what jumps were worth back in those days—I was very naive—but I knew that few women performed the Double Full-Full, which was a difficult jump for the times. I knew that if I could qualify it I'd have a pretty solid set of jumps going into the Olympics, and that's all that mattered to me.

Water ramping is no easy task at any time, but in Whistler's autumn months it's even harder, especially with the frequency I was jumping. The weather was quite cold, with a lot of rain and occasional snow, and the water in the pool quickly developed an icy chill. But the generally grey, wet and miserable conditions didn't deter me from wanting to train every day. My wetsuit was now replaced by a drysuit, one with rubber seals at the neck, wrists and ankles so that the water can't get in. A drysuit feels like a big garbage bag and it's a little more restricting than a wetsuit, but at least you can wear layers of thermals underneath and you don't get wet.

As I've said, each of my training sessions took about four hours, and consisted of: hiking up the stairs, clicking on the skis, performing the jump, swimming out of the pool, clicking off the skis, and hiking back up the stairs. Over and over again. It was hard work, it was cold and I was tired, as it had already been a tough summer before and after the Buller World Cups. I had learned six new tricks and was now onto my seventh. I had fought through injuries—first the cyst, then the migraine—and I was still managing the bruised discs in my back. 'It will all be worth it when you qualify for the Olympics,' I kept telling myself. That was enough motivation for me.

After Buller I had become fixated on getting to Salt Lake and believed I was going to make it. I had come so far in one year and I knew I could push myself a little further. Even though I was a rookie and no one expected much from me, I couldn't help but feel inside that I didn't just want to make it onto the Olympic team—I wanted to do well there. I never wanted to just participate in the Olympics, or just wear the Australian uniform and be a tourist; even from the age of six, those were never my intentions.

Other than the actual jumping, I knew very little about the rules of the sport—how many points each jump was worth, how jumps were judged, how the scores were calculated. I was never one to over-analyse or focus too much on the finer details. To me, if a jump looked good it would score well. The more twists and flips you did, the harder the jump—the harder the jump, the bigger the score.

I also knew nothing about pacing myself, managing injuries or overtraining. I didn't see the big picture: I just wanted to get good, fast. I wanted to win and I wanted to be the best and that was all I could think about. I didn't have a detailed plan of how I was going to achieve that, and to be honest Pete was pretty similar to me, in that we both flew by the seat of our pants.

I often wonder why no one sat me down and said, 'OK Lydia, we need to plan for the future. I understand what you want to achieve, but we need to put some steps in place on how to get there. What are your short-term goals? What are your medium- or long-term goals?' There was none of that. Pete was a workhorse, like me; he pushed me and I never backed down.

Normally, athletes stop their northern hemisphere water ramping in the first week of October because it's really cold by then and they need to have a break so they can start fresh on snow in November. But I was still on the water ramps at the start of November. It was so cold—not in the minuses yet, but freezing when you were jumping into the water. Pete had filled buckets with hot water so I could dip in my hands and boots between every jump, and that seemed to help a lot. My new jump was coming along nicely, and with each one I felt more and more confident. There is no formal process for qualifying jumps on water, but in the Australian team we do enough repetitions to make sure that we are confident, consistent and in control of the trick. Once that's the case, you're ready for snow.

When we finished the water jump sessions in early November I was confident that I had the new trick under control and that I could transfer what I had learned to snow. As I had anticipated, I didn't have time to return to Australia for a break because we were going to start skiing and jumping on snow in mid-November, but I did manage a short rest before heading to Fortress Mountain in Alberta, Canada.

Ah, Fortress, or 'the moon', as I like to call it. The only plus Fortress had to offer was its early snowfall and the fact that we could start jumping there early to mid-November, but otherwise it's a horrible place. It's very isolated, with Canmore, the closest town, 40 minutes away.

There's nothing on the actual mountain apart from an old lodge and a few apartments. No shops, no restaurants, nothing. Just like the moon.

Liz, Jac, Pete and I decided to stay in Canmore instead of Fortress so we'd have access to shops, food and the gym. Even though we had to drive the 40 minutes along winding roads, it meant we could get off the mountain each day and have access to everything we needed.

I didn't own a laptop in those days, so the only way to communicate with my family, friends and Late was through phone cards, postcards and letters. How times have changed! Nevertheless, we were there to train, and other than Fortress being a windy place, the training there has always been productive.

As it was an Olympic season, every other team had the same idea so we weren't alone in Fortress. The Canadian, US, Japanese and European teams were also training there, and before long the jump site became overcrowded. With so many people, we couldn't get a lot of jumps in, so after two weeks, Pete decided to break away from the pack. We drove to Apex Mountain in British Columbia, which had plenty of snow and was willing to accommodate us and build a jump site.

I had managed to add two more jumps on snow to my tool bag in Fortress, a Lay-Full and a Full-Full. I now only had two more tricks to do on snow for the first time before the World Cup competitions recommenced in early January. That meant I'd have three whole weeks to get my jumps done and polished before Christmas. In my mind, my preparation was going great and I was on track. It all seemed like it was going to be easy.

As a gymnast I had always been good at keeping to myself and focusing on what I needed to do. While training at Apex I wasn't concerned with how other people were jumping, but I was always in awe when training with the men. They seemed to have so much confidence and did their jumps so beautifully and effortlessly, and I tried to pick up on the techniques they used.

Aerials had given me a new pulse, a new hunger, and other than the painful knocks and bruises that came with the territory, I loved every part of it. I loved the travel, I loved the adrenalin rush before a jump, and the fear and uncertainty I felt when the wind was blowing or the conditions were tough. I loved the feeling of leaving the jump and being airborne, and most of all I loved the feeling of landing a jump and skiing away.

Every day and every jump needs to be assessed differently and half measures are met with painful consequences. We are human, after all, and we do make mistakes. Some mistakes you only make once, lesson learned. But in aerials, every day brings a new challenge and just when you've conquered one, another presents itself. I didn't know it, but I was about to enter some frustrating times. Times when I didn't love the sport and wanted to give in; tough times that seemed as if they would never end.

We had invited the Belarusian team to come with us to Apex because we needed to have more people to help build and maintain the site. They had accepted gladly as they also wanted to get away from the crowds and train in peace. The Belarusian team at the time included Alexei Grishin and Dmitri Dashinski, aka 'the Rockstars', who had finished first and second respectively at the 2001 World Championships. They were and still are my idols. They jumped with grace and ease, not to mention they went at least a metre higher than anyone else in the world. But it wasn't only their jumping that was special, it was their personalities—they were so relaxed, so confident, such good competitors, and at the same time they were really nice guys. True champions. Also in the team were Vassili Vorobiov, Dmitri Rak, Assoli Slivets—a rookie, like me—and Alla Tsuper, the current women's world number two. Then there was their entourage of support staff: coaches, a doctor and a physiotherapist. It was no wonder they were the strongest team in the world, and it was brilliant that they had come to jump with us.

We all stayed at a bed and breakfast place called the Saddleback Lodge, a warm, beautiful ski lodge that was run by a lovely family, and we had a great time there. It dumped with snow nearly every day, which is good for keeping the landing hill soft, but a real pain because we had to spend a couple of hours every day clearing it away from the in-run and jumps before we could start training.

One day when there was still quite a bit of fresh snow on the landing hill, I lost balance on one of my jumps, caught my ski tip in the soft snow then flipped over and cart wheeled down the landing hill. I didn't even know how to crash properly at that stage because I had hardly crashed any jumps, so I did the completely wrong thing. Instead of pulling my limbs in close to my body, I had them hanging out and I felt a really big tug on the inside of my left knee.

I had never injured my knee before, but I knew something wasn't right because it hurt straight away. We didn't have a physio during training camps, just at competitions, so I went to see a local one at the closest town in Penticton. After making his assessment, he told me I had a grade one strain of my medial ligament, the lowest level of damage, which wasn't as bad as I thought it would be. I just needed to rest it for about 10 days. I hadn't got up to my new trick yet, the Double Full-Full, and time was running out, so I cursed myself for the stupid mistake.

After about a week, the knee was still quite painful and swollen and didn't seem to be improving, despite me doing the exercises the physio had given me. After the 10 days I tried to jump again, but my knee just felt wobbly and was still hurting. Pete saw that I was uncomfortable, so we decided to give it more time. I went back to the physio and questioned his initial assessment, asking why it was taking longer to heal than he anticipated. He didn't have any answers other than telling me to give it more time and suggesting I get fitted for a knee brace. By that stage it was already coming up to Christmas, when we had planned a week off training so that Pete could spend time in Whistler with his wife, Annie (a fellow Aussie), and their two sons, Andrew and Hunter. Just like that, I had lost three crucial weeks.

****

Jac and I flew to Los Angeles for Christmas because Australia was too far to travel for such a short spell, and the cost came out of our own pockets because the OWI didn't cover breaks. I wasn't earning any money and survived off Mum and Dad, who generously footed the bill for my gallivanting. (Fortunately, the next year I was given a full scholarship and I started to have some success, so I was able to pay my way without relying on my parents.)

Jac had a friend in LA who let us stay in his apartment while he was out of town. It felt good to be in some warmer weather, away from the snow, and the apartment overlooked the beach in Santa Monica. We drove to Las Vegas to check out the Strip and down to Tijuana, just so we could say we'd been to Mexico. We spent Christmas Day in

Tijuana, eating in the local markets, shopping and driving around the city to see how people lived. I had no idea at the time how dangerous the place could be, but it sounded pretty cool to cross the border and be in 'Me-hi-co'.

We were back in Apex before the New Year, with only a week left of pre-season training before the World Cup circuit kicked off again at a place called Mont Tremblant in Quebec, Canada. I had a week to test my knee to see if it was more stable and although it wasn't perfect, it did feel a lot better, and with the brace on I was able to jump. I didn't have enough time to do any new jumps, but I did get enough training in to feel comfortable again on my knee after the three weeks off.

Mont Tremblant was a quaint place with awesome restaurants throughout, and is a pretty exciting ski resort for a rookie. I hadn't experienced the French-speaking part of Canada before—it was like a different country.

Bianca, our physiotherapist from Whistler, was also with us that week and I was very keen to have her check out my knee. According to her assessment I still had a grade one tear in my medial ligament, which meant that after three weeks of recovery, the initial strain must have been a lot worse than the original diagnosis of a grade one strain. That explained why the knee felt so unstable and why it was taking longer than expected to recover. I was glad to be in her capable hands.

The Tremblant competition was a double event and on the first day I finished ninth with 163.45 points, which was another Olympic qualifier. But it wasn't a perfect day. In training before the competition I got caught in some soft snow at the bottom of the landing and fell forward onto my shoulder. It was a direct, hard hit and I felt something crunch in my shoulder joint. Nevertheless, I shook it off and continued jumping. I think the adrenalin was pumping before the competition, masking some of the pain, and I competed well. At the end of the first day I only needed one more qualifying result, one more top ten placing.

The next day I woke up quite stiff and sore, but was still able to jump well and I finished sixth with 163.78 points. I had done Lay-Full and Full-Full both days and again, landed all my competition jumps. That was it—my qualification process was done. The top score on the second day was only 173.37 points, so to be only 10 points behind the winner was a great result for me. I was going to my first Olympics.

> Pete: 'Originally they did not want Lydia to return to Canada to ramp after the Mt Buller event, but after her performance I was able to convince them to have her return and continue on the path. Even then I still had to do a pretty hard sell to convince them that she could qualify for the Olympics and that she should continue on the World Cup circuit, and eventually they relented. She was able to get to a Full-Full for Tremblant, and with two more top 10s the deal was pretty much done. It was interesting because everyone along the way kept thinking that it was a fluke—that sooner or later she would fold—but, as with every other stage of her career, when the pressure was on she always did well.'

Mum and Dad were ecstatic when I told them I had qualified for the Games, and I'm sure they were surprised I had got so far in such a short time. I felt excited, but it didn't seem like a surprise for me and it had actually seemed fairly easy. I was just annoyed that I had another setback with my knee that put me behind schedule with my jumps, and I was worried about my shoulder, which had pulled up really sore after two days of competition.

We went out to celebrate that night. Back in those days, there was always a World Cup party at the end of each event, put on by the event's organising committee; everyone would go, and as rookies, there was no way that Liz and I were going to miss out on any fun. But on our way to the party I slipped and smacked my head on an icy concrete step. I'll never forget the sound—it was like stabbing an ice pick into an ice block, and my friends in front of me heard it and rushed to my side.

I had my hand clutched to my head, and when I pulled it away, it was covered in blood. Liz was the first to have a look, and said, 'Lyd, you've split your bloody head open.' Oh, great! Bianca was already at the bar, so I decided to go there anyway to see if she could check me out. Once

I found her we headed for the toilets so she could examine my head under good light. It didn't take long for the word to spread around, and in no time the toilets were full of athletes wanting to have a peak at my split head, their grubby bar hands parting my hair to get a glimpse.

Bianca said I definitely needed stitches, but the resort doctor had already gone home for the night and, to be honest, she was in no state to be doing any stitching up herself. So we decided to leave it be and I stayed on to celebrate in the bar. By the end of the night, most people had my blood on their shirts because I had to show them my head. It was a good night and I enjoyed it in true rookie fashion. The next day I woke up with my head stuck to the pillow because the blood had pooled and dried overnight. I had a splitting headache and I felt very ordinary. I definitely shouldn't have been drinking that night and I could still feel the big lump on the back of my head. I really did need stitches, but we were having such a good time and now it was too late.

The following day, Monday, was a travel day as usual, and we departed for Lake Placid, New York, a four-hour drive. I was not in great form. I had banged up my shoulder and I had an egg on my head, not to mention a throbbing hangover. I felt like crap. The only positive was that I'd be reuniting with Late because the mogul skiers were competing in Lake Placid too.

****

After Mt Buller, Late and I had decided that we wanted to be a couple. We knew we were entering a long distance relationship but we still wanted to give it a go. That had been in September, it was now January, and we hadn't met up at all for more than three months.

Each time we saw each other our bond grew stronger, but because of our training schedules we couldn't be together all the time. So for me, it was like turning off the hot tap when we went our separate ways and replacing it with the cold tap to try to block him out and keep focused on aerials. That sounds cold, but it was the only way I was going to be able to function as an athlete and not get too upset about being apart. It wasn't easy but that's what I had to do.

Late was not having a good season and had missed qualifying for the Finnish Olympic team for Salt Lake. He had all the runs and jumps in training, but just wasn't able to get it together in competition. The Finnish team was very strong, so one off day could be costly—and he had a series of them.

I didn't know Late during his prime, but Jacqui did and she told me how good he was before he got injured. In fact, the Finnish men's mogul team had a lot of phenomenal skiers and is still the only team ever to clean sweep at a World Championship event. At the 1999 Worlds, Janne Lahtela, arguably the best mogul skier of all time, was first, Late second, and teammate Sami Mustonen third. That year, Janne and Late finished number one and two respectively on the World Cup tour. Late and his team were on fire. They dominated.

The following year, 2000, Late was leading the World Cup grand prix, when he suffered a terrible head injury which landed him in a hospital in Japan for a couple of weeks. Mogul skiers didn't wear helmets back in those days, and when he came off a jump unbalanced and crashed, he smacked his head directly on an icy mogul. He was knocked unconscious for 15 minutes and doesn't remember a thing about being in Japan.

Three weeks later he went to compete at the Goodwill Games in Lake Placid. He rode the lift up the mountain and put on his skis and headed for the mogul course. He skied a few metres before he fell over. He had lost his motor control and didn't know how to ski any more! He told his coach, Marko, and they slowly snow ploughed together down the mountain. His season was put on hold and he flew back to Finland to go through a series of tests with a neurologist, who determined that he had no permanent damage, but that his motor control had been affected.

'Imagine your brain as a deck of cards. All the cards are there, but they are shuffled and we need to work on getting them back in order,' the neurologist said.

Late worked through the rehabilitation and fought very hard to come back, which he did. Two months later, he made it back for the World Cup final, the last event for the season, and finished fourth. But even then, he didn't feel right and didn't feel like he was back to his normal form.

ONE BATTERED ROOKIE

Despite the injury and the events he missed that season, Late still finished third in the world on the overall standings. But he never skied as fast and was never the same skier after that. Skiing in a cross-country event in Finland a couple of months later, he wrapped his knee around a control gate and ripped it to shreds. He had already torn his anterior cruciate ligament (ACL) years before, but was one of the fortunate skiers with stable joints who could continue to ski without it. This time he really finished the job. His knee joint basically did a 180-degree turn. He tore everything and had the next season off to continue his rehabilitation.

One of Late's good friends, Jussi Kinnunen, aka 'Legs', was scheduled to coach some Australian development mogul skiers in Silver Star during the winter. But Legs had an accident and, ironically, broke his leg. The injury was so severe he needed surgery to insert a titanium rod into his tibia. He wasn't able to go to Silver Star to coach, of course, so he asked Late to take over the job. That was the series of events that brought us together.

Late was devastated when he didn't make the Finnish team for Salt Lake. At the 1998 Olympics, in Nagano, Japan, he was a rookie and finished fifth. He was still a good skier but he was no longer at his peak thanks to those injuries. I should have taken some lessons away from his experiences and learned to take injuries seriously, but I thought I was invincible back then. Nothing was going to stop me. I didn't understand at the time what he had actually gone through to get back on skis. 'What do you mean? Just ski faster!' He never really talked about it, and he never used it as an excuse, he just kept trying to get better.

I suppose I did take away the message that opportunities don't last forever, and in my mind that translated into making the most of every opportunity. I didn't want to be good enough for only one week at the top, I wanted to know what it was like to dominate and I was going to work hard to make sure I got there. I was not going to leave anything to chance.

****

As a member of the Olympic team, I had extra things I needed to do when I arrived at Lake Placid, such as getting measured for the uniform and having a medical examination. Our Olympic team doctor suggested I get a flu shot, so I did, and being run down, I got the flu. I was really under the weather. Not only did my shoulder feel terrible, my head hurt, especially when I put my helmet on thanks to the egg on my head. Now I also had the flu.

Everything fell to pieces that week. It was just shocking. In fact, the whole lead-up to the Olympics from Mont Tremblant onwards was horrible. My ligament strain was now improving thanks to physio treatment and a knee brace, but my shoulder was a different story. I didn't have a scan so it was difficult to know exactly what was wrong, but I was in a lot of pain and found it hard to hold my arm up on the take-off due to the force of the jump. It would drop to the side on take-off and I started going crooked off the jump. Crooked in the air is not a good thing because it meant I was also twisted coming into the landing. Very quickly, my jumping took a turn for the worse— I went from being this young gun who landed everything to a crooked rookie who could no longer control her body. I felt like I couldn't jump properly and I also started to struggle with my landings because I was coming into them crooked with all the weight on my right leg.

I lost my confidence. Even basic doubles became scary because I wasn't sure what was going to happen off the jump. For the first time ever I couldn't control my body. I thought it might be because I had the flu and perhaps my balance was out of whack, but it wasn't the case. I didn't make finals that week and my results plummeted to 23rd and 15th in the two events.

My nightmare continued for the next World Cup in Whistler where again I didn't make the finals. Up to that point, I was pretty tolerant of pain, but this was about an eight out of 10. Because I was landing crooked, my right side started to get jammed up and sore, and that was the beginning of what I called my 'right-side-itis'. All of a sudden, I was scared to jump and in pain. I wasn't having a good time or enjoying jumping. The Olympics were fast approaching, I hadn't done my new trick yet and time was running out. I couldn't understand why everything turned so bad for me. I went from feeling invincible and able to handle anything thrown at me to being a scared rabbit.

We stayed on at Whistler for another week to train before heading to Salt Lake City. We tried everything with my shoulder, including taping it various ways, but nothing seemed to help. If anything, it kept on getting worse. Arms are so important in aerials, and as I said earlier, they are the levers that help you spin and twist. The fact that I wasn't able to hold my arm up against the pressure of the jump was really bad.

Nevertheless, we decided that I needed to start doing my new tricks. First we'd start with a Double Full-Tuck—a double twist in the first flip and a simple tuck for the second. For that trick I had adopted a take-off technique founded by American aerial legend, Eric Bergoust, which meant that you took off from the jump with one arm up and one arm down. When you left the jump, you'd switch your arms like a scissor action to generate twist momentum and then wrap them close into your body to speed up the twist and complete the double twist. Anyway, it meant I could take off with my sore arm down by my side instead of holding it as I went up the jump and then swing it up as I left the jump. Bingo! I could go straight. It was a more difficult jump but it worked for me with my shoulder injury. Pete and I changed the attack from that point, doing less of the jumps that I was going really crooked on and concentrating on jumps I could do straight.

I did a bunch of Double Full-Tucks that week but ran out of time to attempt a Double Full-Full. I felt more at ease, though, knowing that it would be the same take-off and all I needed to do was add an extra twist in the second flip.

> *Pete: 'Honestly, I don't remember how crooked she was jumping leading into the Olympics, all I remember was how determined she was not to let anything get in her way. She had a pretty tough January but that was to be expected with the number of events we had in such a short period of time, and given how little experience she'd had with her tricks. But she was, and still is, one tough customer—nothing was going to stop her.'*

The World Cup season was over and the Olympics would be the final event of the season. Alla Tsuper had been rock solid all year and deservedly took out the World Cup title. Jacqui Cooper was second, and it looked like it was going to be a battle between them for Olympic glory. Alla didn't have the degree of difficulty that Jacqui had on the Triple, but she was consistent and had excellent form in the air.

Alisa Camplin also had a rocky preparation leading into Salt Lake 2002. She, too, had strained a ligament in her knee and then bruised her heels when she fell short on a jump and landed on the knoll. American Emily Cook had the same misfortune at the Lake Placid event, but actually shattered her heels. She was out of the Salt Lake Olympics, and needed surgery to pin her heels and feet back together. It took her years to come back from that, and even now she gets shooting pain through her heels. It can always be worse, I suppose.

After missing some events, Alisa was back jumping in Whistler. Of the World Cup team, Alisa, Jacqui and I had qualified, but Shannon Leotta had missed out. So it was now time to depart for another new place, Salt Lake City. With all the hype that surrounds an Olympics, it was impossible to not get excited. I was going to be an Olympian at last.

CHAPTER 6

SALT LAKE 2002

In February 2002 we settled into the Salt Lake Olympic Village, with security especially tight following the 9/11 attack in the USA a few months earlier. On arrival, the most exciting part by far was receiving our suitcases full of Australian uniforms and visiting the big food tent that had every cuisine you could possibly desire. Jac and I spent the day exploring the village and everything it had to offer, including free haircuts, manicures and pedicures, the works. Mum and Dad had also arrived from Australia, and I hadn't seen them since September, so it was nice to have them there and to show them around the athlete village and fill them in on what had been happening for the past five months.

The slogan for the 2002 Olympic Winter Games was 'Light the fire within'. At first I thought it was a strange slogan—you'd hope that your 'fire within' was already lit before you showed up to the Olympics in the first place. My 'fire within' had been lit since the day I was born. There's no explanation for why I desire to do the things I do or why I want to push my limits. I just do. I want to.

Since I started aerial skiing I have constantly pushed my limits to overcome fear, pain and fatigue, and just to beat the odds. My training has been full of courage, persistence, spontaneity and drive and I have wanted to make every day a challenge for myself. I'm certain there wouldn't have been many people in the world willing to accept the challenges and the risks that I had to take to get to the Olympics. But I wanted to and I did.

I had heard from so many athletes that marching in the opening ceremony was an amazing experience, something I'd never forget. I didn't really know what to expect, or how I'd feel when I marched into the stadium, led by our flag bearer, mogul skier and friend, Adrian Costa. But I know it didn't impact on me the way people said it would. It was an amazing show but I wasn't swept up in the emotion or hype created by the opening ceremony. I simply didn't allow it. I was totally focused and all I remember thinking about was the competition and the reason why I was there: to perform to the best of my ability.

'Light the fire within' made more sense to me as the Games progressed. One of the best things about the Olympics is the athletes and their stories, which give you hope and really inspire you to go on— stories of overcoming adversity and extreme odds, stories of persistence and courage, and stories of triumph after failed attempts. There are so many athletes competing at an Olympic Games, but so few get to go home with a medal. Sometimes the favourite doesn't win.

Steven Bradbury had a great story to tell after Salt Lake 2002. While I was on the massage table, Steven cruised across the line to win Australia's first ever Winter Olympic gold medal. Some say it was a fluke, but if you knew his story you'd realise he was very deserving of that medal. He put himself in a position to be in the final that day, which was no fluke. He had dedicated his life to speed skating and overcame life-threatening injuries to keep chasing his dream of one day winning an Olympic gold medal. He wasn't the favourite, but he was in the final with as much right to win as his competitors and, at the Olympics, expect the unexpected. It was wonderful to see him win and finish his career on the ultimate high. It was amazing to see how Steve's life changed after winning that medal and I wanted my life to change like that, too. He definitely added fuel to my 'fire within' that day.

I had definitely chosen a difficult road to get to the Games. Not many people thought I'd make it, and really, I'd come from nowhere. All that mattered was that my coaches believed in me and I believed in myself. If I didn't, I wouldn't have taken the risks that I did—risks that had left my body a complete mess.

SALT LAKE 2002

My shoulder was the culprit and I've already spoken about it sending me crooked off the jump and crooked into the landing. It made landing jumps even more difficult and the whole situation really tampered with my confidence. The right side of my body took a pounding and I ached from my shoulder down through my leg. After a few jumps, I'd get a dead leg. It wasn't good. Instead of the fun, exciting sport that I had fallen in love with, I started associating aerials with pain. I was miserable, but I had made it to the Olympics and I wasn't about to back down now—I had to dig deep for another two weeks.

We started training in the second week of the Olympics—aerials is always in the second week—so we moved out of the athlete village and into sub-site accommodation in Deer Valley, closer to our freestyle skiing venue than Salt Lake City and away from the distraction of the main village. Our team had a personal chef who cooked whatever we wanted, Bianca was our physio, and Jac and I were sharing a condo, which we were happy about.

Training got off to a rocky start for me. I thought the short break that week would have settled my body down a bit, but it hadn't and I was still very crooked on my jumps. It really affected my mood and my confidence.

> *Diary entry: 'I was standing at the top of the in-run today about to go, not concentrating, not fired up. I was just hurting and I felt powerless. Pete also knew I wasn't myself, and I think the fact that I knew he detected weakness in me was also tampering with my confidence.'*

I was at a low, I felt underprepared and I still hadn't attempted a Double Full-Full. I was cutting training short because I was frustrated and scared because I was going so crooked. On one jump, I landed crooked and started to ski off to the side. I hit some crusty snow in the area outside the landing zone, lost control and crashed into the fence. I did a double front flip over it and my equipment exploded off me: one ski was buried under the fence and the other was hurled over the other side of the landing zone. My glasses were in pieces and my lenses scattered in opposite directions. My white helmet had a blue rope burn on it from the fence. I lay on the snow for a moment and took stock of my body. Surprisingly, I had survived the crash with no additional injuries.

Pete was down in a flash and just shook his head at me in disbelief. 'What are you doing, girl?' It was a spectacular crash, one that we still laugh about today. It was played over and over again on TV during the Olympics as one of the 'best crashes'. But at the time, I was embarrassed and helpless. I picked myself up, shook myself off and continued jumping. The rest of the athletes couldn't believe that I had done a double front flip over the side fence and that I had come up for more jumping. I'm pretty sure they thought I was nuts.

Just when things couldn't get worse, disaster struck four days before the qualifying round. I remember that day so clearly. It was sunny and I was having a real shocker of a day. I had another spectacular crash and made it onto the 'best crashes' highlights again. I was doing a Double Full-Tuck, which we decided to do as my first jump because I didn't go crooked on it, but I gave it too much rotation on the take-off, and instead of doing two flips I did three and landed flat on my stomach. I picked myself up yet again and tried a couple more jumps but decided to finish training early. I was frustrated; my shoulder ached, my hip and back were sore, and I had a dead leg. Then the lift broke down.

It took about 20 minutes to get the lift working again, and in that time the sun went behind the clouds and the whole jump site was in the shade. The in-run and jumps hardened up and after the break, Jacqui was cleared to jump. She didn't account for the change in conditions and came into the jump much too fast. She crashed onto her back, tumbling and spinning down the landing hill. I'll never forget her scream. I dropped to my knees in disbelief as I watched her clutching her knee in agony. She had blown it to pieces and was out of the Olympics. That was a huge shock. She was my teammate, she had taken me under her wing, and we'd been training with each other the whole year. All expectation was on her—it was meant to be her Olympics, but now she had crashed and it was over. I'm sure a few competitors were rubbing their hands together thinking, 'That's the favourite out of the way,' but my reaction was utter shock and disbelief that the worst possible thing could happen at the worst possible time.

> Diary entry: 'Pete and I were a mess. As Jac was taken away in the ambulance, we hugged each other tight and just cried and cried. I'll never forget that, it was horrible.'

I went back to the condo to pack Jacqui a bag and then went to meet her at the hospital in the athlete village. From the waiting room I called Late to tell him what had happened. He was still on a high from watching his teammate Janne Lahtela take out gold in the men's moguls, but he was sad for Jac and aware that I was upset and struggling. That night I stayed with Jac in a room in the village. She cried herself to sleep, and I was glad I was there for her. The fact that the Olympics were occurring around me and that I had to compete in four days time seemed irrelevant.

When I think about it now, I realise I put my whole Olympic debut on hold to comfort a friend. I didn't even think twice, I just did it. I'm glad I did, it showed loyalty, friendship and camaraderie, all things that are very important to me. I was a bit of a mess, though, and it wasn't just Jac's knee I was dealing with, it was a combination of stresses. It was all too much. But it made me realise that things could always be worse. Sure, I was having a tough time with my injuries and jumps, but at least I could still compete.

The next day, I went back to our sub-site accommodation in Deer Valley and my training was disastrous. I couldn't concentrate. I was tired and emotionally drained. What made it worse was that I knew people had lost confidence in me. With two training days to go before qualifying, I knew that at some stage I was going to have to come around. We didn't have a sports psychologist back then, so no one else was going to help my mental state except myself.

> Diary entry: 'I knew it was time to pull myself together—I had to toughen up and pull through. I went to my room with the intention to 'fix' myself up and put on the theme from Rocky III, Eye of the Tiger, an all-time favourite, especially when the chips are down. I sat in front of the mirror and stared strong and close into my eyes. They

were dull and had lost their spark—the fire, like my dreams and desires, had been blinded by the events that I had to deal with, and I was determined to find them and be back to normal. I stared and stared for hours, just talking to myself, trying to find myself. I was telling myself that no one wanted to succeed as much as I did, no one deserved it as much as I did. Eventually, I found my spark and reminded myself that I was there to do my job, the best I could.'

I trained much better over the next couple of days. I was still crooked off the jump, but I just accepted that and tried to land as many jumps as I could. I wasn't prepared to throw away my first Olympics due to a series of events or excuses.

The qualification round was on the morning of February 16 and I was as ready as I was going to be. In the final couple of days leading into the qualifying, I had kept to myself and tried to block out everything else that was happening around me. With Jacqui down in the athlete village, I had the condo to myself and it helped to be alone.

I chose to do a Double Full-Tuck and a Full-Full for the qualification jumps. These were my best jumps at the time because I was going the straightest off the jump and I could land them. I scored 82.21 points for my Full-Full, which was not a great score, but I'd had a wobble on my landing. I then did a Double Full-Tuck, which has a higher degree of difficulty than a Full-Full, and scored 83.85. I had a really good landing and it was interesting to see how the judges scored it as it was an unusual jump and I was the only person competing it at the time. Since I was third on the start list, I had to wait for the rest of the field to jump before I knew if I was in the top 12. It was an agonising wait, and as competitors came down and scored higher points than me, they bumped me further down the list.

In the end I qualified 10th, a result beyond the expectations of the people around me. I was going to be in the Olympic final. My parents were so happy for me; Jac was there in the crowd on crutches and she was happy too, but it must have been hell for her to watch from the grandstand with a busted knee.

Evelyne Leu from Switzerland easily won the qualifying doing triples with 203.16 points, a new world record. Alisa was second with 183.66, and Alla Tsuper (ranked number one at the time and a clear favourite after Jacqui's demise) was third with 181.37.

> *Pete: 'I remember the crashes at Salt Lake City, including the 'famous' one, but I most remember the absolute clarity and confidence that I had in both Lydia and Jac. I knew we had done all the right things and I knew we were well prepared and that both Lydia and Jacqui believed that too. I think that was what made Jac's injury so devastating— I knew she was a really good chance and the injury had taken that away from her. For Lydia, though, anything was still possible and, as much as Jac's injury was shattering, it only cleared my resolve on what was possible for Lydia. I knew that it was going to take more to qualify Lydia for finals and that we most likely needed the Double Full-Tuck to assist in the 'degree of difficulty' aspect, and we had a lot to do in a very short period of time. That meant we had to keep pushing through training, which was not the normal approach for a peaking athlete, but Lydia was so used to the heavy volumes from what we had done in training that I knew she could handle the load and the challenge. She did her first Double Full-Tuck in competition and she made the final in style.'*

After qualifications, we went back to the condo and Pete and I discussed our plan of attack for the final. We had one more training day before the final and we both decided there was nothing to lose—if the weather permitted, we would go out and train and do the new trick, a Double Full-Full. We went over the video of my training jumps on water to confirm that the trick was good and that I wouldn't have any trouble doing it on snow. I was exhausted and would have loved a rest day, but I knew it was the right decision.

The next day it was quite windy and speeds were hard to read, but I was on a mission to do the new trick. After a few warm-up jumps I went for it. I did three that day. I completed the actual trick successfully in the air, but on all of them, I had too much speed and backslapped them. Nonetheless, I had done it and I was ready to compete it in the finals.

****

The Olympic final was my eighth day in a row of jumping, which is uncommon in my sport. I was so exhausted mentally and beaten up physically, but it was Olympic final day and I wasn't going to give in to being tired. In my eyes, I was jumping to win and would give it everything I had left.

I was focused and alert. I arrived at the athlete tent where everyone goes to prepare, organised my gear (I had spare boots which I left there) and closely observed all my competitors. Alisa had her headphones on and was bopping up and down to music, playing a card game by herself. I'm pretty sure she was either trying to distract herself from what was about to happen or wanted to act as though she was having a great time, oblivious to what was going on around her. Whatever the case, she did look focused and her training had been great.

Training commenced, and on my second jump I again went really crooked and headed for the fence. This time I crashed and skidded into it and one of my skis went flying through the air over another fence.

> *Diary entry: 'I was so embarrassed and angry. Here I was in the Olympic final, for God's sake, and I'm losing my skis during practice!'*

I collected the ski and noticed I had broken the binding on it. Thankfully I had a back-up pair, so I grabbed those and continued jumping. I got to the Double Full-Full, the new trick, and did two in practice, landing the second perfectly.

It was all coming together. Training had finished and it was time for the showcase, where they get all the athletes in the final to greet the crowd by skiing down the landing hill in the order they will jump.

Apart from the ski over the fence incident, training had gone well. I had taken some painkillers for my shoulder and back and felt as good as I was going to feel.

> Diary entry: 'I was really zoned in. I was very composed. My breathing was calm as I went through the jumps in my head.'

My first jump was the Double Full-Full, which by that stage I had dubbed the 'Hail Mary', only because I had done it for the first time the day before and was hoping I was going to be able to pull it off. Once I was in the start gate I bent down to tighten my boots and a cable snapped on my buckle. I have always jumped in a Raichle boot (now known as Full Tilt) and before that day I had never snapped a cable. That's the Olympics: expect the unexpected. There was nothing I could do, as my name was being announced to jump. I refocused and went. I heard Pete call me in the air to stretch but I didn't react in time. I was probably too focused on getting the trick done rather than actually feeling how high I was. I landed it, but had a wobble on landing and scored 84.49. The landing had cost me, and even though I was on my feet, I was disappointed.

Pete raced to the athlete tent in between jumps to get spare parts for my boots. (Since then I always keep them with me in my backpack!) My final jump was a Full-Full. I was a little slow coming into the jump so I had to pull it in for the landing. I scored 84.89 for a total of 169.38 points and I finished eighth in the Olympic final. I obviously knew I could have done both jumps better, but at the same time I was happy I landed two of them under pressure in my first year of competing. It was also my first year doing double somersaults.

Everyone was happy and I had exceeded all expectations. I was happy too, especially because it was all over, but I knew I hadn't competed to my best.

Evelyne Leu, the favourite after the qualification round, unexpectedly crashed out and so did world number one, Alla Tsuper. Alisa put down two great jumps to take the gold medal, which was the first win of her career and a great result for Australia. Jacqui had flown home already and woke up to the news on the operating table.

Alisa's progress was amazing. I had come from nowhere to make the finals, but she really had come from below the radar to win. As well as her new coach, she had also hired a sports psychologist, Barbara Meyer, and from then on she became a different athlete. It was an impressive transformation, but she needed to break out of the shadows to be able to do it. From that point on, she flourished.

> *Pete: 'Because we were at the Olympic Games, Lydia and I knew we had to have a go, so the day after qualifying and the day before the finals we headed off to do her first Double-Full-Fulls on snow, and again she was unshakable. The night before I remember lying in bed and hoping she was going to be able to sleep. I was thinking of how far she had come and how meticulous the journey had been, and feeling fully confident that anything was possible in the final. She did a Double-Full-Full for the first jump and nailed it and then following up with the second really strong jump, I remember being on the knoll afterwards and being so proud of her. I can honestly say that I count what we were able to achieve over that time as one of my single greatest coaching highlights, one of the milestones that gave me the greatest sense of accomplishment.'*

It wasn't until after our event that I could really enjoy the Olympics, as well as the parties and the great things Olympic athletes have access to. I moved from our sub-site accommodation in Deer Valley down to the athlete village in Salt Lake City to be reunited with the rest of the Australian team. That was when the fun started and we partied every night. I don't know where I got my energy from, but I put it down to 24/7 McDonalds and some tasty beverages. It had been a mammoth year; it was a nice feeling for it to all be over, and my body was especially thankful. The closing ceremony on February 24 was definitely a highlight for me. All the athletes from different countries mingled with one another centre stage, and it was so much more relaxed than the opening ceremony. Or maybe I was just more relaxed.

Before I could fly home I needed to go back to our base in Whistler to pack up all the belongings I had left behind after the summer and to collect Jac's things. Liz was there too and it was great to be reunited with her. She had watched the Games on TV. It would have been great to have her there competing with me, but I knew that the 2002 Olympics just wasn't in her game plan. She had opted for the more sensible road, her sights set on the 2006 Olympics.

I was so exhausted I slept for 18 hours straight. The next day I headed for Vancouver airport with Michael Kennedy, our team manager, and 11 bags to check in! At the check-in counter the airline clerk asked for my ticket. I said I had an electronic ticket, but she told me I'd been issued with a paper ticket, which I would need to produce if I wanted to fly. I had no idea where it might be, although I vaguely remembered throwing out what I thought were some old ticket stubs. Great! There I was trying to check in with 11 bags and no ticket. Miraculously, she let me through with no extra charges and I arrived in Melbourne, not with a normal luggage cart but two cargo trolleys. It was good to be home. My family and friends were there to greet me, holding up signs when I arrived. They were so proud of me.

> *Diary entry: 'My Olympic experience didn't turn out to be what I had expected or what I had envisioned as a little girl. It was only afterwards in reflection that I realised the enormity of the Olympic Games and what I had achieved in such a small time. But at the Olympics, I was in the moment—too focused on what I needed to do to absorb other details and experiences. My first Olympic experience was indeed that: an experience. I really put my body on the line to get there and I exceeded people's expectations. But I left there with a hunger. Next time, I'll be ready. If I was able to get as far as I did in one year, imagine what I could do in four years' time. That's how I felt . . . I can be so much better.'*

CHAPTER 7

RIGHT-SIDE-ITIS

I walked away from Salt Lake City battered and bruised. As soon as I arrived home I had to have a shoulder operation and I was in really bad shape physically. It all started with the strained ligament in my knee and that was followed by the shoulder injury, which then manifested itself into related injuries down my right side, leg, hip and spine. I continued to refer to it as 'right-side-itis'.

I figured fixing the shoulder would make everything else better. I was naive, I suppose, and didn't realise the damage I had done. I had a torn rotator cuff tendon and a bad slap lesion, which is a tear in the inner capsule of the shoulder joint. It had been badly bashed up and wasn't going to be an easy fix in itself. Even though I'd had injuries before, I'd never needed surgery or anything that severe, so this was a whole new experience. It was quite painful after surgery. The shoulder is not an easy joint to work with and the rehab is tedious; there are a lot of muscles surrounding the joint and it's not the most stable of joints at the best of times.

No one really knew how much pain I was in during my Olympic campaign because I just battled through it. When I told some of my friends on tour that I had to have surgery on my shoulder, most were surprised because I didn't let on how bad it was. At least that explained why I couldn't hold my arm up off the jump.

RIGHT-SIDE-ITIS

> *Geoff: 'I thought that the big risk of Lydia going full blast to qualify for the 2002 Olympics, as we all agreed, was that she would begin an injury cycle by pushing hard so early. Her maximum intensity in training and competition performance made it possible for incredible early results, such as eighth at the Olympics in 2002, then being ranked second in her first full season of the World Cup. But there was a cost.'*

Normally we'd be back into water ramping at the start of June, but I had the surgery in March right after the Olympics and couldn't start training again until mid-July. Not a big deal, or so I thought.

The first 10 days after the surgery had been the worst. After that I could start to lift my arm and eventually got it above my ear. With the exercises it was recovering fast, and by the time I arrived in Finland to spend some of my enforced lay-off with Late it was starting to feel quite good. That was perhaps the only upside to the injury. Little did I know that during the next three years I'd keep re-injuring it and it would continue to plague me and interfere with my jumping—not to the point where I needed surgery, but enough to need rest and time out. After re-injuring it a few times, I started to learn how to manage it better.

Late was based in Rovaniemi, which is up above the Arctic Circle in the Lapland region of Finland. He'd been living there since he was 15 when he joined a winter sports school. This was my first time to Finland and it was a culture shock. Coming from multicultural Melbourne, I was surprised to notice that with my dark hair and dark skin I stuck out like a sore thumb. People actually stared at me, knowing I was a foreigner. It was the first time I really noticed I was from a totally different culture and world to Late. It didn't worry me though, I just thought it was funny—I wanted to tell people they should see the rest of my family.

Meeting Late's family was a bit intimidating and I was nervous. His parents have a beautiful home about an hour north of Helsinki in a place called Hattula. Late has one brother called Kalle, and let's just say he's a colourful and interesting character. When we first started dating Late didn't really talk about him much, but eventually stories started to come out about his brother's wild adventures and the fact that he has a mental disorder that requires medication. The thing about Kalle is that he's exceptionally smart, borderline genius, but to put it mildly he has no filter. Whatever he thinks, he says, so it was a pretty funny experience to finally meet him. The first thing he said to me as he shook my hand, before he even said hi, was, 'I thought you would be blonde,' in that accent the Finns have.

Late's parents Leena and Erkki were lovely from the beginning and welcomed me warmly into their home. Generally speaking, Finns are quite reserved by nature—until they have a drink and then they all open up a little. Leena is different, though. Her English is perfect, she is talkative and sociable and she reminded me immediately of my mum. Leena was a very successful businesswoman in Finland, a head buyer for Stockmann, which is a big department store chain like Myer is in Australia. His dad, Erkki, is hilarious, a typical Finn. He likes the same things and isn't a fan of change—he only eats one type of mustard, his butter needs to be salted and hard so that he can cut it like cheese, he only drives John Deere tractors, loves everything RM Williams, and he's been drinking the same Argentinean Malbec wine since the day I arrived in Finland 10 years ago. He has two sausages with mustard and potatoes for lunch every day and doesn't like chicken. He also had a pretty good career as a radiologist in Helsinki before they moved to the family farm where he now breeds Hereford cattle. Doctor turned farmer, go figure! Erkki and Leena are polar opposites in that she's really open-minded, loves trying new things, and he's set in his ways and as stubborn as they come.

We stayed with Leena and Erkki first and then went to stay in Late's apartment in Rovaniemi. That was almost a deal-breaker for me. I know how boys can be because I've lived with three of them plus my dad, but Mum's a bit of a clean freak so we've always had a clean house. But this apartment was pretty disgusting. It was a bachelor pad—the TV and sound system were top of the range, but there were dishes everywhere. His roommate, Mikko Patrikainen, was a character and didn't mind his surroundings. Late obviously didn't mind either.

I said, 'If you want me to stay here, I'm going to have to clean up first.' So I spent a day cleaning and scrubbing. I felt better for it and I doubt the boys had seen it that clean before. It wasn't great for my shoulder, but the trade-off was that Mikko was studying to be a physiotherapist—he's now the national team physio for Finland—and so he occasionally treated my shoulder. Shoulder rehabilitation is quite finicky, and involves extensive resistance exercises to strengthen the individual muscles surrounding the joint.

Late and I went to the sports centre in Rovaniemi every day to train. It's a massive complex, all undercover, with running tracks, sand pits, full gyms, a gymnastics hall with trampolines and pits and so much fun equipment. It's a sport Mecca, and as with most things in Finland, you just pay your entry fee, go in and do whatever you want. At that stage I was accustomed to living in North America where you need a waiver for everything, but there were no over-the-top disclaimers or waivers in Finland—if you do something stupid, that's your responsibility. As I said, it is a different kind of place.

I was 20, so I wasn't sure if a relationship with Late was going to work forever, but I liked being around him and we got along really well. Obviously the opportunity to spend a lot of time with him instead of just short bursts here and there was a bonus. It was the first time we enjoyed a long stretch together, about eight weeks, initially in Finland and then on a trip to Thailand. It was a good time.

Life was pretty easy for me back in those days. Aside from the injury, I was travelling, I had a boyfriend, I was managing my studies and I really didn't have a care in the world. I even had my first legitimate sponsor, Bollé, which has been a great supporter of mine for the past decade and made my life much easier. It was a great lifestyle for a 20-year-old, because I didn't have any responsibilities other than to jump and get my body and mind right.

Life's a bit more serious nowadays, but at that time it was unreal. Late and I used to joke about it, and when we'd wake up each morning we'd say, 'Every day is a holiday.' We both loved what we were doing.

But when our holiday was over we parted again. I was heading to Park City, Utah, for water ramp training and Late was going to Mt Buller to train and coach. We would rendezvous at Buller in August when I arrived for the World Cups that would kick off the 2002/03 season.

In the meantime, significant changes were occurring in our program, which usually happens after the Olympics. Pete was no longer my coach, and I was sad about that because I really loved him and it was going to be a big adjustment. We'd spent so much time with each other he'd almost become a father figure for me while we were on the road, and he had so much coaching experience in the sport. Jacqui was out injured from her crash in Salt Lake City and Alisa had won gold, so the OWI hired her coach, Todd Ossian, as head coach and fired Pete. Obviously, it would have been too costly to keep both coaches on the books, so Pete was out and Todd was the man. As a rookie along with the rest of the juniors, I didn't have a say in the matter. I was sad to lose Pete, but at the same time, I knew that Todd was a great coach and we would be fine with him.

> *Pete: 'It was difficult when I was replaced in a number of ways. Firstly, I knew that I had done all that I could and more to make the program the best it could be and I felt disappointed. I had been very loyal to the program (the US came to me in the fall of 2000 and offered their head coaching job, but I turned it down because I had a team and I could not leave my girls), even to the point of operating the parallel programs in the face of significantly difficult team dynamics. I knew I had been fully committed and the outcome was very good. I think probably the biggest disappointment was knowing that I was not going to have the opportunity to keep on the path with Lydia. I knew there was something special inside Lydia, something that inspired me as a coach and that this was only the beginning for her. I remember very clearly discussing with OWI staff, and many others subsequently, that given time she would be able to do tricks that the guys do, that she would be able to do a Lay-Double Full-Full, and that I could see her doing a Double-Full-Full*

and a Full-Double Full-Full, only to be told that this was not the best path for her. I guess her audacity eventually proved them wrong and me right.'

I didn't really know Todd well enough to make a judgement on whether I liked him or not and I didn't know if he really wanted to work with me or if it was just a job. I didn't even know if he actually liked me. We'd barely communicated before he took on the head coach job, so it was a bit strange at first.

It turned out that he was a fantastic, enthusiastic coach with fresh energy and we got along straight away. That northern summer season of 2002 Alisa was dating Canadian aerialist Steve Omischl and training at Lake Placid with the Canadian team so she could be with him. That left Todd to coach Liz, Bree, Lainie and me. Bree and Lainie were a year behind Liz and me, and were at the stage where they were ready to start jumping on the water ramps.

The four of us stayed together in a tiny, grotty apartment but we really had great relationships and got along well so there was no cattiness. Two more gymnasts coming into the aerials program from the same gymnastics culture with a similar mindset was a blessing to us. Everyone was cooperating and working together and it was a proper functioning team. We respected each other and treated each other as equals. We had so much fun together and I have great memories from that summer.

****

While the team dynamics were great, it was one of the toughest summers ever for me both physically and mentally. I'd come from being an athlete who could always fix the problem to one who had no answers. When I got back into training my shoulder felt quite good and I could hold my right arm in the air, but my hips and my back were still so damaged and unrepaired that I was still going crooked off the jump. I was experiencing terrible pain in my back and hip and I continued to get a dead leg during training sessions.

Because I had been landing heavily on my right for so long,

the muscles on that side started to shut down and there was no protection for my joints, which started rubbing together, causing arthritis. In spite of the fact that I was feeling the pain, I didn't spend enough time early on worrying about my hip and back. Any time my body was in a slightly arched position I'd wince in pain, and even going over a speed bump in the car would hurt. It was a major problem, but at the time the priority was my shoulder.

It was a vicious cycle and a complete nightmare. Here I was trying to steer my body to go straight off the jump, but because my right side was so messed up I would leave the jump crooked and land heavy on my right side, making it worse. We tried everything possible to get me straight. I even tried skiing up the opposite side of the jump, but nothing was working.

We still didn't have a physio travelling with us when we were training and it was really hard to try and figure out what was wrong. I can't believe how naive I was back then. I knew about the body but I didn't know the damage I was doing—I didn't realise that putting up with the pain and fighting through it could lead to further injury, I thought I could just jump through things and it would all get better. There was no one there to say, 'Your back is messed up, we need to get this ironed out.' I'm sure if we had a physio there it would have taken less time to heal or the injury wouldn't have become as bad as it did in the first place.

I finally went to see a back specialist in Salt Lake City who told me, 'You're a mess from your neck to your tail bone. You're all crooked and out of whack.' He said it had been that way for such a long period it was going to take some time to fix the problem. But once we knew what was going on, we could start to deal with it. The muscles supporting my spine and vertebrae had become so weak that each time I landed everything got whacked out of place again. So he gave me a series of corrective exercises to do after every jump to realign my back and hips, and I did these in my ski boots and wetsuit before walking back up the stairs to do another jump. It was hell. I'd be crying after every jump because I knew I'd come in crooked, and then I'd be crying as I climbed back up the stairs. Then I'd have to watch the whole thing on video after training.

RIGHT-SIDE-ITIS

I did about a thousand crooked Back-Lays that summer before I actually started to ski off the jump straight. There were so many times I wanted to quit. The worst part was that I couldn't feel myself going crooked until I was off the jump. If I couldn't feel it, I couldn't change it. It was the most frustrating summer of my life to that point.

Todd could tell how frustrated I was, but he had never coached me before and he didn't really know what I had dealt with in the lead-up to Salt Lake City until I told him. He was left to pick up the pieces and try to solve my problem. I don't think he doubted my ability—nobody could have come as far so quickly on luck alone—and he shared my frustration and disappointment and wanted to know why this was happening.

It was tough. I was really exploding inside because I knew I could be a better competitor if my body was in better shape. I thought that I was doing all the right things and was just frustrated that the problem persisted. Let's face it, demands of the sport and the impact it was having on my body was going to make it really difficult for me to heal from injuries, let alone get on top of them, especially without a full-time physio. I felt like I was wasting time. I wanted to progress and move on to the double, get new tricks done and perfect them. If I had got as far as I did to make the Olympics in such a short time, imagine what I'd be able to do the next year—I'd just smash everyone, and that was my intention, so the whole situation was devastating.

Papou, my Greek grandfather, was diagnosed with lung cancer that summer and that added to my stress levels. He was in his early 80s but it was really the first time that cancer had affected my family or someone close to me, and it was hard to be away from everyone. Before that I hadn't ever thought about leaving home—it was simply, 'Yeah, see you later! Woo-hoo, I'm off!' But this was different. At one stage my hair started falling out in clumps. Apparently I had a bald patch on the back of my head that I couldn't see. Liz noticed it, but she didn't want to tell me because it would stress me out even more. It was a hell of a summer, though Liz and I joke about it now.

Eventually my back became stronger and more stable and my jumps started to straighten out. Finally, I could start progressing as I knew I could and I no longer wanted to quit, I wanted to conquer. Battling this problem had been a big lesson for me—to be smarter with my body and never let it get out of control again. The after-effects of the injury still trouble me today and I still get the occasional bout of right-side-itis, but I know what exercises I need to do to keep on top of it.

****

We competed at the Mt Buller World Cups in September 2002, about seven months after Salt Lake, and I got my first podium in the opening competition, despite a less than ideal lead-in and not feeling 100 per cent. The weather was horrendous once again, but I stayed on my feet and finished second on home soil in front of my friends and family, which just made it all that more special. To be honest, though, I had such a crazy mindset that I really *expected* podiums at that stage, even though I had the injuries. I was really hard on myself and I knew I could be better than I had shown so far.

That was the problem—I was so hungry. I would do anything to be in a competition and it would have taken a very serious injury to make me miss a World Cup event. I would find a way around the limitations of any injury. If it was just pain that was easy, but if it was affecting my jumping that was a different story.

After the two Buller events I went back to Park City for a final camp of water ramping. It had been a trying summer but I had come out of it okay and got to where I needed to in the end. I was able to add two triple-twisting double somersaults to my kit bag and have them ready for the rest of the 2002/03 World Cup season.

I returned to Australia in October for a quick break before heading back to North America and the next events on the tour. I went to see my Papou, because at that stage his condition had deteriorated and he was in hospital at Lorne. That's when I got really emotional and started to tear up, because I knew I was heading overseas again and it was probably the last time I would see him. He passed away in December when I was on a training camp at Fortress. It was difficult hearing that news because we were just about to start the World Cup again. After my coaches told me I spoke to Mum and Dad on the phone. I said I'd come home,

Me as a baby on the beach at Lorne, my favourite place. My earliest memories are of sand, sun and salt water.
PHOTO: PHYLLIS IERODIACONOU

As a family, we have always loved the outdoors. This is at Wilsons Promontory National Park, where we had to carry our own sleeping bag. It seemed so big and heavy back then.
PHOTO: ANGELIS IERODIACONOU

From the moment I could walk I loved to test my limitations.
PHOTO: PHYLLIS IERODIACONOU

As the only girl, I always wanted to be like one of the boys when I was growing up. This didn't change once I became an elite athlete, although I did stop sneaking into mum and dad's bed with my brothers. PHOTO: PHYLLIS IERODIACONOU

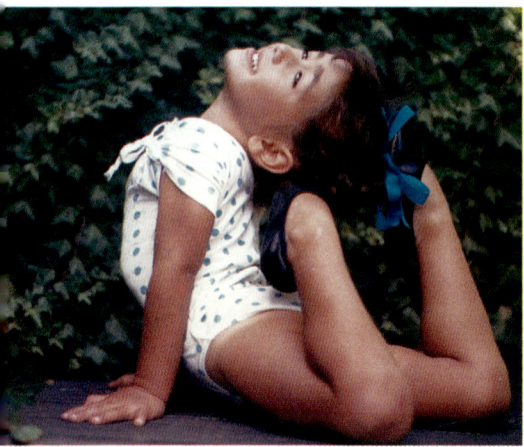

This is me as a flexible three-year-old. I loved gymnastics and even back then I knew I wanted to be an Olympian one day.
PHOTO: PHYLLIS IERODIACONOU

I have always been ultra competitive and I loved winning races at school. Completing the double is my best friend (in blue) from Primary School, Carol Diaz.
PHOTO: PHYLLIS IERODIACONOU

I always liked the view from the top. On this occasion I had just won the 1995 Level 8 Championships as a 13-year-old. PHOTO: PHYLLIS IERODIACONOU

Me and my great friend Lainie Cole with our swag of medals and trophies at the Niddrie Gymnastics Club. PHOTO: PHYLLIS IERODIACONOU

I had just successfully landed my bars routine at the 1997 Level 10 National Championships. That year I was the National Champion as a 15-year-old. PHOTO: PHYLLIS IERODIACONOU

From gymnastics champion to beginner skier. This was my first ever day skiing at Mt Buller, and, judging by my lack of beanie, gloves or goggles I clearly had a lot to learn! PHOTO: PHYLLIS IERODIACONOU

Liz Gardner and I getting ready for our first flips on snow at the Mt Buller World Cup in 2000. We loved our matching white suits. PHOTO: MARK ASHKANASY

I had my first World Cup win in 2003 in the Czech Republic. Celebrating with me are coaches Todd Ossian (back left) and Dustin Wilson; at the front I'm joined by Liz Gardner (left) and Alisa Camplin. PHOTO: PHYLLIS IERODIACONOU

This is me face-planting in the World Cup Final in 2003, which cost me the overall title. I finished second behind my teammate, Alisa Camplin.
PHOTO: AP VIA AAP/PETR DAVID JOSEK

The view from underneath the jumps. There are so many volunteers that help prepare our jumps and landing hills for World Cup competitions. I guess their hard work grants them the best views! PHOTO: GETTY IMAGES

I was so excited to record my first victory as an aerial skier on home soil at Mt Buller in 2003.
PHOTO: MARK ASHKANASY

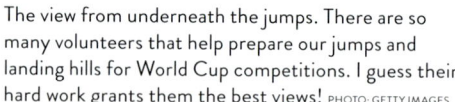

'Focus Lyd.' Here I am preparing for take off at Lake Placid while all the other skiers wait their turn.
PHOTO: GETTY IMAGES

Here I am in the middle of performing a double twist at Mt Buller in 2004.
PHOTO: LUCAS DAWSON PHOTOGRAPHY

PHOTO: GETTY IMAGES

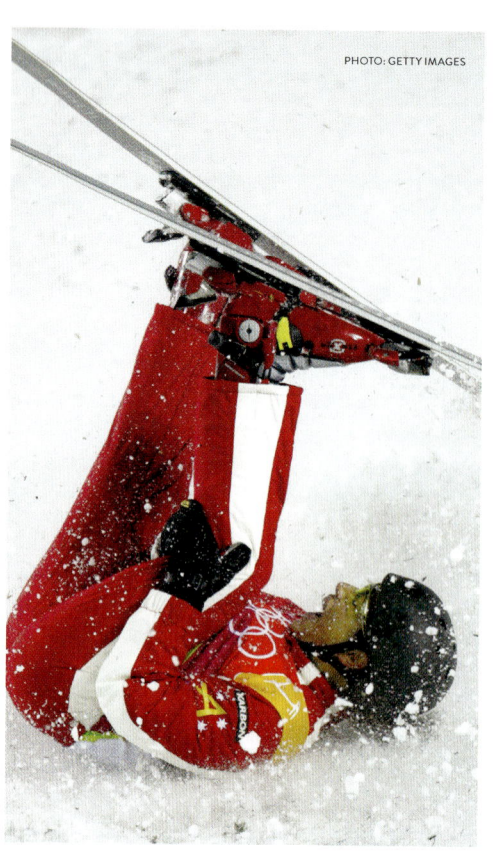

The Torino Olympics in 2006 were supposed to be my moment to shine. Instead, it all ended in heartbreak when I re-injured the ACL in my knee after crashing out in the qualifying round. I was thankful my mum was there to accompany me as I was stretchered off and taken by ambulance back to the hotel.

PHOTO: GETTY IMAGES

PHOTO: AAP IMAGE/DEAN LEWINS

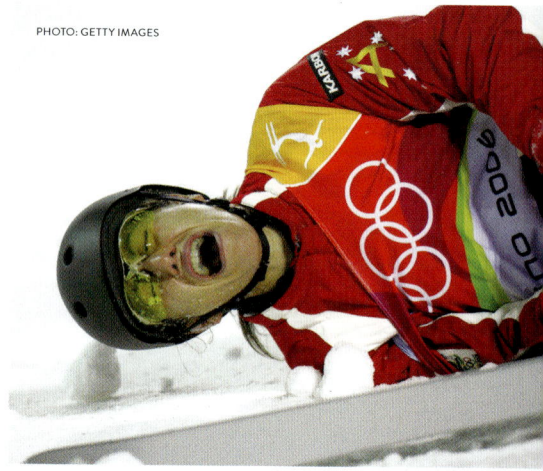

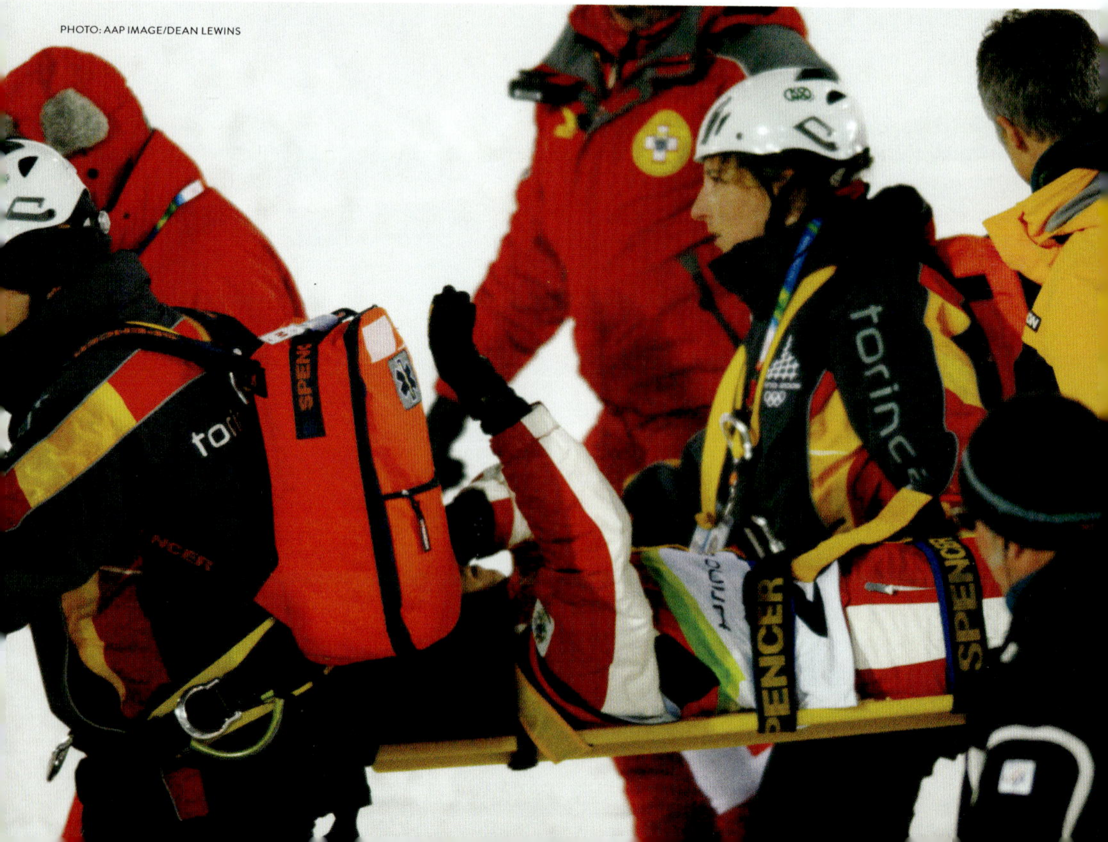

but Mum said, 'No, what can you do now? You just stay and do what you need to do.' I think Mum was starting to understand what I needed to do to succeed, but it was hard missing the funeral. Late was in Finland at the time, but I had my teammates around me and it was important to have them there for comfort and support. Sometimes you just need a hug.

Friends and family from Australia often say to me, 'Gee it must be wonderful gallivanting around the world most of the year doing what you do,' and for the most part I would agree, but people don't understand the sacrifices we make to realise our potential and get the best out of ourselves. I loved what I did, despite injuries and setbacks, but losing a loved one when you're far away was a different pain and I wasn't around my family when I really wanted to be. It didn't help that I was in Fortress, a godforsaken place miles away from anything.

Aerial skiing for Australian athletes is quite odd. We are a small team and we live with each other nine or 10 months a year. You need to be tolerant of everyone's differences to be able to function properly. We are a team but we compete as individuals. Ultimately, those closest to you are people you need to beat, but you develop a different set of boundaries and a respect for them as people. If you are lucky, you actually develop good friendships. What happens on the field of competition is just that, and when you walk away after the battle you need to at least be able to show respect. If someone has a bad day and you've had a great one, you're not going to rub that in their face. You have to understand that they need to reflect on what happened that day, and you've got to celebrate in your own way. I have always admired sportspeople who can remain considerate and humble no matter what has happened. I've also known a lot of champions in this sport who don't behave like champions—they want to win at any cost, which looks great on paper, but at the end of the day, they've lost the respect of their teammates, coaches and competitors. They've been happy to trample on everyone on their way up to the top and most of the time they are so delusional they don't even realise how they've conducted themselves to get there. I've never admired people like that. In fact I vowed to never be like them.

******

Pre-season training on snow was once again a battle. While the shoulder was manageable, my back and hip were terrible and I had to cut back my hours on the jump site. We still didn't have a physio with us and my body started to break down again with the impact of jumping on snow. The pain led to inhibition in my muscle, I'd get the dead leg and then I'd go crooked off the jump. That was the pattern again. I was taking handfuls of Advil painkillers and when I wasn't getting any relief from those any more, I started taking Voltaren, a stronger anti-inflammatory. It didn't take long before I stopped feeling the effects of those, too.

So nearly every day I travelled to Canmore, 40 minutes away, for treatment. I was trying anything to get better. I was seeing an acupuncturist, a massage therapist, a physiotherapist and an osteopath—anyone I thought could help me really. I jumped when I could but it wasn't often enough. No one else seemed to have the same difficulties, and the fact that my teammates and competitors trained with no drama really got to me. It just seemed so unfair. I'd never wish anyone to be injured, but I did wish for less drama in my training and preparation. One pain-free day or one day without having to worry about being crooked off the jump would have been a blessing.

But somehow by the time we left Fortress I had done my new jumps on snow, and while I hadn't done a lot, I had done them well. I had two triple-twisting doubles ready, even though I had taken a roundabout way of getting there.

The first World Cup for the northern winter section of the 2002/03 season was at Mont Tremblant, Canada. I competed a Full-Double-Full, which was my new trick for the winter, and a Double-Full-Full, the first time I had done both jumps in competition, and I landed them really well. So did Alisa, however, and she won the event while I came second. Aside from winning the Olympics, that was her first ever victory and she was definitely on the rise at 28 years of age.

It was only my second season on tour, and I was fairly green in terms of experience. I knew there was a World Cup Grand Prix champion at the end of the season but I didn't understand how the points were tallied up after every event. I also knew that the World Cup leader wore the yellow bib, but I didn't really pay much attention to it. I didn't really think it was that significant, I was more interested in the individual events, which is why I didn't know how the points system worked.

I knew the World Cup Grand Prix meant a lot to Alisa because she needed to prove that her win in Salt Lake City wasn't a fluke, but to me, the overall title meant nothing. I came second a lot that season to Alisa and also had two other top six results, and when we came to the final stop on the tour, in Špindlerův Mlýn in the Czech Republic, I was second on the Grand Prix standings behind her.

It was a double event in Czech that year, and even my parents and brother Peppi had flown over to see me. It was so nice to have them there, especially as they got to see my first win. In the first of the two events, I jumped a personal best score to beat Nina Li, with Alisa coming in third.

So I was number one and Alisa was number two heading into the World Cup final the following day. On my first jump in the final, I copped a really big head wind and came into the jump way too slow. The Spindle site had quite a long transition leading into the jump and the wind has a bigger impact there than at other places. I copped a sudden gust as I was going into my Full-Double-Full, couldn't get the trick around and landed on my face.

I hurt my neck and had a decent headache, so I decided to pull out of the competition. What I didn't even realise at the time was that if I had done a really basic jump and got a result instead of zero points for not finishing the competition I could have won the World Cup tour. Whoops! I was really stupid because I should have paid more attention to that kind of thing. I was just more concerned with winning events; because I landed on my face I wasn't going to win, so I pulled out. I finished second overall that year. Number two in the world was a good result for my second year on tour, but I was the bridesmaid. I had also apparently made it to number two in the world faster than anyone else. I was happy, but I wasn't really.

****

The World Cup title is a big thing, I realise that now—especially after coming second four times and winning the trophy only once. It is a title that recognises a whole season, whereas the Olympics and the World Championships are just one event. The World Championships are held every two years and I've competed in three, but each time I've failed to make the finals. Each time there have been different circumstances that led to a poor performance, including my first one in 2003.

The 2003 event had been held in Deer Valley, USA a few weeks before the Czech World Cup final. My back was at its worst and physically I was still a battered mess. I'd had some very good results leading into it despite my body feeling like it had been through a train wreck every day. However, in the week of the Championships things were so bad that I couldn't hold my skis in the landing position coming into the landing. That position, with the weight of my skis and boots, was killing me and I couldn't land my jumps. I exploded like a bomb every time I touched the snow for landing, so those first Worlds were a complete disaster for me and I didn't make finals.

The next week we went to Steamboat Springs, again in the USA, for another World Cup event and I went to see another back specialist who had been highly recommended. He scheduled an MRI on my back, the first time I'd ever had it scanned. Peter Hogg, the team physiotherapist who was with us that week, suggested the scan because he thought that all the pain I was feeling might be the result of a stress fracture. There was no fracture, but the scan did show arthritis and a cyst growing in the facet joint, the part of the spine that looks like wings on the vertebrae. The cyst had been compressing my nerves, which explained the constant pain and why I was getting a dead leg all the time.

As I sat with the specialist I joked that I was suffering from a bad case of right-side-itis, but he didn't really find that funny. He said, 'You have some serious damage on your right side. What we can do is—' but I interrupted him and said, 'Hang on, can I compete this weekend?'

'Well, what we can do is give you a temporary nerve block in your back so you won't feel the pain and you'll be able to jump. But we can't do that until the day before the event for it to have its effect properly, and you shouldn't jump until then.' That was a typical story for me, missing training, and I had done that before—but at least I could jump in the event. And at least now we knew what was actually going on in my back.

Normally a patient needs to be sedated for this sort of procedure, but I wanted to train on the day before the competition, so that wasn't an option. Women's training was in the morning so I was going to miss that, but of course I'd already asked the chief whether I could join the men's training session and he had agreed.

So on the day before the event, 'Hoggie' and I went back to the specialist for the procedure. I lay face down on the bed while he injected the nerve block into three different points in my back and also managed to pop the cyst with the injection at the same time. I felt everything and it was very uncomfortable. I could hear my heart beat on the monitor and I distinctly remember trying to keep my heart rhythm the same to pretend that I wasn't stressed and that I was tough. That's what I focused on. Then they gave me an apple juice.

It was a bit crazy. 'Yeah, got it,' he said, but I wasn't allowed to move for at least half an hour. I had my apple juice and watched the clock because training was due to start in half an hour. As soon as they released me I did a few tests and I felt really good—I couldn't feel any pain!

We raced back to my condo, I put on my jumping gear and joined the guys' session. Bingo! I could land again and was pain-free. The next day I was back on the podium in second place. Pity we hadn't done the procedure the week before at Worlds!

****

So with minimal training and juggling of injuries I finished that 2002/03 season ranked second in the world. Most weeks I couldn't jump much because I'd get too sore so I'd just do the competition. I competed well but I hated the pattern I was in, and I wasn't going to jump like a man with that training regimen—I felt like I was always jumping with a handicap, always playing catch up.

Getting home to Australia at the end of the season following the Czech final was interesting in itself. While the rest of the World Cup teams were flying out of Prague, we were going out of Munich for some reason. So we went from the competition venue to the hotel, packed our gear, and climbed into the rental van to drive six hours to Germany for a 6am flight. I had my jumper wrapped around my neck as a brace because it felt like I'd broken it and the poor coaches were drinking Red Bulls all night to keep awake and get us to the airport on time. It was quite dangerous and an unnecessary risk, just to save a few bucks, it seems. Yes, we had jumped and we were being chauffeured, but the coaches had worked hard all week shovelling snow and chopping our landing hill. Having to drive a car full of athletes throughout the night to make an early flight from Munich was just stupid. I was disappointed at the OWI for that decision and voiced my opinion, but I doubt they listened. I was very vocal right from the beginning about things like that, but because I wasn't number one I probably wasn't taken seriously.

When I did arrive home, I wanted my injuries to heal. After the Olympics, I had become a scholarship holder of the Victorian Institute of Sport (VIS) and had access to all their services, including doctors, physios and trainers. I started going to the VIS to see if they could help me fix my body. Our team doctor, Peter Braun, was also based in Melbourne, and he put me in touch with a back specialist who took one look at me and said I should stop jumping. It was a significant injury in his eyes and he saw two options—a permanent nerve block or giving up aerial skiing. I didn't like either alternative, so my instinct was to look for a second opinion and a third and a fourth until I got the answer I wanted to hear. I was seeing another team physiotherapist at the time, Randall Cooper, so I told him what the specialist had said. I was devastated and was hoping he had a better solution. He said, 'Lyd, your back is really unstable. Don't worry about the nerve block, don't worry about what this specialist has said because that is not an option for us. Let's start doing some work with one of the Pilates instructors on the machines here and see how you go.'

With the Pilates program in place I also started working with Dee Jennings, a trainer at the VIS. I went to a doctor who practised Chinese medicine and did a lot of acupuncture, and prescribed all kinds of disgusting herbal concoctions I had to drink. I was undergoing three or four different kinds of treatments at the same time and I was open to trying anything and everything other than surgery, nerve blocks or illegal substances.

Everything I was doing was right and the Pilates was helping me strengthen those stabilising muscles that had been switched off for two years. All the treatments were beginning to work and I began to regain control, but I decided to delay my departure for summer training again. I went in for a meeting at the OWI and said, 'I can't go away in June, I'm not ready—my back still needs some work.' They were quite surprised and shocked—'Really, it's that bad?' So I stayed home, rehabilitated it as much as I could, and continued to feel a lot better and a lot stronger.

The physiotherapy, the Chinese medicine and the VIS all helped get me back on track, but the Pilates was my real saviour. To this day, I still travel with a Pilates machine whenever I can. I have one in Finland and one in Australia so that I'm covered on both sides of the globe. I know my back will never be perfect again because of the arthritis, but at least I know how to manage it now. It was not the most economical way for me to rehab but at that point I was fed up with being injured and just wanted to get better. That's why I was willing to try anything and found a combination of therapies that worked for me.

In the 2007/08 season, the OWI finally supplied us with a full time physiotherapist, which was a huge relief. I am certain that my injuries got out of hand earlier in my career because we didn't have a medical professional monitoring and treating me. Today we always have a physio with us when we are training, which makes sense given what we do. It's made a huge difference to my body and ability to train.

In earlier days, I managed the pain and injuries on the road by myself. I had all these injuries and no one to treat or manage them. Our on-snow training camps—which essentially go from November until the first World Cups in December—are a critical part of every aerial skier's development. Apart from the lead-in to the Vancouver Olympics, my injuries meant that I never completed one of them.

CHAPTER 8

IN THE SHADOWS

In the summer of 2003 I was finally on top of my injuries and performing better. I was still doing triple-twisting doubles, and with Todd's meticulous coaching style my jumps had become more polished. We also had an assistant coach, Dustin Wilson, who was employed as our 'top guy'. A top guy stands with us at the top of the in-run before we are about to do a jump. He's the one keeping an eye on our speeds and giving us advice on where to go from. He also communicates messages to our coach on the knoll, Todd, and they relay information back and forth to each other.

In the 2003/04 season, I won twice and had seven podiums in 12 events. In the World Cup in Fernie, Canada, in January, I missed the podium because I knocked myself unconscious, which then kept me out of training for a week. The next World Cup was in Deer Valley, USA. My coaches wanted me to miss that event because of the concussion, but I felt good and through a series of tests with our physio I convinced them I was fine to jump, which I was, and I finished second at that event.

Alisa had another great season that year and she took the crystal globe and I finished second again. She really peaked after the Olympics and she became a fierce competitor. With Jacqui still injured, Alisa was the star of our team and I was in her shadow. I felt I was good enough to be number one and was jumping really well, but I had made mistakes, and missing the event due to the concussion really set me back. It was a familiar situation. I was getting sick of always fighting off the back foot and didn't want concussions and the like to impede me any more.

My teammates used to joke with me, saying, 'You don't need training, Lyd, because you jump better when you don't train.' It was a terrible pattern and one that I was desperate to get out of. I wasn't going to improve if I couldn't train. Being ranked number two in the world should be considered a great achievement, but knowing I wasn't jumping at my best really frustrated me. With Alisa being number one, in many ways I didn't feel important. She demanded so much attention and energy from the coaches that I often held back in asking them for what I needed, fearing I would be taking up too much of their time. Number two was my place and it was exactly how I felt.

From the beginning, as I've said, I've always wanted to do triples. At that time, triple-twisting doubles were enough for you to win major events—they still win events today—but I wanted to do big jumps, and to jump like a man. Others thought, 'Why bother? Why take risks when you can win doing triple-twisting doubles?' No one understood my motivation, which was not only to win, but to dominate and leave my mark on the sport. Most importantly, I wanted to reach my full potential.

Being a more experienced athlete, I had smartened up and it was the right decision to compete in 2003/04 with a solid season of doubles to get my body right before I started pushing for new tricks. I wanted to make sure my technique was perfect with doubles before starting to do triples.

But in the northern summer of 2004, I started doing triples on the water ramp. From the beginning they were impressive and I wasn't afraid to launch myself off a four-metre-high jump. The feeling was exhilarating. I was on top of my injuries, and my body was feeling fit and healthy. Todd was still our coach in Park City, but Dustin had since become the head coach of our major competitor, China. I loved Todd's coaching style and his eyes were tuned for perfection. He knew my aspirations and I'm certain he wanted to be around to see them through. We had also acquired a new assistant coach from Canada, Daniel Murphy. With Alisa and me ranked one and two in the world for the second consecutive year we had earned an extra coach but still no full-time physiotherapist.

At the end of August we headed home for the World Cups at Mt Buller. It was the first time since the beginning of my career that I felt 100 per cent fit. I had a bag full of fantastic tricks by then, including two triple-twisting doubles, and I had started triple somersaults. We decided not to do my new triple somersaults for the Buller events because there wasn't going to be enough time to train them, so we opted for two triple-twisting doubles instead and decided to wait to start triples on snow in the northern hemisphere winter.

The Mt Buller World Cup in 2004 was the first event when I wasn't battling from behind and jumping with injuries. I won both World Cup competitions that weekend and scored a personal best. I was on fire.

After the World Cups we returned to Park City to finish training on the water ramps, a period of fine-tuning my tricks to make sure they were ready for snow. By the end of the summer, I got up to a triple-twisting Triple—a Full-Full-Full—and my first ones were unbelievable. They were perfect! Even the guys were impressed, and no doubt the girls were worried. My new jumps looked great on the water ramps, but now it was a matter of transferring what I had learned to snow. I knew that wasn't going to be easy, and would take some time, but I was prepared to take the hits. It was all part of the plan: start doing triples now and they'll be ready for the Torino Olympics in 2006. I don't think anyone doubted me at that stage. Unfortunately, while it looked fantastic on paper, it didn't quite work out that way.

****

I was super fit leading into the northern winter season of 2004/05. My right-side-itis was under control. I had become a Pilates fanatic and I knew the exact exercises I needed to do to keep my back in check. I had a new training program in the gym, which involved a lot of plyometrics, and I was in great shape. I also started reading books that would help me with my mental training and stumbled across a book called *Sportsmind* by Jeffrey Hodges (a fellow Australian), and I loved the book so much that I bought his CDs too. From the beginning, Hodges' material had a different style and I felt a connection with it. His workbooks and material made sense to me and raised my awareness of myself and my behavioural patterns. They made me really think through the issues I was facing. I listened to his many relaxation CDs repeatedly and his voice became familiar and comforting to me. He was my escape. Little did I know that I'd continue to use his material for the rest of my career and someday his influence would be my secret weapon.

Fortress Mountain in Canada, where we normally did our pre-season training, had stopped operating, so we decided to train in Park City. From the first day of training on snow I was jumping great and nailing everything, but after about 10 jumps I started to feel a sharp pain in my kneecap. I thought it was strange because it was a pain that I hadn't felt before, and by the end of the session it had become quite sharp. I hadn't done anything to set it off other than jump, so I was a bit annoyed. The next day, I could hardly walk up and down stairs. I went out and started training but this time the pain was worse. I tried to suck it up and I continued jumping. I was going so well and had already got up to triple-twisting doubles, which is rare for the second day of pre-season training. But the pain was excruciating and I wanted to collapse to the ground after every jump. I couldn't believe how fast my kneecap had flared up. Just like that and out of the blue.

I went to see Dan Ivey, a local physiotherapist, who diagnosed a bad case of patella tendonopathy, commonly called 'jumper's knee'. I had never had patella pain before and here it was getting worse jump by jump. I couldn't figure out why it had happened so quickly. I felt as strong as I had ever felt and I was landing all my jumps. Dan asked me what other activities I'd been doing outside of jumping that could have over-loaded the tendon so I told him about all the plyometric training I had been doing in the gym. 'Oh, well that's your answer,' he said. 'You've been loading up the tendon quite aggressively in the gym, so with the additional impact from jumping, the tendon has flared up.' His advice was to rest it.

My old nemesis—injury—had returned and I couldn't jump. If I was going to be doing triples I needed time, but my knee was not improving and time was running out. The coaches and I decided that I would do just one more day of pre-season training before the Christmas break. And with one day, we would go for my first triples on snow. I wouldn't be able to do many because of my knee, but the point was just to do them. My doubles were perfect, so in my mind it was time to move on.

The next day I was pumped and ready. It was one of those key moments where I felt quite similar to the way I did in Vancouver years later. I was so zoned in and focused that I felt like I could do anything. I did my first triples and landed them and the coaches were ecstatic. Very few male aerialists land their first triples, so it was pretty impressive for a girl to land her first ones. And in all, I'd only had three days of pre-season training, hardly ideal preparation.

I decided to fly home for a short Christmas break for shockwave treatment on my kneecap. Shockwave therapy is like a mini jackhammer is placed on the source of pain on the patella tendon. Tendons don't have a good blood supply, which is why they heal slowly, so the idea behind the shockwave treatment is to stir up the tendon so that it bleeds and starts to heal itself. It's a very painful procedure.

Mum picked me up from the airport when I arrived back in Melbourne and she seemed weird. Something was wrong. Straight away, I asked what was up and she began to cry. Dad had cancer and so did his brother and sister, Uncle John and Auntie Yvonne. So I came home for a short break to treat my knee and three people in my family were battling cancer. I was devastated and that was a tough Christmas.

My family had known about Dad's cancer for a couple of weeks and didn't want to tell me while I was away. Although the diagnosis was only recent he'd had it for some time. For about six months before he was diagnosed, he was having dreadful pain in his back between the shoulder blades. He'd had physiotherapy, which often made things worse, and he'd stay up all night in front of the fireplace trying to ease the pain. He didn't bother to get it checked out any further and just tried to deal with the pain. (I guess I inherited my stubborn tolerance for pain from him.) Eventually he ended up going to a back specialist, who examined him and said, 'Buddy, there's nothing wrong with your back, but you've got to have a gastroscopy.' The specialist's intuition was right, because the gastroscopy showed Dad had stomach cancer. It was radiating up his oesophagus and producing the pain in his back.

I was scheduled to leave Australia on December 24, Christmas Eve, to compete in a World Cup in Canada in the first week of January. Dad had surgery on the day I left and it was the first time in my career that I really found it hard to leave. I was on the plane while he was in surgery and my mind was racing, hoping that he was going to be OK. My summer had been great, my triples were ready, but now everything seemed to be going wrong again.

I thought about staying home and having the season off, but I felt like I needed to go back to work and get the job done. It was a hard season because I was forever calling to see how Dad and my uncle and auntie were going. They had cut out two-thirds of Dad's stomach and removed all the cancer, which meant he didn't need radiation or chemotherapy. They had got it in time. My uncle John was not as fortunate and he died from lung cancer complications a year later. My auntie Yvonne did beat that bout of cancer, but unfortunately it returned and she is still fighting it. She has an amazing spirit and is determined to beat it.

In spite of everything that had happened, when the season re-started in Tremblant, my knee had improved and I was still jumping well. I won the event, making it three in a row counting the two Mt Buller competitions, and I was well into the lead in the Grand Prix.

The next week we were in Lake Placid, USA, for another double event. The weather was shocking all week and we couldn't train, so we decided not to start triples yet and opted for doubles. On the first day of competition the weather was still foul and we kept getting delayed throughout the day. It was getting late before the weather became stable enough for us to jump—so late in fact that they changed the women's format to a one-jump competition and cancelled the men's event.

Of the 30 girls on the start list, I was second last to jump. The sun was going down and the light was disappearing fast. By the time it was my turn it was nearly dark, and if it hadn't been for a small glow coming from the lights in the judges' stand I wouldn't have known where the jump was. This was going to be interesting. I jumped and somehow I picked up the landing and skied away on my feet. Five minutes later it was completely dark. I finished second that day and Nina Li, from China, won. It was one of those days when I was just happy to land safe and sound. The following day I finished second again to Nina, who was proving to be my toughest opponent.

The only glitch in the season came the following week in Fernie, where I finished fifth.

Todd and I decided it was now time to start triples on snow because I needed experience landing them and you can't achieve that without numbers. It would also mean I would sacrifice some results—and maybe the World Cup title—because my triples would need time to be consistent. It was a tough decision. I had come second overall in the previous two seasons and wanted a World Cup title of my own, and here I was leading the World Cup with three wins and two seconds after five events. But it was a move I had to make if I wanted to compete triples successfully at the Torino Games in 2006.

Triples are quite different to doubles and it takes time to adjust. You ski into the jump about 10km/h faster and the take-off jump is four metres tall instead of three; you do three flips instead of two, which takes about three seconds, and in that time you need to calculate and read how high you are in the air and how fast you are dropping into the landing. It's a completely different ball game to doubles. You hit harder and the risk is increased.

I started the triples in Deer Valley, USA, after not doing them since that one day in Park City during my three days of pre-season training. I landed them all week in training, however, and in my first event doing triples I finished third. It was my sixth podium in seven events for the season, but Nina won the event and we now shared the lead in the Grand Prix.

The next World Cup was in Shenyang, China. We had planned to continue doing triples there but on that particular site, the in-run was long and flat and I couldn't get enough speed for triples so I had to revert to doing doubles. I finished third, another good result, but by now Nina had a narrow 20-point lead over me in the race for the title.

We had another competition in China the following weekend at a place called Changchun. Unusually, the girls were scheduled to open the site for training, so essentially we were the guinea pigs who had to check what speed was needed for the jumps. Normally the men open the jumps, but for some reason we did it that week. I trained a few doubles and everything felt fine, so we decided to speed check the Triple. Generally, for a basic Triple you need speed in the low-to mid-60km/h range, but it changes with every site depending on the steepness of the in-run and length of the transition before the jump. No site is identical and it always takes a bit of time getting used to a new venue—something we have to do week in, week out. We didn't know the exact speed needed and it's always a bit of a guess. Also on the Triple in those days was Jac, who was back from injury, Swiss skier Evelyne Leu and China's Guo Xinxin. All three girls were very experienced in doing triples and had been doing them for a long time, but none of them was prepared to go first, and there I was, the most inexperienced triples jumper of the lot.

I had done a few speed checks and was ready to go. The speed felt and looked okay and Todd agreed, so we decided to jump. I led the way and I came in too slow, missed my take-off, panicked in the air to try and get the trick around and pulled it through onto my back. It would have been a normal hit, but the landing hill had some hard chunks of ice in it and I hit one, which knocked me unconscious. In hindsight, it was a stupid decision and I should have waited for someone more experienced to go first. You don't send the girl who is leading the World Cup tour to test a jump she has little experience on. It was just a dumb move on all accounts.

I couldn't compete that week in China or the week after at the World Cup in Torino, Italy—the site of the next Olympics—because I was still experiencing symptoms of concussion. I missed two events, and in that time Nina Li stretched her lead.

I had to regain my confidence after the crash and get back up on the Triple. You're always a bit timid and shaky getting back on the skis after a concussion and there's always a part of you that second-guesses yourself and wonders whether all the marbles are lined up properly, but I was fine and built back up from doubles to triples, preparing for the final two events of the season.

However, my triples were not yet consistent and I was really using the final competitions as training to get more numbers under my belt. Nina Li charged ahead with her meticulous triple-twisting doubles and won the Grand Prix. Despite the mishaps, I finished second in the World Cup for the third consecutive year. I had gone from being on fire to being the bridesmaid for the third time in a row. I could understand why, though—I had only three days of pre-season training due to my knee flare-up, and even though it was a good three days, it wasn't enough to produce consistent triples. It certainly wasn't good enough compared to the six weeks of pre-season training in Mongolia that Nina Li and her team had enjoyed. The Chinese team had a clear advantage with a healthy pre-season training regimen and it showed in their results.

****

The World Cup tour for 2004/05 was over and our last stop was Ruka, Finland, for the 2005 World Championships in March. At that point I had two options: I could do my consistent doubles and have a good chance to come away with a win or a podium, or I could give triples another go. I chose the latter. I just felt that if I wanted to compete triples at the Olympics the following year, I should give myself the best chance possible to gain experience in doing them.

Mum, Dad and my brother George made the journey to Finland to watch. It was a big trip for my dad, having undergone major surgery in late December. They stayed with Late's parents and by now they had a fantastic relationship. The World Championships were going to be Late's last event before retiring and it seemed fitting he would end his career on home soil.

World Championships have the same format as an Olympic Games: a qualifying round and then a final. You get two jumps in each round and the top 12 make it through to the finals. I'll never forget the feeling of being so completely underprepared going into the qualification round. I'd been short on preparation before but I was doing triples now and that was a whole other level. I didn't have enough experience to just wing it like I normally did. My training jumps were inconsistent due to the lack of numbers I had actually done on snow and I was still learning how to read triples. I hadn't yet managed to transfer what I had learned on the water ramps to snow because we were on a new site every week, and there just wasn't enough time.

I remember standing at the top of the in-run ready to go, knowing I wasn't really ready. I didn't have confidence and I was too focused on the fact that I was underprepared rather than on the job at hand. On my first jump, I landed with my chest too forward and somersaulted forward down the landing hill. We call that a 'punch front' or 'going over the handle bars' and the deductions you get on your landing points are disastrous. I landed my second jump, but I was out of the final 12.

Another World Championships down the drain. I was devastated. Late's parents were there and my parents were there, supporting me and happy I was safe and sound and had survived my first season of triples relatively unscathed, but all I wanted to do was get out of there and hide. It just wasn't good enough and I was disappointed with myself. I questioned whether it was worth doing triples at all.

Why was I risking myself for so much disappointment when I could easily be successful with doubles? The answer was simple and came from within: I didn't just want to be good; I wanted to be great.

On the upside, I had survived my first year of triples, I was ready for a big summer of water ramping, my patella problem had settled down, and as far as I could tell I was pretty much injury free. I had done my triples on snow and some had been good while some had been bad, as expected. The point is I had done them—the next season was the Olympics, and success there was the real goal. What I needed more than water ramping was more time on snow to get my triples consistent. And I needed to do that in a stable training environment, not on tour in a stressful competition environment where the jump site changes from week to week.

It was essential that we find a new training site that could provide us with early snow. As far as we could tell, the places cold enough for early pre-season jumping were Mongolia, where the Chinese went, or Ruka, which was way up north in the Arctic Circle. Ruka was a good option for us and it is a great resort. The only downside was that in winter it is dark most of the day and can be very cold. That didn't bother me as long as we'd have good training. I presented the option to the coaches and the OWI and they seemed interested, but I'm fairly certain that they weren't keen on going, preferring to stay in the familiar territory of North America, even if it meant that training would be compromised. In the end, it didn't matter. My plans were about to be turned upside down.

****

In May 2005 I headed to Lake Placid, USA, with the rest of the team and a group of strong juniors who were starting to jump on the water ramps. We had decided to make the switch from crowded Park City so that we could train with more flexible hours and get in more jumps.

For some reason I was suffering from a bit of jet lag from the flight. Normally I don't get jet lag, but this time it was significant and I hadn't had a good sleep. On the second day of jumping, my body clock was still out of whack and I was tired, but for that session I had only planned to do basic single flips, which is what I normally do at the beginning of a water ramp season. I had intended to mount bindings on some new skis, but on that day I was using the previous season's skis. They felt a bit shaky because they were old, and moisture from the constant jumping in water had got into the core and warped them. I figured I was only doing singles and could just use them for one more day then mount up a new pair the next day. But the skis weren't tracking well and felt quite unstable. On one jump, both skis popped off on the landing, which sometimes happens when you are water ramping. I normally had straps connecting the skis to my boots, so that if they did come off they wouldn't sink, but because this was the start of the summer, I hadn't put the straps on yet. So I had to dive down to retrieve the skis and, since the pool is more than four metres deep, to do that you need to take everything buoyant off—helmet, life jacket and boots. I grabbed them, but as I was swimming back up I lost my socks and they also ended up on the bottom of the pool. I thought, 'I'm not diving down again to get my socks, I'll just jump without them'.

Without the socks there was a bit more movement inside the boots.

I went up to do another jump, but as I skied down the in-run, I caught an edge, got off-balance and my knee twisted up the jump at a 45-degree angle. I hit the edge of the jump with my hip and ended up landing on the concrete at the side of the pool before toppling into the water. My knee was very painful straight away and I knew something was wrong.

I had failed to listen to the alarm bells that day—jetlag, unstable skis and losing my socks—and had set myself up for disaster, which came in the form of a torn ACL in my knee. Unfortunately, however, it took a while for the doctors to figure that out.

I went to see a doctor in town and he said, 'Your ACL is fine. You've strained your lateral ligament a bit and you will be fine to jump in about two weeks.' I was surprised because the knee had swelled up a lot and felt quite ordinary, but I was relieved to hear his good news. After about 10 days the knee hadn't improved so I had an MRI scan. I wanted to be certain about the extent of the damage, even though at that stage I had seen two doctors and they had both said my ACL was fine. When I went to get the results of my scan and the doctor told me I'd torn my ACL, I broke down in tears of disbelief, knowing the consequences of that diagnosis. For 10 days I'd been thinking everything was okay and I'd be back in two weeks, and then the doctor said those terrible words: 'Your ACL is gone and you need to go home and have a reconstruction.' It was rough news to digest and I was a mess. I had so much to do that summer before a big winter leading into the Olympics, but now my plans were going to be drastically changed.

My question now wasn't what sort of form would I carry into the Olympics, but could I make it at all?

That 2005 summer was a weird one for our team, one that seemed to be cursed. I blew my knee first and then five of our juniors also sustained knee injuries. There was nothing structurally wrong with the jump, but it just kept happening. It was like a really bad dream. It's unusual to blow your knee on a water ramp, so for five of us to do it was truly bizarre and inexplicable. The coaches checked the surfaces of the ramps over and over but found nothing to indicate that there was a problem with the jumps. It was a terrible summer, not only for our injured team members, but also for the athletes who were left standing, wondering if they would be next.

I flew home to Australia and met with knee surgeon Hayden Morris to discuss my options, keeping in mind that I wanted to make it to the Torino Olympics. Option one was to leave the knee as it was without repairing the ACL. Given that the knee was quite unstable, I'd run the risk of doing further damage, so that wasn't really a good option. Option two involved a traditional reconstruction using my own hamstring tendon. Recovery time with this procedure is normally nine to 12 months, and Hayden believed the timing would be too tight because I'd need to start jumping on snow in December in six months' time. Option three was to use a cadaver graft (a tendon from a dead person) to replace the torn ligament. This procedure was the least invasive on my own tissues because, instead of taking the graft from my own hamstring tendon, he would use the donor tissue. This meant a faster recovery time, which would improve my chances of making the Games.

Three days later we went with option three and I had the operation. That was the start of a desperate, rushed and ill-prepared campaign to make it to the Torino Olympics. Success was possible, but I was going to have less training and needed to revise my plan of attack.

CHAPTER 9

TORINO AND THE BIG BLOW

Hayden used a donor Achilles tendon to replace my torn ACL. His first preference was to use a patella tendon because it has a piece of bone at each end of the graft that act as anchors and allow the graft to be securely fixed and heal quickly inside tunnels drilled in the femur and tibia, but unfortunately there wasn't one available at the time so we settled on an Achilles tendon, which only has bone on one end. We needed to get the operation done as quickly as possible so that I could start with my recovery. He made quite a thick graft as my new ACL in the hope that it would hold through the seven months I needed. If it lasted a little longer that was a bonus.

Any kind of surgery involves risk, but when you're using a donor graft—called an allograft—there are the additional risks that your body will reject the tissue or you'll develop an infection. I was counting on Hayden's reputation and expertise and I felt comfortable that everything was going to be fine. The surgery went well and I stayed an extra day in hospital so that the nurses could give me a good dose of antibiotics to limit the risk of infection.

Knee injuries go hand in hand with skiing—it's not a matter of *if* you'll need knee surgery but *when*. If you make it through your career escaping the knife, then you should thank your lucky stars, but where there's one athlete who hasn't had knee surgery, there are dozens who have had multiple knee operations. That's just the nature of the beast. I was hoping to become a one-timer.

Generally, returning to the top of your game after a traditional knee reconstruction takes nine to 12 months because the graft is harvested from your own tissue, such as your hamstring or quadriceps tendon, which also needs time to recover. When you're using an allograft, the recovery time is shorter because the surgeon doesn't take any of your own tissue to create the graft. The downside is that it loses some of its tensile strength when it is frozen to preserve it, and therefore won't be as strong as your own tissue.

In seven months I needed to be competing at the Olympics and I had to be in peak form. It was going to be a challenge, not only for me, but also for the team of physios and trainers that had never rehabbed an allograft surgery before. There were a lot of unknowns about how it was going to respond and recover. Once again I was the guinea pig, but I had nothing to lose. This was my first knee operation and it was quite different to shoulder surgery. It was so swollen straight after the surgery it didn't look as if it belonged to me, but with constant ice, elevation and compression, it started to resemble a knee, and once the rehab started it improved by the day. It's funny, I didn't ever think about having a dead person's tendon inside me and I wasn't at all spooked by it. What I did feel was grateful that someone was willing to donate their tissue to a stranger who needed it. I signed up as an organ donor straight away after surgery.

To help me recover, my rehab team included Dee Jennings from the VIS and Randall Cooper, one of our team physios attached to the Olympic Park Sports Medicine Centre, who had both worked on my injuries back in 2003. There was also my surgeon Hayden, of course, and a collection of massage therapists from the VIS. Before the surgery, Late and I moved from Diggers Rest on the outskirts of Melbourne's west into the Eureka Tower in Melbourne's CBD, which was fully equipped with a gym and swimming pool and only a short walk to the VIS, where I would be doing all of my rehabilitation. Rehab involved three separate sessions a day in the gym. The morning session went from 9am till midday when I'd go home for lunch. I then had a swim and a powernap before heading back to the gym at around 3.30pm for another two-hour session followed by an ice bath. I also had three or four physio and massage sessions a week to keep my hardworking muscles loose and free of tension and to help flush out any swelling.

That was my routine. I was doing everything possible to give myself the best chance to recover and make the Olympics. Because I was a scholarship holder at the VIS, all the services provided there were free, which was a huge financial help, but there was no other financial compensation. No work cover or loss of income insurance, and with the schedule I was keeping there was no time to get a job or earn money. I basically threw all my savings into rehab and rent. I didn't even think twice about it at the time—it was just what I needed to do.

Other athletes from different sports started to take notice of how fast I was rehabbing and what I was able to do in a really, really short time. Dee had me doing plyometric exercises at six weeks, including running, skipping and hopping drills, and we learned fairly quickly when we could push. It was trial and error. Even though I was training hard, we still took the right precautions and planned when I could start skiing on snow, when I could start jumping on the water ramps and when I'd be ready to jump on snow. We had a good plan and I was on track.

To replace my actual jumping, I included at least one hour of mental training and visualisation every day. In the past I had read a lot of books on sports psychology and ways to gain a mental edge in the past, but I found none that were as powerful and effective as Jeffrey Hodges' books and CDs. Since discovering his material, I had been to see him for a session at his base in Queensland and found his techniques to be amazingly powerful.

So while I was rehabbing my knee, I worked intensely on my mind. I visualised myself jumping, I visualised competing in the qualifications and finals of the Torino Olympics, I visualised my knee healing, I did relaxation and breathing exercises and I constantly filled myself with positive thoughts and affirmations. I had done this kind of mental training prior to my knee injury, because I was often injured and on numerous occasions had to replace physical jumping with mental rehearsal, but never at this level of intensity. It took on a new meaning and purpose because I wasn't jumping at all.

I started skiing at Mt Buller two months after surgery, which was scary at first. But after a few runs I felt more confident and my knee was coping fine. I was obviously not doing anything too dangerous—it was really just getting back on skis and into my boots, and testing my confidence in something other than runners. I didn't pull up too sore, so that was a good sign. I obviously had to miss the 2005 Mt Buller World Cup that year and instead I took on the commentary role for the event, which was something different and I really enjoyed it.

It was strange to be on the jump site knowing I wasn't part of the event and it was also weird to see my teammates and coaches again, as well as the rest of the competitors. I had purposely distanced myself from everything other than my rehab and my training up until then. I hadn't been concerned with how anyone else was going; I was in my own world. So to see everyone jump and to see that their Olympic preparation was going smoothly was hard. They had all been water ramping, getting new tricks and polishing their skills while I had been pedalling for hours on a bike, lifting weights and sitting in ice baths. I couldn't help but feel behind the eight ball. But those were the cards I was dealt, I suppose, and there was nothing I could do about it.

Nina Li dominated the Mt Buller event, winning both days, and unfortunately we didn't have any Australians on the podium that weekend. One of my good friends, Deidra Dionne from Canada, had a bad crash and had to be airlifted back to Melbourne in a helicopter. She over-rotated on a jump and basically landed on her neck, then lay there completely motionless. It was a horrible crash and looked really bad from where I was sitting in the judge's stand. She said later on that she had been conscious the whole time, but had felt something was wrong in her neck and didn't want to move. Smart girl! She had, in fact, broken her neck and needed emergency surgery at the Alfred Hospital in Melbourne. The doctors took bone from her hip to put into her neck to act like a cradle and stabilise the joints, and her parents flew from Canada to be at her side. She has two pretty mean looking scars now, one at the back of her neck and one across the front. She stayed in

Melbourne after the surgery until she was cleared to fly home and she was constantly being stared at because the scar at the front of her neck looked as though she had tried to cut her throat. What a story! Deidra and her mother stayed with me for a few days, which was nice, even if we were both lame ducks. Again, her situation was bad and it reminded me that things could always be worse.

It's serious stuff when injuries are that severe. It does give you a sense of mortality about what you are doing. This can be a dangerous sport, but it is also addictive. Deidra did in fact make a return to aerials and competed at the Torino Olympics five months after neck surgery. It was an amazing and inspiring effort.

****

Late September 2005, three months post-surgery, I passed a series of fitness tests and was cleared to start water ramping. I felt great, my knee felt great and I was happy that I was on schedule. It felt like a bonus to be able to get some water ramping in, and even though I had missed most of the water ramp season and wasn't going to be able learn new triples in time for the Olympic season, it was better than nothing and a good way to test how my knee would pull up after a few jumps.

I didn't go back to Lake Placid where I'd hurt myself, deciding instead to train at Park City where I felt more comfortable. Todd flew over to join me and I started jumping, even though it made him uneasy. At that time it was unheard of for someone to come back to jumping three months after ACL surgery, but I was doing fine. I jumped in a brace and kept my numbers to a minimum, and after a couple of days on the single I started doing some doubles.

Todd suggested I go to see a top knee surgeon in Salt Lake City, just to make sure I was OK. I was really uneasy about it and told him, 'No, it's not necessary, I'm doing fine and I don't want strangers poking around at my knee.' He said, 'Peace of mind, Lyd, just to make sure we're on track, that everything's good.'

So I reluctantly went to Salt Lake City to see this knee specialist and he was negative from the beginning. 'I can't believe you're jumping after three months. You're really taking a risk of hurting yourself even further,' he told me. This was not what I wanted to hear at all. He said he wanted to test the laxity, or looseness, of my joint and then I became even more uneasy. He strapped me into this machine that specifically tests the laxity of an ACL by forcing it to its end point and calculating how much movement there is. It's a really aggressive machine and I said, 'I don't think this is necessary. I have an ACL. It's fine. We don't need to be doing this. I don't care if it's a little loose. It is what it is.' By that stage, I was sweating and in tears. When the test was over, the specialist indicated that my ACL was a little loose, but I don't know how he came to that conclusion seeing that he didn't compare it to my other knee. Who was he to know how tight or loose Hayden had made the graft? I didn't need someone like that tampering with my confidence either.

I cursed myself for letting someone external to 'my team' experiment on my knee. The graft was only three months old and didn't need to be tugged aggressively like that to prove a point. The specialist was much more aggressive in his examination than Hayden had ever been. In any case, Hayden was the one who had tested my knee before and after surgery, so only he could tell if it had changed or not. That night my knee was really sore. It had been aggravated by the stupid machine and it was swollen. I was absolutely gutted and traumatised. By now Todd had gone back to Lake Placid and our other coach, Daniel Murphy, had come out to Park City to join me. I rang Todd and told him what had happened, that my knee had flared up and it was all a really bad idea. I couldn't jump for a couple of days after that, and even then it was still swollen. I ended up going home early after about seven days of water ramping and I had only done up to a Full-Full. It was not what I'd planned and I was so angry.

When I got back to Australia, I went to see Hayden straight away and told him what had happened. He was ropable. 'You did what? You got into what machine? Why did you do that? Those machines are aggressive and should only be used to confirm an ACL is torn.' The episode had set me back about a month and had taught me a lesson. To this day I don't let anyone touch my knee unless there is a good reason.

Dee and Randall were also frustrated, of course, and once again

I needed to revise my plans. Up until that point I thought there might be a slight chance I could still do triples at the Olympics if I could get some done on water. Now that option was looking very unlikely, so I shifted my focus back to doing what I knew, which was triple-twisting doubles. Theoretically, if I did those as well as I knew how, I could still win or at least podium. It was disappointing not being able to do what I wanted at what I thought would be the pinnacle of my career. I had big dreams for Torino. I was going to do triples there that no woman had done before. Now I was struggling just to make it to the Games.

I continued with my rehab throughout October and November to get my knee functioning properly again. While I was in Park City, Alisa also blew her knee on a landing into the water. She had done the same thing the year before and it seemed like the curse was continuing. She now joined me in rehab and in the race to make it back for Torino. She, too, had allograft surgery where they basically took out her old graft from the previous year and inserted the donor tissue.

****

After more rehabilitation and a series of fitness tests, I was cleared to go overseas on December 20 and headed to Apex Mountain in British Columbia to start jumping on snow. At that time, Lainie, Bree and Liz were in China competing at World Cups, so when I arrived it was just me and Jacqui, who was there training with Todd, trying to get her triples right. I trained for a couple of days, my knee responded well and it was great to be jumping again. Unfortunately for me it was Christmas, so Todd nicked off for a break and Jacqui bailed too, which left me alone in Apex Mountain for Christmas without a coach. I knew it was Christmas, but it was also an Olympic year, and seeing I had missed most of the year because of my knee and had flown over to start jumping, I thought someone would stay behind to coach me. That wasn't the case, however, and in a lot of ways I felt abandoned.

I rang Alisa's former boyfriend, the Canadian aerialist Steve Omischl, who lived in a nearby town and who was also on a Christmas break. Steve was number two in the world in men's aerials at the time, and surprisingly he agreed to come and coach me for a few days in Apex starting on December 26. It was really nice of him to do that, seeing that my own coaches couldn't make themselves available. Unfortunately the weather turned foul for the three days he was there and we didn't get much jumping done, but the gesture was nice and I was grateful for his help.

The team wasn't scheduled to return to Apex until the first week of January so I needed to find someone else to come and coach me. After the New Year, Deidra Dionne was coming back from her broken neck and was heading to Apex to jump. My old coach Peter Judge was working with her and they both offered to help me, so we formed a little team—the comeback team! It was great to be back with Pete. He realised Deidra and I were a bit nervous and possibly a bit fragile being back on snow, but he was so good with us—'Come on girl, you can do this,' he'd say, which was exactly what I needed. So Deidra and I faced our fears together and Pete guided us through it. We were all cautious, of course, but it was nice to know he cared and was still there for me when I needed him.

The Canadian team arrived back in Apex a couple of days later. By that stage I'd already jumped a few days with Pete and was starting to gain confidence on the double. Pete had to leave, so then I joined the Canadians who also agreed to help me. That's how good the sport is sometimes—when I really needed help my competitors were there to support me. It was a fantastic display of sportsmanship.

That whole period of coming back to jumping was testing. I was nervous, not sure how my knee was going to feel, and being very careful not to crash and inflame the injury. I remember landing and feeling no pain, which allowed me to build my confidence, and once I had that it felt good to be back. In spite of hardly any water ramping for the season, I didn't feel like I had lost much in terms of the feel and quality in my jumping. Because of my good results from the previous season, another positive was the fact that I was the only person on the Australian team who had already qualified for the Olympics, so I didn't have to worry about getting any results to make the team. We could only send four girls and we had six who had a chance of qualifying, so two were going to miss out, which was always going to end in tears.

The rest of our OWI team returned to Apex after the break and I finally had Todd and Murph back coaching me. By that stage I had already got some doubles under my belt, I was up to Full-Full and my knee was fine. We only had about 10 days before we had to depart for the Deer Valley World Cups, which would be a double event. Alisa had miraculously returned to jumping less than three months after her surgery, but she, too, had to qualify for a spot on the Olympic team, and with only a handful of events to do it, the pressure was mounting. Jacqui was in the same boat—she had been missing events to concentrate on training, so she had enormous pressure to pull something out of the hat and qualify for a spot. Liz, Lainie and Bree had already racked up some top 12 results between them, so it was pretty cutthroat in the Australian camp at that stage and I was just glad I didn't have the extra stress of having to qualify.

The training went well; I got up to my triple-twisting doubles and was off to Deer Valley for my first World Cup of the year. I didn't want to do too many events before the Olympics but I wanted to get back in the start gate and compete. My knee was now feeling quite good and I was regaining my confidence. I had some trouble initially adjusting to the Deer Valley site because I had been jumping at Apex for a month, but by the competition day I felt ready.

I landed two solid jumps and I won my comeback event. I felt like I was back where I left off. All the mental training I'd done and the physical rehab had paid off. Even though I wasn't doing triples I was still jumping well, and if I could win a World Cup, I could win the Olympics. I hadn't lost much in terms of skill because I'd rehearsed my jumps so many times and I realised how powerful my mental training and visualisation had been. It was the perfect comeback, and I let my competitors know that I was back and as determined as ever.

I pulled up a little bit sore after the first day of competition in Deer Valley and decided not to compete in the second World Cup. I could have, but I wasn't about to take any risks. I was very conservative for the first time in my life!

******

In an Olympic year, the World Cup takes on a different role. Winning the Grand Prix isn't the priority. Everyone is focused on being ready for the main event, the Games. It's a stressful period with athletes trying to qualify for a place on their Olympic teams. Everyone feels it, from the athletes to the coaches to the support staff, and when people are stressed they tend to behave differently, a bit on edge. They get 'Olympic fever' and it's so important to remain focused on your own program and keep your eyes on your own plate. I was on track, right where I wanted to be, so I just tried to stay in my bubble and not be distracted by what was going on around me.

But the rest of the team were still fighting it out for spots in the Games team. Alisa still had to jump, Jacqui had to jump, and so did Liz, Bree and Lainie, and the battle came down to the final pre-Olympic event in Lake Placid. I had great training all that week but on the competition day, the weather turned foul and I decided to pull out— I didn't need the result and I didn't need to take any risks in bad weather.

The selection process for the aerial skiing places in the team for Torino stipulated that one spot was discretionary, and at that point our coaches were in a quandary: do you give it to Jacqui Cooper, a three-time World Cup champion, or do you give it to Alisa Camplin, the reigning Olympic champion? Luckily, at Lake Placid Alisa saved the selectors from having to make that tough decision by qualifying in her own right. Jacqui didn't have a good result, but was granted the discretionary spot. Liz also made the grade and Bree and Lainie missed out. It was pretty tense for us all, but I was just trying to be in my own zone. I didn't want to get involved in the politics of who qualified and why. I had my spot and I was trying to stay out of the way. But it was very tough for the two teammates who missed out. Four years is a long time to wait for another chance. Lainie retired after that.

After the final World Cup we had a few days off before a pre-Olympic training camp. I wanted to get away, as did most people, so Alisa, Randall and I decided to drive to New York. It was good to get out of Lake Placid and clear my head for a few days. I had never been to New York City, so it was really cool to see the sites. We walked constantly, we shopped and we went to a Knicks game, museums and exhibitions. It ended up being a good mini-break, the last real break before the Olympics.

Before we knew it we were back in Lake Placid for the pre-Games camp. Everything was going smoothly for me. I was landing everything, my jumping was back to normal, and after the year I'd had I was now on schedule and right where I wanted to be. I was really happy with my knee, too. It wasn't perfect and I would get a little bit of pain and swelling after training, but that was to be expected. With ice, spinning on the bike and physio treatment I managed to keep it under control.

We had all planned to depart as a team for Torino before the opening ceremony, but Jacqui and Alisa were still scrambling to get their tricks done and under control. I was ready and as cool as a cucumber. Liz was also under control, so we both left for Torino while Jacqui, Alisa, Todd, Murph and Randall stayed in Lake Placid for a few more days of jumping.

When I got off the plane in Torino my knee felt a bit swollen, but I figured it was just the flight and was no big deal. Liz and I settled into the Olympic village in Bardonecchia, where we'd be staying until we could move into our sub-site accommodation up in Sauze d'Oulx, where our jumps venue was located. The Torino Olympics was a very different set-up compared to the Salt Lake Games. The athlete accommodation was spread over three different locations and the food was very average, which surprised us given it was Italy. But that was the least of my problems.

After a couple of days the swelling in my knee hadn't gone down—in fact it had increased. I was taking anti-inflammatories, I was icing constantly and I was wearing my compression stockings, but it still wasn't getting better. Randall was still in Lake Placid with the coaches and I was having a bit of a freak-out. I wished they were there, just so I could tell them what was happening and they could help me. As the days progressed my knee deteriorated and began to make all kinds of clicking and grinding sounds, something I hadn't experienced before. For some reason it was angry. As I walked and flicked my leg forward, it would lock up. I started to panic. I even decided not to go down to Torino to march in the opening ceremony, instead watching it on the big screen in the village while I iced my knee.

The rest of the aerials team travelled up to Bardonecchia after the opening ceremony and I rushed off to see Randall to find out if he could shed some light on what the hell was going on with my knee. I told him how bad it was feeling but he said there wasn't anything more we could do other than what I was already doing. I also saw our team doctor, Peter Braun—or 'Doc' as we called him—and he was just as perplexed. All he could suggest was to increase my dosage of anti-inflammatories. So I kept up the icing, the compression tights, the exercises, the physio treatment and spinning on the bike.

Then about three days before our event, I was on the bike and my knee locked up while I was strapped in the pedal. I screamed with pain and just broke down in tears. I couldn't understand why it was happening. Why now? I hadn't crashed and I had been so careful. I felt helpless. I was gulping down I don't know how many anti-inflammatories but they didn't seem to be having an effect any more. We didn't have much training time before our event so I started jumping, and as expected it felt very ordinary but I was managing. It felt horrible with the knee grinding and clicking, but I could still jump the same and I managed to get my tricks ready. From the outside I looked fine—I was jumping well and I was landing. But I knew something was brewing—I just hoped I'd last a few more days.

The night of the qualifications was a blizzard and after an hour of training they were postponed. None of us had expected that to happen, but again, it's the Olympics: expect the unexpected. The qualifications would now be held the next day so I raced home to ice and recover.

I remember my physio treatment with Randall the next day. My knee was obviously struggling so I asked him if I was going to be OK, was I going to make it? Stupid question, really, and I don't know why I asked it but his response was positive—'Yes, Lyd, you're going to make it, you'll be fine.' I guess I just needed to hear that.

That night, I was focused and I was ready. On my first jump I did a great Double Full-Full. I scored 101.52 points with a perfect landing score and I really couldn't have done it better. After the first round of jumps I was sitting in third place behind Jacqui and Chinese jumper Guo Xinxin, with one more jump to go. I was 19th on the start order, so I faced a long wait for my turn in the second round. About about 20 minutes of waiting, my knee began to stiffen up. I kept on moving to try to keep it warm, but the standing and waiting around in my knee brace and my ski boots was not doing it any good. I kept telling myself I just needed to hang in there for one more jump.

I skied in on that final jump, Todd called 'stretch' in the air and I responded, but as I came into the landing and my skis came in contact with the snow, I felt that familiar snap as the knee gave out. I knew instantly that I'd blown my knee. It was such a significant snap that even today I remember every detail of it. I screamed and I clutched my knee in agony as I slid to the bottom of the landing hill. I wasn't in agony over the pain, but because I knew instantly what had happened. My Olympics were over.

Nothing had gone wrong in training. I took precautions, I was jumping fine, I was landing well and I hadn't crashed many jumps. There seemed to be no reason for what had just happened. It was such a difficult time and I know everyone was feeling my pain. I was just so disappointed that my Olympics had ended like this and all the effort to come back and recover was undone in an instant.

I was carried off on a stretcher and taken inside a mini clinic, with OWI boss Geoff Lipshut with me the whole time. Doc followed and Pete, my old coach, also rushed in to see me. Even though he worked for Canada now, he was clearly upset. Soon Mum and Dad came in with Late and his parents. My cousin Miriam had come to watch me, as well as an old gym mate, Bronwyn. I was sorry they had to witness what had just happened, and see me in the state I was in, but at the same time I was glad they were there. We were all a mess.

Doc cut away my suit and peeled off my ski boot. He removed the brace and began to test my ACL. Through tears I said, 'It's gone.' I knew it, I had felt it snap. I was then taken in an ambulance to our hotel. The media was camped outside, but thankfully I was protected by team officials and didn't have to face the cameras and the questions.

I was in shock and I hardly remember the details from when I was carted off the snow on a stretcher. Much of it was all a blur except the crash and the instant I felt the snap inside my knee. Unfortunately for me, those particular memories haven't yet faded.

My Olympics weren't supposed to end the way they had. It wasn't what I had visualised. I envisioned a fairytale ending of triumph over adversity. But the reality was totally different. My family and Late followed me back to my hotel room. Everyone was distraught, and I was still crying, hoping I was in a nightmare and I'd wake up. Doc continued to test my knee—all the other ligaments seemed intact but it was difficult to say what other damage had occurred. I declared in the room straight away that this wasn't going to be the end of me, telling everyone, 'I'm not done yet.' Everything else in my life, other than the obvious, was perfect. I had a wonderful family, which included Late's, I had great friends and I was in love. All I was missing was an Olympic gold medal.

ACL grafts, and particularly allografts, go through cycles of strengthening and weakening. Mine had obviously been irritated by the flight to Italy and didn't recover. If it were a normal event I wouldn't have competed, but when it's the Olympics you don't pull out.

****

The Olympic final was the next day. Jacqui had qualified first with a world record score and was looking for redemption after what happened four years earlier in Salt Lake City. Alisa had scraped into the top 12 even after crashing one of her jumps. Liz had missed out on the finals and I was in 14th place. I tried to steer clear of Jacqui and Alisa so they could concentrate on the final. Jac popped her head in and gave me a hug to say how sorry she was. Alisa was in the room next to me, but walked straight past my door. Perhaps she didn't want to even entertain the thought of injuring her own knee and her way of avoiding that was to pretend I didn't exist.

I went to the final on my crutches, although it was painful to watch. My family and Late were there for support as well as other staff and officials. One of our team physios, Hoggie, stood by my side the whole time. It was a strange feeling watching the final and I experienced a flood of different thoughts. Somehow I couldn't believe it was going on without me. I felt sorry for myself and embarrassed at the same time, and I felt like I'd made a fool of myself. I would have preferred to have blown my knee in the final, then at least I would have been one step closer to contending for a medal.

Jacqui, the favourite after her record score in qualifying, crashed her first jump and was out of contention. Alisa won the bronze medal in what I thought was an amazing performance only three months after surgery. It seemed she got the fairytale ending I was hoping for. Her preparation had been far from perfect and on many occasions in the lead-up she'd had some crashes where I thought she had re-injured her knee, but she had survived and she is as resilient as they come.

Evelyne Leu from Switzerland won the gold, which was her redemption from Salt Lake 2002, and Nina Li won the silver. I left Torino needing more surgery, wondering if I was ever going to get a break in this sport and if I was ever going to reach my potential.

> *Geoff:* '*Given her determined nature, I thought Lydia would return due to unfinished business, but I was worried she would return with a 'Why me? ' chip on her shoulder. I have thought many times of how unfair that outcome was—the question I ask myself is, 'What if the strategy had been just a safe Full-Full for the second jump after a great score on the first. Would it all have been different?' I was always of the thought that Lydia would be the best jumper in the world. My vision was doubles for 2006 and after that triples. I thought Lydia would do triples technically well—no female triples jumper had ever been able to win regularly jumping triple-twisting doubles, but I felt Lydia could. I did not agree with Lydia swapping to triples when she did, though. She was easily number one in the world in season '04/05 after three consecutive wins and jumping some of the best doubles in history.*

I would have preferred her to keep on winning as long as possible doing high-end doubles (like Nina Li), and then to gradually move to triples—move on when people beat you rather than beating yourself. No one was even close to her at the start of the '04/05 season.'

****

When I got home from Torino I went back to see Hayden. He was perplexed as to why my knee had flared up when it did. It's funny—I never thought about having a dead person's tendon inside me until I damaged it again. I felt sorry that the part of that person I had kept alive was dead again. I told Hayden I wanted to continue jumping and he had no objections to it, so we made a plan about what type of surgery was needed and how long it would take to properly recover.

I had already decided to take a year off and was in no mind to rush the surgery or rehab this time. I didn't need to; I had four years. We decided to go with a traditional ACL procedure using my own hamstring tendon, but because the allograft had been quite a thick graft, it left big holes in my bone where the screws were. Redrilling through the same holes wasn't going to work, so the ACL reconstruction was going to have to be done in two stages. First Hayden removed the old graft as well as the screws that had attached it. He then plugged up the screw holes with bone from my hip. I had to let the bone graft heal for three months before I could go ahead and have the reconstruction. Again, my leg wasted away to a stick and I had to rebuild the muscle through hours in the gym and on the bike. I had also damaged some cartilage so I had to avoid taking any impact through the joint for quite some time. It was a drawn-out process, but at least I had time on my side. When the bone had healed, I went back in to have the reconstruction. This time Hayden did what is called a 'double bundle' graft, which was very innovative at the time. Instead of using one large graft, he used two smaller grafts, requiring two additional bone tunnels, to better replicate the function of the normal ACL.

With all this going on, I tried to distract myself as best I could from what happened in Torino. Knowing I was having a year off, I distanced myself from the sport as much as possible and tried not to think about it. I wasn't bitter; I just didn't want to know. I didn't want to know that the World Cup was going on without me and other athletes were going on as normal. I suppose I wanted to pretend that everyone was having the year off and I just concentrated on my rehab and getting better.

I got busy, and in a short time developed my own business called Body Sphere. The idea had come to me as I was icing my knee in the athlete village in Torino before the closing ceremony. I had a bag of ice on my knee that kept leaking and slipping everywhere and I was so fed up. I said, 'Someone should bloody well design a decent ice-pack!' On the long flight home from Italy, I sketched some designs and started brainstorming. I knew what I wanted to create because I had so much experience in trying to ice injured body parts. I wanted to design a product that I could have used and would have needed during my own rehabilitation. I wanted to create designs that could allow people to target any injured area with ease without having to manually hold the ice pack in place. I wanted the ice bag to be cold enough and to stay cold for a long period of time and I also wanted it to function as a heat pack.

I chose to couple the traditional ice bag with joint-specific neoprene supports that strap onto an injured joint or body part with a good level of compression, allowing it to stay in place. I called my new product line Body Ice. The next step was to find a suitable manufacturer and make up some prototypes. After my initial surgery and as soon as I was able to walk properly, I travelled to China and Taiwan with Dad and my brother Peppi to visit a trade fair and meet with some manufacturers that I had sourced. I had sent each manufacturer my designs so they could make up some samples for me to evaluate. From that point, I chose the best quality design and proceeded with manufacturing. Each step was an incredible learning experience and extremely fulfilling because I was creating a business of my own from scratch and learning everything from manufacturing, shipping and freight to sales and marketing.

Burying myself in my new business was the perfect distraction because it gave me something else to focus on. Most importantly,

I was being constructive with my time off and making a positive out of a difficult situation.

On 10 May 2006, I went to see Hayden for a review and to find out if my bone had healed enough to go ahead with the ACL reconstruction. He decided that it wasn't quite ready and we should give it another month. I was in no mind to question him, but at the same time I was frustrated because I just wanted to get on with it and have a new ACL so I could start the rehab properly.

I got home and broke down on the couch. Late tried to comfort me, saying everything was going to be all right, and then suddenly he was in tears as he got down on one knee and pulled out a box from his pocket. I was in my tracksuit pants with a Body Ice prototype on my knee and looked an absolute mess, and he was asking me to marry him! In between sobbing uncontrollably, I said yes. The poor guy did have a plan on how he was going to propose. He was going to do it two days later on Mother's Day at a family lunch, where he would ask my dad in the good traditional way. But after seeing I was so upset, he decided to dump his plan and cheer me up instead. It was so cute and it worked a treat! We put on some nice clothes, bought a couple of bottles of Champagne and drove to Diggers Rest to tell my family, who were equally excited. After a few glasses, it seemed everything was going to be all right and I forgot about my knee.

Now I had Body Sphere to develop and a wedding to plan, so there was plenty going on in my life to keep me occupied. On 6 June 2006, I went in for surgery and finally had my ACL reconstructed, and then began the long process of recovery and building back my muscle. By October I received my first shipment of Body Ice stock and Body Sphere was up and running.

I tried not to dwell too much on the past and the time off gave me a new perspective on life. Aerial skiing didn't define who I was. I loved it and wanted to come back, but I found out that there were other things in life that could be just as fulfilling.

My injuries have left scars, but time healed a lot of things.

CHAPTER 10

RETURNING TO TURMOIL

I took a full year off to recover from my knee reconstruction in June. While the year seemed to fly by, the break was great in so many ways. It gave me time to heal physically, emotionally and mentally—each as important as the other.

I developed my Body Ice product line and saw the business grow quickly to a level that started providing me with some income. My main clients included orthopaedic surgeons, hospitals, physiotherapists and sports teams. There was a lot I needed to learn about running a business successfully and my absence from sport left a void that needed filling. I craved learning, so I investigated options for further study. I wanted to do a course in business studies, but I knew that when I returned to aerial skiing and life on the road my ability to attend lectures or physically be present at a university would be limited, so my only option was some sort of distance education. I discovered many options for studying online and enrolled into a business degree with Open Universities Australia. They offer a range of courses online and I found a suitable business degree that would help me run Body Sphere. In no time I was learning skills I could apply to my business and my mind was being challenged again.

I also had time to plan our wedding—or should I say weddings!

Late and I had decided that we would get married during the summer in Finland in July 2007 and then we'd have another 'celebration' in Melbourne that October. It was quite the challenge organising both weddings, although my future parents-in-law, Leena and Erkki, basically did all the work for the one in Finland.

I continued rehabilitation at the VIS under the watchful eye of Dee Jennings. Although my rehab schedule was still intense, this time around I had time on my side and didn't push or rush through my progressions. I was careful and cautious, especially in relation to who gave me advice, who I let treat my knee and who was inside my rehab team. My rehab routine consisted of hours on the exercise bike, lunges, squats, Pilates and balance exercises, to name a few. With time, I introduced running, hopping and jumping drills. Body Ice was a great addition and I routinely had one strapped to my knee after my workouts.

My knee progressed and started to feel better and so did I, and I started to develop a hunger to get back on my skis again. My mind had also evolved during the rehab, and I was absolutely committed to no more mistakes. I had to listen to my body and I had to cut the injuries. It was time for me to change my luck.

During my year off, our team had secured Barbara Meyer as our team psychologist. Barbara had previously been Alisa's psychologist and had obviously been her secret weapon, part of the team that transformed Alisa into a great competitor. When she retired after Torino, Barbara was offered a position to work with the remaining Australian team.

At first I was hesitant. There was no doubt that Barbara brought out the best in Alisa and she became a champion, but in some ways she also brought out the worst in her. She brought out her extremes, which sometimes imposed on us as teammates. Pressure often does that and Alisa was under pressure to perform. You always knew when Alisa was on the jump site. Her intensity would hit you like a tonne of bricks. Everyone could feel it, from the coaches to teammates and competitors. But that is how she needed to be to get the best results from herself. Alisa and I are two very different personalities, and just because Barbara worked for Alisa it didn't mean she was going to work for me or for the rest of the team.

Barbara hadn't had any involvement with the rest of the team at all so I didn't really know her. I didn't know if I would even like her.

> Barbara: 'My initial thoughts on Lydia were formed before I started working with her. Alisa Camplin was always a bit concerned about her as a competitor and so I knew she had to have something special. Alisa would not have offered that sort of compliment lightly. '

As a team, we discussed the option of having Barbara on board. The OWI obviously thought she was a guru but I wasn't ready to put a halo around her head. Instead of me wanting to work with her, I fired the question back, 'Does Barbara want to work with me?' And that was the question I posed to her in an email. We laugh about it now and she often uses it as an example in her lectures because she thought it was interesting. Sure, our team needed and wanted a sport psychologist, but I didn't want to work with her just because she was successful with Alisa. I wanted her to work with us because she *wanted* to work with us.

> Barbara: 'I still have that email and all of the others we ever exchanged. And I think about that particular email quite often, especially when I am considering work with a new athlete/team. Accepting the job as sport psychology consultant for the entire Australian Aerials Ski Team did not come without a lot of forethought and soul-searching. The offer was on the table for quite a while before I accepted.'

Every athlete is different, with a different set of needs, and I wanted Barbara to know that I didn't come from the same mould as Alisa. If she was going to work with me, she would need to think outside the box. I wanted to make sure that I wasn't begging for her services, that she actually was interested in helping me achieve my dreams and goals. I really wanted to know if she was interested in working with us instead of our team feeling 'lucky' to have her. In the end, she proved her genuine interest and the OWI brought her on board.

Barbara: '*While many people assumed it would be easy for me to get right in there and get to work given my history in, and knowledge of, the sport, I knew better. First, I didn't really know any of the athletes. I didn't know if my professional skill set would mesh with their needs. I had observed them from afar for years, but never really paid the kind of close attention necessary to understand strengths and weaknesses. Second, if there was a professional fit, there was the matter of personal fit. Could I connect with each member of the team and they with me in such a way as to develop mutual trust, respect, and affection as people? While I don't have to like the people I work with, it certainly helps.*

'*I realised that there were two major barriers to the personal fit piece: firstly it was my history with a former teammate and competitor; secondly it was my ability to work with a team of athletes who were, in some cases, each others' biggest competitors. Could I give each of them what they needed to succeed without sacrificing any of the needs of the others?*

'*I had numerous friends and colleagues try to talk me out of taking the job. During the decision-making process there were times when I thought I didn't want the job, but I also didn't want anyone else to have it. I didn't want them to have it because deep down I knew I was the right person for the job—I knew my approach was a great match for the individuals on the team. At the end of the day, I couldn't back away from the challenge.*'

Although I didn't really know Barbara, she had obviously been observing me for quite some time, as I was one of Alisa's main rivals. When we first started working together I was still rehabbing my knee and we started planning not only my return to aerials, but also the next three years leading into the 2010 Olympic Winter Games in Vancouver.

Straight after Torino I knew things had to be different, and I told Barbara that I felt my career had been punctuated with setbacks and injury and that I was sick of the up-and-down pattern in which I had found myself. Obviously I was doing something wrong, but at the time I didn't know exactly what was holding me back. All I knew was that there was no more room for mistakes and bad luck. Only I could change my luck, and that's where Barbara's knowledge and expertise would come into play—she would be of great help and a key player in my support network. I shared with her how frustrated I had become, because I knew my potential was greater. I knew I was good enough to be number one in the world and was tired of being a bridesmaid. I told her of my aspirations to win Olympic Gold, to be number one in the world and to break world records. I told her I wanted to jump like a man and compete with triples that women hadn't done before. Even though it was risky and dangerous, I had decided that was the path I wanted to take.

Barbara and I are very different, in some ways polar opposites. She is very logical, analytical and clinical in her approach, rarely expressing her emotions. I, on the other hand, am a feeler. I love structure, but I often fly by the seat of my pants and rely on my emotions and passion because that is what drives me to excel. Barbara was quick to point out my strengths, but also weaknesses that up to that point I had been unaware of. First she told me I was too focused on outcome, too focused on winning, and that I didn't pay enough attention to the process of achieving the things I desperately wanted. Secondly, after hearing about my aspirations she said, 'Lydia, it's great you want to win and achieve all of these things, but this is the last time I want to hear you talking about medals and records. What you are going to focus on now is the process of achieving these goals, one step at a time.'

Barbara then introduced the concept of 'delayed gratification'. I didn't really understand the term at first, but then she said, 'Lydia, do you want to win World Championships now, break a world record now and be number one on the World Cup tour now, or do you want to win the Olympics in three years' time?'

That was a no-brainer for me: my response was, 'I want to do it all.'

I couldn't imagine going out to compete without wanting to win every time. But that was a mentality Barbara said I had to change. And at first, it didn't sit well with me. 'Really? So you're actually encouraging me to not want to win?'

'No. Out of all the goals you want to achieve, I want you to pick one goal that matters to you most. Is it World Championships next year or is it the Olympics?'

'Of course it's the Olympics. That's what I care about the most.'

So that became the priority and we worked backwards in developing a plan and strategy of the steps I needed to take in order for me to be in the best position to win in Vancouver in 2010. Everything else, as scary as it sounded to me, had to be secondary. If I was going to win the Olympics with the intention of doing tricks women hadn't done before, I had to change my focus from outcome to process. I was going to have to learn how to sacrifice immediate results for long-term gain. That's delayed gratification.

> *Barbara: 'In addition to Lydia's very candid email asking me if I wanted the job, I remember a lunch we had in Melbourne in April 2007. It was in a Thai restaurant and we were talking about goals and the approach to 2010, and I suggested that Lydia couldn't win a gold medal from a hospital bed—she needed to be smart and methodical in her approach, not desperate and rush it. She didn't like that, and gave me the silent treatment for a few weeks. I learned quickly that when I hit a nerve—aka when Lydia knew I was right—she needed time to think about it.'*

I spent a good chunk of my aerial skiing career thinking I was seeing the big picture, but Barbara pointed out that I wasn't really getting the concept. I've always set myself goals but they were just destinations with no map. I had a lot to learn about being patient—which was clearly one of my biggest weaknesses—and trusting there was a process in place to succeed. I was desperate to achieve my goals, but I didn't really have a plan in place for how I was going to get there, or at least not the detailed plan Barbara had in store for me. It became pretty clear to me that even though I had come across some bad luck, I had brought on a lot of the 'things' that kept happening to me myself.

> Barbara: 'I have frequently observed that Lydia's greatest strengths are at times her greatest weaknesses.'

I had to prepare myself for some failures and trust that in the bigger scheme of things I was working towards my goal. Learning new tricks, especially triples, takes time and I couldn't put too much pressure on myself to land them in every competition. If I fell, I had to suck it up, know that it was for a good reason and just let it go. It was a conscious act for me to not worry about winning and I had to remind myself that I was building towards something that was going to have a longer term benefit. Those are the concepts Barbara started me on, and once I was committed to the big picture, we worked on breaking down the big goals into small goals, sub-goals and the strategies to get me there.

I took on board every single thing Barbara suggested to me. I didn't want to be embarrassed again. I wanted to go into the next Games with no mistakes, and if that meant sacrificing World Cup wins and World Cup globes and World Championships, then so be it. I was prepared to take that chance, and I had never felt that way before. I had to stay disciplined and focused on building towards the Olympics, not the rest of it, because in reality none of that mattered. It was good to have Barbara on board.

****

After Torino and during my season off, our coaching staff had gone through some significant changes. Todd had left our team and was privately coaching a couple of athletes, one being Jacqui. Murph had also left, going back to his home country Canada to coach, primarily because Vancouver was hosting the next Olympics and it was a great lure. We were sad to lose Murph, but at the same time we understood the opportunity he had been given.

At the time, there was a shortage of coaches available to replace the ones we had lost and the OWI was really scrambling to find someone suitable and with enough experience—not only for the World Cup team but also our development athletes. We picked up a younger coach, Ryan Snow, a Canadian aerialist who had retired and started coaching, but his experience at the time was limited and he wouldn't have been able to handle the World Cup and development teams by himself.

And we were not only battling a shortage of quality coaches, we also had to deal with a bad reputation. A lot of coaches had left our team dissatisfied with the lack of control they had over the program they were employed to manage. While they loved working with the athletes, they were very frustrated that all the shots were being called from head office in Melbourne and they felt powerless to make program decisions. We were the most successful team in the world, but word spreads fast in the freestyle community and no coaches wanted to work with our federation. So I went into the OWI to have a frank chat with Geoff Lipshut. It wasn't an easy conversation, but it was honest and had to be done. The OWI had provided great support during my injury and comeback, but our program was without coaches and this was very unsettling for me.

'Geoff, we are in a very difficult situation here,' I told him. 'We've lost some really good coaches because you have too much control over the program. Now we are struggling to get new coaches and no one wants to work with us. How are we going to fix this? I've worked my butt off to come back from injury. Do you think it's fair for me to come back to no coach and the program in a mess?'

He didn't really have any answers, but at least he knew what I thought and what I had heard from other coaches. I've always been a straight shooter and we had a real problem. Geoff asked me if I still wanted to work with Todd and I said we should try to convince him to come back and work with us. But by the time I was ready to start jumping again we still hadn't found a suitable coach, and Todd was still considering the offer.

In the meantime, Barbara and I had developed a plan for my return. We decided that in my first year back, we'd be slow and conservative without putting too much pressure on me to win. I would do my stock standard triple-twisting double somersaults and focus on staying healthy and injury-free, and use the year to regain my confidence, particularly with my knee. It was a different approach to the one I normally took—it would be the first year that I would compete without wanting to outdo myself or push beyond the boundaries.

The plan for the second year was to start triples on water and then on snow. We knew that they would be inconsistent at first and I probably wouldn't be able to land them in every event, but the point was to do them and gain experience and confidence on snow without worrying about results. Then, the next year, I'd have done enough of them on snow to be consistent and have them ready for the Olympics.

We had a timeframe of three years and a clear path I could see that would lead me forward, and that was the process I had to learn to trust. I knew it would be hard, because I could easily go out and compete triple-twisting doubles and have a chance to win World Cups every week, but triples were a long-term investment, and if I did them well at the Olympics I would almost be guaranteed a win—and that was the kind of return I was after. The plan looked good on paper and I was committed to following the process, one step at a time.

I started back on snow in May 2007 at a ski camp on the glacier in Whistler with my teammates Denita Mudge, who was also recovering from knee surgery, and David Morris, our only male aerialist. With us was our new aerial coach Ryan Snow, and we'd also be working with our national mogul coach, Steve Desovich. I had trained with Steve before and really enjoyed it, so I was looking forward to that. The moguls would help improve my technical skills and, having been off my skis for a year, that was going to be critical before heading to Park City for water ramping.

During that time, we were still trying to convince Todd to come back to work with us, and although we had Barbara on board we still didn't have a full-time physiotherapist, which was something I had stressed we needed to the OWI on many occasions over the years. I didn't feel like the program was moving in the right direction or that my feedback and recommendations to the OWI to improve the program were being listened to or taken seriously, so I started to assess my options.

I couldn't afford any more mistakes and I didn't want my plans and goals to be jeopardised because I wasn't getting what I needed. I wasn't asking for much. All I expected was to have a decent, experienced coach I could trust with my life and a physio to make sure that what had happened to me in the past with injuries wouldn't happen again.

You would think that, as the most successful women's aerial skiing team in history, we had earned the right to be looked after. Coming back from injury was hard enough, and all I expected on my return was for my basic needs to be met. Instead, I felt unimportant, like I had been left on the scrap heap. I had to figure out a way I could get my needs met. I wasn't about to throw a tantrum and make a fuss, so I endeavoured to remove myself from the situation and find opportunity elsewhere.

Finland had asked me to consider jumping for them a few times before because of my relationship with Late and also because they didn't have any aerial skiers. I had never taken the offer seriously before, but now, given the circumstances, I started to think about it. When an athlete chooses to defect to another country the decision is often scorned; I was aware of the criticism I might get, but weighed up the advantages and disadvantages. If I did move to Finland, I'd basically have my own program with the coach of my choice and a physio. I'd have everything I needed and wouldn't have to deal with the politics of the Australian team any longer. Finland is a winter sport nation, and given my string of previous results, I'd be well supported there. On the other hand, if I did move to Finland, I would have been criticised heavily in Australia and seen as a traitor.

Conversely, I wasn't convinced that if I stayed with Australia the program would provide me with the best chance of succeeding in Vancouver. I couldn't afford to take that risk, couldn't afford to leave my career to chance. I had worked so hard to recover physically, emotionally and mentally from Torino, and I wasn't about to throw away all that effort.

In essence, I had to do what was right for me. I started contacting the appropriate people in Finland to start the process. I was going to face many obstacles and one of them was that Australia could ban me from competing for up to two years. I contacted the International Ski Federation and negotiated with them that, because I'd already had a year off due to injury, then that would at least count as one year, and if Australia would let me go quietly, I could resume jumping for Finland the next year. It was pretty heavy stuff.

If I did jump for Finland, I would train with 'Team Europe' in Switzerland under the coaching direction of Michel Roth. 'Mich' was the Swiss national team coach, but over the years had also taken on a number of athletes from other European nations, which is why we had dubbed it 'Team Europe'. Mich was the most successful aerial skiing coach in history. In the four Olympics that he had coached to that time, his athletes had won four individual medals—three gold and one bronze. It was an impressive record and I figured he must be doing something right. The chance to work with him started playing on my mind.

In the meantime, I told Barbara about my concerns and my thoughts of leaving. She was very surprised, but although she understood my frustration and where I was coming from, she urged me not to make any hasty decisions. After the ski camp in Whistler we headed to Park City to start jumping on water. For the first couple of weeks of my return to jumping Ryan had been my coach, and although he was relatively inexperienced I really liked him. He knew what he was talking about when it came to technique. But that still wasn't going to solve our problem of not having enough coaches to service the World Cup and development teams.

Todd eventually accepted the offer to come back and coach us, but he was a different Todd. Something had happened to him and he had changed. He used to be so enthusiastic, so meticulous and we had such a good coach-athlete relationship that I thought it would be the same. Instead he seemed uninterested in the sport and uninterested in me. In hindsight, if we weren't so desperate we wouldn't have hired him, but at the time we had no other choices.

****

In early July we had a training break and I flew to Finland for my wedding. A lot of long distance planning had taken place and Leena and Erkki had been wonderful in helping me, organising nearly everything.

About 30 guests from Australia also flew over, including my immediate family, friends, cousins and aunts and uncles. My bridesmaids were three of my best friends: Erica and Taryn had been friends since my early gym days and Courtney was my friend from high school.

It was great having everyone in Finland and I was glad they had a chance to experience the country I had fallen in love with. For the hens' party, 10 girlfriends and I took a boat to Tallinn in Estonia where we spent the night shopping and dancing the night away. We had an awesome time.

The wedding itself was absolutely beautiful. We were married at a castle called Vanajanlinna in the gardens overlooking a picturesque lake, and it was a magical ceremony. Then we headed to Late's parents' farm, where they had transformed their old barn into a reception centre. It was amazing. We partied all night under the midnight sun and didn't get back to our hotel room at the castle until 6am! It was a memorable wedding for everyone and a day Late and I will never forget.

The honeymoon was postponed until October, and a week after the wedding I flew back to Park City. Nevertheless, we were married and I was now 'Mrs Lassila'! I got back into the routine of jumping, everything was going to plan and my knee was coping well. But with Todd not himself, it didn't take me long to realise that the set-up wasn't going to work, reinforcing my intention to defect to Finland.

There was a water ramp competition in Switzerland that summer and I flew myself over there at my own expense to do the event. At least that was the reason I gave everyone in my team. My real intentions, however, were to see how 'Team Europe' operated and to see if I could train in Switzerland and work with Mich.

When I arrived, I told Mich everything that was going on, and told him that I was basically there to see if I could work with him and find out whether he wanted to work with me. I told him how serious I was about switching teams and jumping for Finland and he was really good about it. While Finland's mogul team was really strong, they didn't have an aerial team, so it was going to be a great thing for the sport to bring another nation into the game. Mich was keen to work with me and excited about my plan for the next three years. Everything about him felt right for me, so I asked him, 'If the situation with the Australian team gets worse, could I come and join your team for the winter?' He had no objections and that's where we left it.

In mid-September Todd went to a wedding in Denver and didn't come back when he was supposed to. He didn't ring or text us to tell us where he was and basically left us to fend for ourselves for more than a week. At that point, we really came together as a team and decided that, instead of not training, we would take it in turns to coach. One half of the group would jump for half a session while the other half coached and videoed jumps, then we'd swap. The US, Chinese and Canadian teams were also training in Park City but we pretended they weren't there and just got on with business as usual. They were confused as to why athletes were coaching each other and asked where Todd was, but we simply said we didn't know. It was great that we pulled together as a team and figured out a way to handle the situation, but the whole time I was thinking about how ridiculous and unacceptable it was. So I decided it was time to tell Geoff Lipshut about my intentions to leave the team.

Once again it wasn't an easy conversation. I told him how fed up I was with the program and how I couldn't afford to waste my time. I needed to do what was right for me and I wanted to be removed from the situation and the drama. My job was to be an athlete and I gave 100 per cent effort every day. Neither the team nor I deserved the stress that was created by a dysfunctional program and we gave too much of our lives up to be treated like that. I was clearly unhappy and I let Geoff know.

Obviously he wasn't expecting me to say I was considering jumping for another country, but when I explained and justified my reasons, there wasn't much he could say. By the end of our conversation, I gave him an ultimatum: fix the mess or I'm gone.

> *Geoff: 'I felt it was partly a hangover from the Torino injury and the difficulty of being in Alisa's and Jacqui's shadows—up until Olympic Winter Games 2006 we had either the best or close to the best program for female athletes ever with Todd and Murph.*

> *'I did feel that we needed to change the program after Torino and start over again to a certain extent—in the last days of Todd being head coach with Murph in '05/06, the behaviour and standards had gone out of control. The coaching staff were more absorbed with themselves than with the athletes. With the benefit of hindsight we should have kept Murph and paid the additional money to make him the highest paid coach in any team, but I wasn't sure Murph would step up and throw off the example set by Todd.'*

Meanwhile, Barbara was trying to locate Todd, and instead of being our sport psychologist, her role changed to team mediator, mostly trying to figure out the psychology of our coach rather than spending her time on us athletes. Todd eventually came back and naturally we asked where he'd been. He said he'd been really sick with fever and we pounced on him, asking, 'Were you too sick to text us, just to let us know where you were?'

We called a team meeting without Todd to decide what we were going to do with him. I said we should get rid of him straight away because we couldn't afford for this to happen in the middle of the season. Jacqui was on the same page as me but Liz wasn't sure because we didn't have anyone else. Denita and Dave were working with Ryan and were really happy with him, so they were immune to the predicament we were facing. It was really up to Liz, Jac and me to decide, so we called a meeting with Todd.

We didn't beat around the bush. 'Todd, you either want to work with us or you don't and you have to make the decision now, because if you don't want to work with us we need to get rid of you and find someone who might want to.' He was strangely startled and really defensive.

'So you're going to fire me now?'

'No. We just want to know if you're up for the job and if you're not, you need to leave and we need to find someone new.'

He decided that he still wanted the job and that he was sorry for abandoning us. So we gave him another chance and finished off the summer as per usual.

At the end of September I went back home to Melbourne to prepare for our second wedding celebration. Before I left, I told Todd that I would see him in Apex at the start of November and we went over some brief plans for the winter. We left on good terms and that was that. Apart from the coaching dramas, my summer had been great. I was jumping triple-twisting doubles and back in form, I was married to a great man, my knee was doing fine, and I was ready for the season.

I flew home and had a lovely second wedding with all our family and friends who couldn't make it to Finland. I arrived by horse and carriage to Treasury Gardens in Melbourne, where we had a short ceremony confirming our vows to one another before heading to the Hotel Windsor for a reception in the beautiful grand ballroom. Late and I then went on our honeymoon to Tahiti and just had a great time relaxing and spending time together as newlyweds, which was something we hadn't yet been able to do.

At the start of November the team departed for Apex Mountain, and for the first time ever we had a full-time physiotherapist, Ashley Merkur. That was one positive change that had come about after my threat to leave the team and I was relieved to have her on board. Given the injuries I had sustained and unnecessarily put up with throughout my career, it was very comforting to know that I'd be in the care of a medical professional. But then the unthinkable happened. Todd didn't show up.

We called him to find out where he was and he said, 'I'll be there in a week,' but that week passed and he hadn't arrived. After two weeks of waiting around in Apex, we finally got an email telling us he was resigning. He didn't want to coach us any more, he was sick of the lifestyle and the travel, and that was it. It was the worst situation our team had ever been in. I was returning to snow after recovering from a knee reconstruction and our coach just decided to not show up. It was embarrassing for us to have been abandoned like that yet again, and for Ashley who had just joined us, it was a rude welcome.

Geoff: 'The second hiring of Todd in April 2007 was a disastrous move with only limited options. Our thoughts were that Todd was capable of doing a very good job in the summer living in Park City, but would struggle in the winter with travel and pressure. This is when we decided to employ Ashley for the first time to provide physio support and manage the athletes, and with Barbara in place off site, we were confident we would manage the situation with Todd. As it happened, there was no winter with Todd, who left in November 2007 without a jump on snow.

'The idea of Barbara and Ashley was to support the welfare of the athletes both physically and mentally with a volatile and less-than-perfect coach situation. In retrospect this period made us all better, and we all learned from the poor choices we made first!'

At first, we didn't know what to do, but again we pulled together and started to brainstorm our options. We couldn't coach each other like we had done on water, because on-snow training is very different and we rely on a coach who has experience to call you in the air. We needed someone, but we didn't know who, so we started calling every single coach and ex-coach we knew, to see if someone—anyone—could help us out.

It wasn't easy. The Canadians, who were also in Apex, couldn't do anything for us because of the commercial implications. Canada was the host nation of the next Olympics and had sponsors that had invested a lot of money into their programs so they could have the best chance of winning medals. There was no way they could help their competitors, which was completely understandable. The Americans weren't in Apex but said they may be able to help us out in the opening World Cup events of the season in China, but we would need to find something more permanent after that. It was not even an option to ask the Chinese for assistance, given their team was now coached by our ex-coach Dustin Wilson. We knew the answer would be no so we didn't bother.

I don't know how many people we rang, but we just kept getting shut down. Then we started looking into some ex-aerialists who might want to coach. We were really clutching at straws just trying to find someone. Jac rang the former Russian jumper Dmitry Arkhipov, the 2003 World Champion and World Cup Champion, and surprisingly, he said he'd take on the job. The only problem was that he couldn't come straight away because he needed a visa. Russians need a visa for nearly every country, so we handballed that job to Ashley and she started planning for the visas he would need during the World Cup season.

I was at a point where I could have easily said, 'OK, that's enough. See you later guys, I'm going to work with Mich Roth,' but instead I rang Mich and explained the situation. 'Remember how I said I might be joining you in November or December if the situation got worse? Well, the situation couldn't be any worse. Can you consider taking on Liz and Jacqui as well?'

He couldn't believe what had happened and said, 'I am sorry for you guys, and it's okay for you to come Lydia, but I will need to ask the rest of the team about the other girls.' At that stage he was the only coach for nine Swiss and other European athletes, a big team for one coach. With us it would be 12 and that was a tough call. The only carrot I could offer him was that we could bring Dmitry with us as an assistant to help.

The Russians are renowned on tour for being lazy and not working very hard on the jump site. They often show up when all the work and preparation has been done, and while they have some good athletes, when it comes to picking up a shovel, doing work and having initiative, they tend to be as lazy as they come.

Mich was sceptical straight away. 'Dmitry Arkhipov, really? I don't know. He's a good athlete but I'm not sure he likes to work very hard.'

'I know, Mich, but he's all we can find unless you have anyone else in mind.'

'OK, first I need to ask the team and I'll get back to you.'

It was an anxious wait hoping that Mich and his team would say yes. The Ukrainian team was training in Apex at the time, and instead of sitting on our backsides, we asked their coach if she would be able to look after us for a couple of days. She was very obliging, said yes, and that was my return to jumping on snow.

I was nervous, not only because we were jumping with a random coach, but also because of my knee. I had been fine on water but I wasn't sure how it would be on snow. After a few basic jumps, however, I was okay.

After a couple of days, I rang Mich and he said yes, he would take on the whole team. It was a huge relief for all of us and, really, he was our saviour. Team Europe was training in Switzerland on a glacier in Saas-Fee, and after a couple of days of jumping with the Ukrainians, we hopped on a plane for Zurich. It was just crazy, but somehow we managed to find humour in our circumstances and did what we needed to do.

I was really happy knowing we were going to be coached by Mich and instantly felt relieved. Everything was going to be all right.

> *Mich: 'I could understand it was a terrible situation and I wanted to help. I was surprised because it happened fast. For me it was not a difficult thing because we had done it in the past with other nations. I knew Lydia was a good jumper and it would be a good chance to work with her. We just needed to work out how we were going to do it.'*

It was a great outcome for all of us. We had a new coach, one that I wanted, we had a physio and we had Barbara, and that was all I really needed. We had miraculously 'fixed' the situation, and although I was prepared to remove myself from the team, I was so relieved I didn't have to. Even though Todd's 'no show' was the last straw and I was fed up and could have easily picked up and left by myself, I didn't. I felt a strong obligation to my teammates and there was no way I could leave them stranded in Apex. If it wasn't for my trip to Switzerland during the summer, where I developed a good relationship with Mich and semi-prepared him for what I thought may happen, we may have been in real trouble.

All I wanted was to have a simple program in place. All I was asking for was a decent coach and a physio. It wasn't as if I was demanding the world on a silver platter. It had taken a lot of effort for me to work through rehabilitation and back into good shape, but when I got back to jumping, I felt that the ball had been dropped by others and there was no one there to support me. I felt like there was nothing there for me and that is why I seriously looked to defect.

I was committed to not making any more mistakes, and coming back from a year off with injury to resume training without a coach would have been a problem. My energy should have been focused on jumping and being the best athlete I could be, not worrying about administrative issues, but the reality was that I cared about the program and the athletes who were being affected. If I left for Finland, I'd be running my own program because I'd be the country's only aerial skier and I'd have the things the way I wanted, which did seem beautiful. I would live most of the year in Finland and I could spend more time with Late, which was a great option. But, in truth, I didn't want to do that. I wanted to jump in the green and gold and sing the Australian national anthem when I won. I wanted to jump for Australia.

****

Switzerland was very different for us, as I had already discovered in the summer. We were used to training and living in North America, so when we arrived in Switzerland we really felt like we were on a great adventure. To get to Saas-Fee, we drove through never-ending tunnels under the mountains, we travelled along narrow streets through tiny villages and we even had to drive our car onto a train that transported us through a mountain. It was a totally new experience for everyone and was a bit surreal.

Ashley, our new physio, had also become the de facto team manager, responsible for booking flights, vehicles and accommodation and arranging how we were going to get to and from places. She had organised Dmitry's visas, but because of time restraints he couldn't join us in Switzerland so ended up meeting us at the World Cup openers in China. Given our situation, we were glad Ashley was with us and we would have been lost without her. I'm sure she was wondering what she had landed herself into. On top of physio treatments, she was our video girl and team manager, a really massive job in her first year.

After arriving in Saas-Fee we jumped for three days straight. We tried to blend into the team as best as we could, but it wasn't easy. The Swiss do things in a certain way, which was different for us, but we tried to be compliant. They had come to our rescue and the last thing we wanted to do now was make waves.

It was a strange situation. We were the biggest threat to Evelyne Leu, the reigning Olympic champion. We were her competitors, and now we were being coached by her coach in the same team. The Swiss could have said no to us like the rest of the countries did, but thankfully they didn't. They are led by a coach like no other, one of the most respected on the tour. Mich's passion is aerial skiing and it's not difficult to see that. I was so happy to be coached by him.

> *Mich: 'I really like working with people that want to work hard and Lydia had high goals. The fact that she wanted to do difficult jumps was exciting for me and it was clear that she was able to do those jumps. She really wanted to do something big and she was motivated to do it. I think she did a good job to show them she could do it.'*

Finally everything was okay. I had the coach I wanted, I was jumping and, importantly, I was still doing it for Australia.

CHAPTER 11

THE A-TEAM AND THE SILENT PARTNER

We entered the 2008 northern winter season with a new coach, a new physio and new ways, just two weeks away from going to our first World Cups in China. Training on the glacier at Saas-Fee happens at an altitude of 3500 metres and it took two gondolas and one train ride up through the mountains to get to the jump site from where we were staying. It's an incredible place, very majestic, and the beauty of the mountains took my breath away every day.

Jumping was going well and in three days I was already up to Full-Fulls and landing everything. I decided to wear my brace for jumping, but after a few days, a problem I'd experienced during a ski camp on the glacier in Whistler in May 2007 re-emerged. I had worn the knee brace during the camp for peace of mind and also to give my knee more stability, but because I'd had a hamstring graft on my second reconstruction, the brace rubbed against the hamstring and felt uncomfortable. After a couple of days of skiing in Whistler, I had what resembled a golf ball behind my knee. My instant reaction was, 'What the hell is this? What now?' I got it checked and I had developed what's called a 'Baker's cyst'. It was quite ridiculous, really. I'd had a year off to recover and had done all the right things and then two days after going for a leisurely ski, I'd developed a growth behind my knee.

I had ditched the brace back in May because it was aggravating my hamstring tendon and had probably caused the cyst in the first place. But now it was back, bigger and fuller than ever. It got to a point where I was having trouble walking, so I took some days off to rest it. It felt like my knee and calf had become one and it was a complex problem for Ashley to deal with, but I was glad she was there and I was in good hands.

Ashley and I gave it a name—we called it 'Popeye', and Popeye was really getting on my nerves. It was an uncomfortable fluid-filled sac right on the back of my knee, which made it difficult to straighten and bend the knee properly. There was nothing we could do to treat it other than get it drained or surgically removed, and in most cases drained cysts reappear within days. So we treated it with massage and my trusty Body Ice hoping it would vanish as quickly as it had reappeared. But the result was that I didn't get to jump much before we went to China, and I also decided to start using tape instead of the knee brace.

In spite of the limited training, in my first World Cup back from injury in Lianhua Mountain in China, Popeye and I came second while Jacqui was first. Jac really had reinvented herself after her injury in Salt Lake City, polishing up her form and technique to become a different jumper. It's funny how setbacks can so often bring out the best in an athlete, and in Jacqui's case it was certainly true.

It was an exceptional result for Australia and my return to competition, especially given the dramas we had recently experienced. By that stage we had finally sorted out Dmitry's visas and he joined the Swiss-Aussie team as Mich Roth's assistant. We were happy we were able to contribute something to the Swiss team, but after a few days Mich's prediction ran true—Dmitry wasn't used to working hard, he lacked any kind of initiative and had to be constantly told what to do. He was lazy and the relationship wasn't working, and Mich indicated that he wasn't happy.

In fact I think he had made that decision when we first mentioned the option to him, so after the World Cups we put Ashley up to the job of telling Dmitry that we didn't need his services any longer. I felt bad, but if that was what Mich wanted we weren't going to question it. Mich had in mind his own Swiss assistant, an ex-aerialist named Misra Noto, so we got rid of Dmitry and brought in Misra instead. I'm fairly certain Mich just wanted a Swiss assistant.

We left China with Jac and me number one and two in the world respectively and it was great to be back. Barbara had also been in China and she was really happy for me, but she reinforced my plan. 'Don't place too much focus on results this year, Lyd, just keep focused on your process one jump at a time.' It was good to have her around to keep me under control and, without me knowing it, my A-team, which included Mich, Barbara, Ashley and Misra at the time, was starting to form.

> *Barbara: 'I remember my first competition with Lydia in China in 2007. It was her first event back after her second ACL reconstruction. I think we bonded over me holding her glasses and helping her dig the snow out of her jacket. She podiumed at that event.'*

For Liz and me, Mich was a dream coach. For the first time in our careers we felt like we were receiving the attention we needed, even with 12 people in the team. It was the most attention we had ever been given. Everyone in his team was treated equally and no one got extra attention because they thought they were special. It was like being back in gymnastics. Mich is the fairest coach I've ever worked under.

With so many athletes it was a massive job and he was worked to the bone, but he never once complained. His door, as he put it, was 'always open' to go over plans or watch some jumps on video. Even when he was clearly tired, his response was 'I can always sleep after the season.' His passion for what he was doing was awesome, and I felt like he was perfect for me.

Mich knew I had talent, and talent mixed with a burning desire to succeed was pretty obvious to him. He was enthusiastic about my plans and dreams and I hadn't felt that excitement reflected back to me in a while, probably not since Pete. Not everyone in the team was happy, though. Jacqui was having a phenomenal season and was ranked number one, but she wasn't getting the kind of attention she was used to, so by the end of the season she had already sourced her own private coach, American Jerry Grossi. Liz and I were happy to continue training with Mich and the Swiss team, and he agreed to work with us right through to the 2010 Olympics. It was nice to know we would have stability in our coaching arrangements for the next two years and, with Barbara and Ashley on board, we liked our whole set-up.

****

In terms of performance I had a reasonable 2008 season. I didn't have any wins, but I collected a string of podium finishes, which was good considering it was my comeback season. I was only doing doubles, so I didn't feel out of my comfort zone at all and I was regaining my confidence, which was the whole point of the season. I finished second overall in the world behind Jacqui, a great result for Australia, and I was satisfied that I had made a successful comeback.

The only issue for me that season was Popeye. Although the cyst didn't stop me from jumping too much, it was annoying and wouldn't go away, so I decided to have it surgically removed when I got home. I went to see Hayden after I landed in Melbourne and booked in for the surgery. He said he had removed Baker's cysts before and it was a fairly basic procedure with quite a short recovery time. In my case, though, Popeye had grown a root deep inside my joint, and Hayden had to dig deep through my tissue again to reach the source of the cyst, take it out and stitch me back up.

It turned out to be a longer recovery than expected; my muscles wasted away just like they do after a reconstruction and it took me three months to return to normal. During rehab I reflected on my comeback season and my plan moving forward. Even though I now had the coach I wanted, physiotherapist and a sports psychologist, I still felt something was missing in my preparation—particularly with my mental training. What I worked on with Barbara was helping. She kept me in control and disciplined with my thoughts and kept me thinking on a logical and analytical path, which was what I needed. But somehow, I didn't feel connected to the plans and strategies I had written down on paper. I'm not sure I entirely believed what I was writing. I hoped it would all work out but I still felt that I was reacting to events and, at times, I felt out of control in some ways. The recent surgery had also got me down and, again, I wondered why it had even happened in the first place. I felt that I was still in an up-and-down cycle.

Throughout my whole career I'd carried Jeffrey Hodges' *Sportsmind* book with me and listened to his relaxation and visualisation tracks. Even when working with Barbara, I kept going back to his material and, in many ways, found comfort in just hearing his voice.

I already had a sports psych in Barbara, but I thought that there must have been a reason why I continued to go back to Jeffrey's material—that there was something else I needed, something that only he could offer. Barbara was also the team sports psych, so in essence she was trying to get the best out of all of us, me and my competitors. I felt like I needed someone just for me: a silent partner, a mentor. So I decided to call Jeffrey.

It was funny hearing his voice over the phone. I was so used to it already and I felt I had known him for years. He agreed to meet with me and was coming to Melbourne anyway so we arranged a time to sit down and discuss my options.

I told Jeffrey about my up-and-down career path, about how things kept 'happening' to me and that I didn't want to make any more mistakes. I felt like I was always reacting to events and often didn't feel in control of my future. He took it all in and I could tell he was reading me like a book. He went through his program with me, outlining what it would involve and cost. Initially it would take three months to complete, and if I wanted to, we could continue with its next phase for a further three months after that. He said it was an intensive program and was going to take a major commitment from me otherwise there was no point in doing it—it would be a waste of time for both of us, not to mention the money.

It was expensive but I considered it a good investment, and deep down I knew he was the missing link for me, so I started his program.

> *Jeffrey: 'I thought Lydia was sincere and committed and very frustrated at how the ultimate success had eluded her, despite all her efforts and striving. Two things stood out that I knew we would need to work through. Firstly, she had a very strong fear that what had happened before when so close to success would happen again. I knew it was imperative to stress that 'the past does not equal the future' over and over. One of the key techniques used to drive this home was to put her in contact early with her own successful future self, and to establish a very close relationship and regular communication with her as Lydia's ultimate coach and guide, rather than me. Secondly, her subconscious belief that in order to 'win' she would have to become like another competitor who she thought was selfish and not a nice person. It has been wonderful to see that she didn't have to become a selfish person to succeed at the highest level. I am very proud of the fact that Lydia has maintained her own 'self' and integrity throughout the journey.'*

Jeffrey wasn't kidding: the program was intense. We spoke for at least one hour over the phone or on Skype twice a week for three months. I had exercises to do, workbooks to complete and CDs to listen to every day. Each week I'd fill out an achievement log, which included my mission statement at the top, my short-, medium- and long-term goals, and what I was doing on a daily basis to be able to meet those goals. It was detailed and it took a lot of time and work from me, but I was committed and believed it would pay off.

I didn't tell anyone I was working with Jeffrey, not even my teammates or Barbara. She still played an integral role in my A-team and I didn't want to replace her. But what made Jeffrey different to Barbara, who is very logical and analytical, was that he dug deep into my emotions and belief system. It was as if he peeled back every layer that made me and revealed who I really was. I developed an extraordinary conscious awareness of myself, and he tapped into my unconscious mind.

He corrected the language I used and my explanatory style, teaching me to focus on nothing but the positive. For example, instead of, 'I'm always injured,' or 'I've never been patient,' it became, 'In the past when I had some injuries,' or, 'In the past, I've had a tendency to rush'. No one had ever broken me down to that extent before. I'd never shared these kinds of thoughts, beliefs or feelings with anyone else before—not even Late. Instantly, I was transforming.

> *Jeffrey:* '*Lydia was the perfect client. She did all I asked of her and consequently got the result. Some clients say they 'want' it, but then self-sabotage by not doing the processes properly or losing momentum/interest. What I most liked was Lydia's trust in me and the Sportsmind processes. That was important.*'

When I started back on the water ramps in late June 2008, a month after the rest of the team, I was already a month into Jeffrey's program. Instead of Park City, we were now in Switzerland with Mich and the rest of the team, which was a nice change. It felt more private in Switzerland because not as many teams trained there, and even though it was going to take some getting used to, I liked the new set-up. Being in Europe would also make it easier to see Late, because he would spend most of the summer in Finland, just a short flight away. Still, it wasn't easy to catch up with him; I was already behind because of my knee and I wasn't able to take much time off.

When you're living the lifestyle we do as Australian aerial skiers, it's important you have a partner who understands what you are trying to achieve. Late has always been great. He understands the sport and the commitment it takes to be the best because he'd been there himself. He also understood it wasn't forever and that the next two years were so important. To be at peace with myself I needed to reach my potential, and Late knew that and had always supported me. I tried not to get upset over the time we would spend apart, it was hardly the norm for a married couple, but those were our circumstances and the sacrifice we had to make. Thanks to the advances in technology, Skype has made keeping in touch a whole lot easier, even when juggling time zones.

When I started jumping on water my knee was still not quite right and I was getting a lot of pain on impact. There was nothing wrong structurally with the joint, but it was still recovering from surgery and the muscles still weren't functioning properly. Ashley wasn't going to be with us for the summer, which was a real shame because I really needed her and had to miss a lot of days jumping because my body was once again struggling. My summer got off to a rocky start and it wasn't until mid-August that the knee settled down and I could start doing triples.

I tried not to dwell on my body too much and focused on what I could control. I worked hard mentally and had already noticed a change in my training. I was more consistent, I was able to focus more clearly and I had better emotional control. I started triples in late August; it had been three years since I had last done them and it was good to finally be back doing them again. Mich and I aimed to do Lay-Double-Full-Full, a triple-twisting triple that no woman had done on snow before. As I built through the tricks on the Triple, I hardly missed a take-off, and they were high-quality and consistent. Even the boys started to give me compliments.

By the end of the summer, my triples were ready and I had qualified not only Lay-Double Full-Full, but also the Full-Full-Full, another triple-twisting triple. My preparation for Vancouver was on track. It was now a matter of transferring what I learned on water, to snow. Again, the plan looked good on paper.

After my first three months on Jeffrey's program, I had decided to continue working with him for another three months, taking me to mid-October, right before the winter season kicked off. I was confident that I had learned some valuable techniques from him and he was confident I now had the skills to implement them. I was sad that his program had come to an end. We had been working so intensely together and I wasn't sure how I'd go without him. He reassured me that I would be fine: I had Barbara, I'd done all the hard work, and if I needed him, he was just a phone call away.

****

I began jumping on snow in mid-November, once again up on the glacier in Saas-Fee. It was a bitterly cold training camp that year and we often had temperatures less than 20°C below zero. At 3500m altitude with wind, it was miserably cold. One day my feet were so completely numb that I burnt the soles of my feet and the skin peeled away. My feet have never been the same since and are always cold—whenever the temperature drops now, I'm lost without my Therm-ic boot heaters!

On my fourth day of jumping in Saas-Fee, it was cold, windy and foggy. The light was flat and it was difficult to see. I was doing a Full-Full and I caught an edge as I skied up the jump. I got completely disoriented in the air—with no sense of which way was up or down—and crashed heavily, tweaking my knee. Luckily Ashley had now joined us and she rushed over to see if I was okay. I was panicked and crying. It's a scary feeling not knowing where you are in the air and that crash really shook me up. I was also worried about my knee. It hurt a lot and I struggled to put weight on it, but I managed to get up and slowly skied back down to the lodge.

We got inside and Ashley made a thorough assessment. I was shaking and worried that I had torn my ACL again, but after her tests, she confirmed it was still there. I was so relieved, but I had definitely done something to it, so we decided to get an MRI scan. The results showed I hadn't done any major damage, but there was a slight tear in my meniscus cartilage, which is essentially a shock absorber inside the knee.

And that was the end of my pre-season training. It was definitely not what I had planned or prepared for. We had World Championships that season, and even though results weren't my priority, I still wanted to do triples and perform well there. I had so much work to do and I felt like I was back into the same pattern I had so desperately tried to get out of. I had worked so hard mentally, my summer training had been excellent and I felt totally ready and fired up for the season—I just couldn't understand what I was doing wrong. What more could I do? The first World Cups of the 2009 season were going to be in China in late December, so we decided to not jump until then and give my knee a chance to heal.

On the first day of training in China my knee wasn't good at all, and as I started to jump, I was in so much pain that even doing a simple speed check was agonising. I was down and miserable and, for the first time in my career, I thought about quitting. I rang Late up and said, 'I can't take it anymore, I'm in so much pain, I'm done. I just can't cope anymore.'

He said, 'Don't be silly. You are one year out from the Olympics, you're not quitting now.'

I rang Barbara as well and said, 'Barbara, I think I'm done.' She said, 'OK, let's not make any hasty decisions and let's just get through the weekend. If you can compete, compete. If you can't then don't, and we'll revise and work it all out.'

The next day there was a blizzard for the event. I still wasn't sure if I'd compete, but after my first training jump and some painkillers I decided to go ahead. I landed my first jump and went into the lead. The weather continued to get worse, so they cancelled the second round of jumps, which meant I had won the event.

Barbara rang me straight after and asked, 'Do you still want to quit?' I said, 'No way.' Winning eases pain.

I jumped again the next day and came away with bronze. I'd had four days of pre-season training, a banged-up knee and I still managed to perform. Unfortunately, it was a typical situation for me.

I flew home from China for a quick Christmas break and my dad's 60th birthday. I also had more scans on my knee and continued with the rehab. Before the New Year, I was back in Switzerland for a 10-day training camp before the World Cup tour resumed. I had lost so much time in the pre-season and I was desperate to make up some ground and get some triples off. But I continued to struggle with my knee so I had to limit the number of jumps I did per day and just focus on quality. By the end of the camp I had three days of triples completed and I'd landed a few here and there. It wasn't enough to make them consistent but at least I had now done them.

The next World Cup was in Lake Placid, USA. I trained triples all week, but crashed my first jump in the qualifications and didn't make the top 12. The next week we were in Mont Gabriel, Canada. On the first day of training, I over-rotated on a jump and smacked my head hard into the landing hill and concussed myself. I wasn't able to jump all week and every day did tests with Ashley to see if I was improving. By the day of the event, and after a series of more cognitive and physical tests, I was cleared to jump. Obviously, we couldn't take the risk and do triples, so I opted to do doubles. I landed both jumps and won the event. Bouncing back from a concussion, and with no training all week, I had managed another win and was still leading the World Cup.

From Mont Gabriel we went back to the USA, this time to Deer Valley. Training had gone well and again I was back up on the triple but my landings weren't consistent. The visuals are so different compared to doubles, as is the speed going into the jump and the height of it, and I hadn't done enough in the pre-season to get the hang of it. Again, I crashed my first jump and failed to make the finals, but still managed to hold on to the leader's bib. However, the gap was closing and a string of Chinese competitors were breathing down my neck.

The next stop on tour was Cypress Mountain, the site of the 2010 Winter Olympics. The organisers decided to make it an Olympic test event, which meant that it would follow the Olympic format: one day for qualifications, where each competitor would get two jumps, and another day for the finals. I wanted to have a good week there and do triples. I wanted to leave there with a good feeling because in 12 months' time it would be the Olympic stage and my time to shine.

But on the second day of training I crashed on the Double and my ski dug into the snow, twisting my knee around. I thought I'd blown it again and was rushed off to the clinic to be checked. To my relief, my ACL was fine, but in the process of the fall, I had also twisted and sprained my ankle. Again, I was on the sidelines, frustrated and fed up with how my season was playing out. I was unable to train all week, which meant that triples were once more out of the question. I decided to do doubles in the qualifications, and after a solid first jump, I misjudged the second and crashed. Again, I missed the finals.

The last World Cup of the season was in Moscow. I was still leading overall, but only by five points in front of China's Nina Li. The pressure was on, and although my focus was not on winning the grand prix, with one event to go and after four times of coming second, I wasn't about to give it up. You receive 100 points for a World Cup win, 80 points for second and 60 for third, etc., so we decided to stick to doubles—all I had to do was finish in front of Nina. In the end, the season came down to one final jump. I did a Full Double-Full, a triple-twisting double, and I nailed it. I finished third and Nina Li was fifth. I had finally won my first crystal globe. I was finally number one in the world and it was a good feeling to get that monkey off my back. I had also qualified for the Olympics and that was a big bonus.

****

Even though I won the World Cup overall, I was dissatisfied with my season. Too much had gone wrong in the pre-season and I didn't do as many triples as I would have liked. I also had to be careful with my knee, which limited the number of jumps I could do.

The World Cup season was over, but we had one final event, the biennial World Championships, this time in Inawashiro, Japan. I hadn't been successful in my two previous world title attempts, and even though in the big picture the Olympics took priority, I still wanted to do well there.

We planned to compete triples because it was our last chance for the year to do them. In the air they were good but I was still struggling with landings and wasn't consistent. During the training week, I practised both doubles and triples and decided to do doubles for the qualifications and triples for the finals. On my first jump, I landed with my chest a bit too far in front and somersaulted forwards over my skis—a 'punch front'—and even though the jump was great in the air, the judges crucified me for the landing. I did land my second jump, but it wasn't enough to get me through to the finals. Another failed World Championships. I was ranked number one and I wouldn't be in the finals. I was devastated. My season had been up and down like a yo-yo and I was crushed to finish on a low.

There and then, I started planning. I wrote down what I did right that season and what had gone wrong. Other than my knee, which needed some serious attention, the main issue was my lack of pre-season training on snow—I'd only had four days and that wasn't enough time to transfer the skills I had learned on the water ramp to snow. On the water ramp my jumps were great. They were so consistent and polished, but that hadn't transferred to snow, purely because I lacked the numbers. On the other hand, the Chinese, my toughest competitors, had been able to get eight weeks of pre-season training in Mongolia, where they start jumping on snow in October.

Clearly something had to change and I brainstormed ways I could get more time on snow. We could do a Mt Buller training camp during the Australian winter and we could start jumping on the glaciers in Switzerland mid-October. Jumping on the glaciers is hard work at 3500m and you can't sustain it for eight weeks, so while that would be good for a couple of weeks we needed to find a more suitable training site that had enough snow in November. I knew a place: Ruka, Finland.

I told Mich my ideas and he seemed to take them on board, but he also had to consider the rest of his team. When I got back to Melbourne I presented the idea to Geoff Lipshut. He understood where I was coming from and agreed that I needed to maximise my on-snow time if I was going to succeed in doing triples. He worked on making the training camp at Mt Buller happen and I started looking into training in Ruka because I had the Finnish connections. So that was the plan: May to August on the water ramps, August on snow at Mt Buller, September back on the water ramps, October on the glacier in Saas-Fee, and then mid-November and all of December in Ruka.

There are usually two World Cups in China before Christmas, but I had already decided I would miss those to get in more training time. It was a good plan but it had one limitation: we couldn't convince Mich to come to Mt Buller and coach because he had to be in Switzerland for water ramp training. Also, who would stay behind and coach me while the China World Cups were on?

We needed another coach.

We really didn't want Mich to spread himself too thin and we thought it would be good to have someone just for us, someone employed solely for Australia. That's when we brought in Cord Spero, an ex-aerialist from Canada with a meticulous nature. His role would be to assist Mich and fill in the gaps when Mich had commitments elsewhere. His role gave us the flexibility required to carry out the plan. He was the final addition to my A-team.

Geoff: 'When I spoke to Cord Spero on the telephone for the first time in March 2009, he said, "I want to help you guys win at the Olympics." I was impressed with his vision and did background checks, which were very positive, so I was very keen to have him join us.

'Training at Buller was a really good idea of Lydia's and I was more than happy to facilitate it. Rino Grollo and Nick Whitby at Mt Buller did everything they could to make it happen, and that was a big tick for us. Ruka was also a great idea—the OWI has run many great camps there with the mogul program over the years, so we did that too.'

Cord: 'Being part of the Olympics has long been a goal of mine but I didn't want to simply experience the Olympics, I wanted to win. I was excited with the idea to coach the Australian team and I truly believed that Lydia was the best female jumper in the world and I wanted to work with her. It doesn't always work out that the best jumper wins the Olympics—things can happen and mistakes can be made—but the opportunity to help see it through was all anybody in my position could have asked for. So when the opportunity arose I jumped at it, but the fact that Lydia invited me in with open arms and then put her trust in me meant that I was probably as committed as she was. I had seen everything Lydia had been through, and I wanted to see her win gold more than I can explain.'

Barbara agreed with my ideas. She understood what I needed to do to meet my goals and together we formulated a plan. I discussed it over and over with her, and while I couldn't have avoided some of the setbacks I'd had the previous season, there was no room left for error. I had to change my luck. Barbara knew by now I was committed to the big picture. My ultimate goal was to win the Olympics in Vancouver doing triple somersaults that women hadn't competed before. Barbara helped me to create a plan on how I was going to do that and we started working on my 'goal map'. She asked me what my purpose was beyond winning the Olympics, 'Why are you really doing this sport and why does it mean so much for you to succeed?'

I wrote down my purpose: 'To be the best female aerial skier that has ever lived.'

From there she said, 'Pick a milestone goal that would bring you one step closer to achieving your purpose.' I wrote: 'Winning Olympic gold.' The next step was to break that down into smaller sub-goals, called 'challenge goals'. She asked me, 'What are you going to need to do in order to win gold in Vancouver?'

Mich, Cord and I had already predicted I was going to need about 210 points to win the Olympics in Vancouver, based on past results and history. Alisa had won the 2002 Olympics with 193 points doing double somersaults and Evelyne Leu took the 2006 Torino gold with 203 points doing triple somersaults, so scores were increasing by roughly 10 points at each Olympics. To score those 210 points, I would need to do triple somersaults rather than doubles. In order for me to do triples as successfully as the ones I was doing on water, I was going to need to increase my on-snow time so that I could get experience and confidence doing these new tricks on snow. To be able to do that, I needed to sort out my knee and be healthy and injury-free and perhaps even smarter with my body.

Under each of these challenge goals, Barbara then got me to put strategies in place for how I was going to achieve them. Those are called 'goal achievement strategies', and they included: making the most out of each training session; staying disciplined with positive thoughts and behaviours; staying motivated with positive self-talk; being diligent with my mental training and visualisation; being smarter with my body by getting on top of any niggling injury, making sure I was having enough rest and not taking unnecessary risks.

With this goal map in place, I realised very quickly that winning the Olympics didn't seem overwhelming any longer—I had a plan in place to get there and had broken it down into achievable steps that I could concentrate on, one task at a time.

Cord: 'Lydia's strengths are obvious. She is amazingly determined. I first saw it in Switzerland when Mich was gone for the day and Lydia and I were the only ones training. She missed a Full Double-Full and ended up landing backwards, which would have rattled most people. I remember thinking about how to handle the situation before approaching her, that she might have been shaken. I think I said, 'It's okay sometimes we just miss.' She looked at me and said, 'I don't miss,' and walked away. She didn't see it, but I was smiling ear to ear—I knew right then that she was going to win.

'Her weaknesses are a little tougher to spot. Like any good athlete, she hides them well. I think the biggest thing to overcome was some of the issues of the past that still haunted her—like making finals in a major competition, which was weighing on her pretty heavily.'

The plan looked excellent on paper but it was now time to make it happen and I wasn't going to leave any stone unturned, so I rang up Jeffrey Hodges and said, 'I know I won the World Cup, but my season still didn't go to plan. I'm not going to take any chances and I want you on board for the whole year, right through to the Olympics.'

Jeffrey was happy to continue working with me, and I was more relaxed knowing I had access to him whenever I needed him. Just hearing his voice put me at ease, and I wanted to be able to call him when I needed to. Because I had already done his Sportsmind program, he had to be rather experimental with me and he created a lot of new ways for me to keep improving mentally. In particular, we started hypnosis training sessions—they were like relaxation sessions but they took me into 10 times the state of relaxation—and then he would make positive suggestions to me. I found it to be amazingly powerful. If I was home in Australia, I would try to do the sessions face to face, but most of our sessions were done over Skype—he would even play music in the background.

Jeffrey: '*After she had already done my program, I wondered if I had more to offer Lydia, since she had already learned everything I thought I had to give. When she wanted to continue, it was a turning point in the whole journey because it forced me to develop a totally new program: the training of the unconscious mind. This is something I am continuing to work on even now, and I expect to expand Sportsmind coaching in future to include a combination of both conscious and non-conscious mental training techniques through 'altered state training'. This was a wonderful example of the student pushing the teacher—rather than vice versa! The ideas had been there for many years within me, but Lydia forced me to bring them out and turn them into practical application.*'

When I started working with Jeffrey again, he made me write an Olympic timeline. At the top of my page was me winning the Vancouver 2010 Olympics on 24 February with more than 210 points. I not only described how I wanted to feel and what I wanted to think, but I visualised it and felt it happening. From there, I wrote down each of the milestones I needed to reach to give me the best chance of winning.

I worked my way down through qualifications at the Olympics, the World Cup season, right through pre-season training camps, and lastly the water ramp training. Under each of these, I wrote down and visualised exactly where I wanted to be mentally and physically with my jumping and what I needed to do to be able to meet each of the milestones. As you can see, I'd come a long way from just setting a goal for myself. My plan was systematic, it was realistic and it was achievable, and I made it feel real. And rather than reacting to events, I was creating my future and things started to happen exactly how I planned.

Another interesting concept Jeffrey got me into when I first started working with him was to imagine my future self—the person I wanted to be, the person that had already won an Olympic gold medal—and then he would get me to ask her for advice and basically have a conversation with her. I thought it was weird at first, and my future self seemed very distant and far away, but I persisted. Periodically, I'd 'check in' and ask her if I was on track, and as time drew nearer to the Olympics I felt like I was becoming her: the future self I wanted to be.

Another issue of high priority was to sort out what was going on with my knee. When I arrived home in March 2009 after the World Cup season I went to see one of my best friends, Erica Whitfield, who over the years had established herself into a very fine physiotherapist. I told her the trouble I was having with my knee and she took me through some tests. I couldn't even hop on one leg without extreme pain and I had very little control when doing a single-leg squat. My problem wasn't structural, but she thought a lot of it had to do with muscle imbalance and poor neural control. It was a complex case, so she recommended I go and see Craig Phillips at Clinical Pilates in South Yarra. She told me that he could fix problems that most people couldn't, so off I went.

I had been doing Pilates ever since my right-side-itis, so I was familiar with the techniques and the special Pilates machine, the reformer. Craig certainly had his own interesting theories and techniques and I was in pretty bad shape when I first went to see him—as I said, I couldn't hop or squat properly because I was in so much pain, so he couldn't believe that I was able to jump! Yet in one session he had me hopping and squatting nearly pain-free, and I progressed really quickly. He likened his techniques to a rewiring process and he linked the problems with my knee with weakness in my back—and right-side-itis was the source. Within two months of doing my Pilates program two to three times a day I could jump, hop and run without pain, which was something I hadn't been able to do since my knee reconstruction.

By May, I was ready to start the water ramp season, pain-free and with no injuries. I took my Pilates machine with me to Switzerland so that I could continue doing my program. Craig had rewired me physically and I had Jeffrey and Barbara rewiring me mentally. Ashley would be with us for the summer, which was a great relief, and Cord would join our team to assist Mich. At that point I had everything I could possibly need.

My northern summer of 2009 was awesome. I got off to a great start and was on the Triple by June. I had a few niggles with my body, but with Ashley there full time nothing got out of hand. I had the triple-twisting triples done and ready for snow.

In August I flew to Mt Buller for our on-snow jumping camp with Cord, Liz, Bree and our junior team (coached by Jerry Grossi). Mt Buller is a great jump site and it's a pity we haven't been able to find sponsors for the Mt Buller World Cup in the past few years, but we'll start work on that soon. It really feels like home and everyone on the mountain was excited to have us back and jumping on home soil. The mountain staff made sure we had everything we needed and Cord and Jerry shaped the jumps to perfection. It was going to be a good test for Cord, who had never called jumps on snow, but because I wasn't doing difficult tricks I felt comfortable with him and it was a great time for him to gain some confidence. It was a really productive three-week camp. We didn't aim to do triples, but chose to focus on consistent take-offs and landings while doing basic doubles. It was just nice to jump without the pressure of competition and to get some more kilometres on snow.

> Cord: 'I was nervous coaching the girls on snow for the first time, but the fact that Lydia had confidence in me made me feel better. I worked hard to show my confidence in Lydia as an athlete, and while I was surprised that both Lydia and the OWI placed so much trust in a first-year coach, I wasn't going to let her down.'

I flew back to Switzerland in September to finish off the water ramp season. My triples were looking great. They were consistent and polished and I had even included a new jump to my repertoire: a Double-Full Double-Full. Four twists in two flips. Going into the Vancouver Olympics, we wanted to make sure we had contingency plans. If the weather on the night of the finals was shocking, as it can be on Cypress Mountain, we wanted to have the option of doing doubles, which is why I trained my triple-twisting doubles, and now added the quadruple-twisting double as well.

After a quick break in Australia, I then headed back to the glacier in Saas-Fee. We jumped there for two weeks and, compared to the year before, it was perfect weather with mild temperatures. I had very productive training, and with the Mt Buller camp I had already done quite a lot of jumping on snow and was feeling comfortable. For once I was ahead of schedule—especially compared to the four days of pre-season I'd had the year before—and everything was going to plan.

> *Jeffrey: 'I noticed a real transformation in Lydia. I especially have a very strong memory of the time we met at Melbourne airport when she was about to fly out to her training camp before the World Cup. I have never seen anyone who looked so 'ready' for success—she was fit, strong and radiated an overwhelming sense of personal power that was tangible to anyone walking past!'*

At the start of November we headed for Ruka, which would be my base for the next two months. Apart from the darkness, Ruka is the ideal training set-up. We stayed in modern apartments, we had internet (which was a must for my Skype sessions with Jeffrey and Barbara) and there was a great gym where we could work out. I also brought along my Pilates machine, which was an important part of my daily routine and something I'd struggle without. I stayed in an apartment with our junior team and I also flew Erica over to be my personal physio, so she stayed with me as well. With the junior team plus the World Cup team, Ashley was going to have her hands full, which is why I brought in Erica to make sure I'd get all the physio treatment I needed.

> *Cord: 'In Ruka I was nervous, but by that point I knew Lydia more as a jumper. The goal was to keep her safe and training. Being careful as to what days we actually trained triples was the biggest obstacle—we only really pushed*

> *hard one day and the goal on that day was to help her to understand that she could jump in difficult conditions.'*

My plan hadn't changed. When it was time for the Chinese World Cups in mid-December I stayed behind in Ruka with the junior team and just trained, a luxury I could afford because I had already qualified for the Olympics. Cord also stayed behind and filled Mich's role while Mich went with the rest of the team to China.

The junior girls were just doing singles so I was the only one doing doubles and triples every day. It's not easy being the only person on the Triple, or even the Double for that matter, because I had to 'guinea pig' the jumps every day. From one day to the next, conditions change and you never really know how the first jump of the day will be. Will my speed be okay? Will it feel the same as yesterday? You just don't know for sure until you get that first one out of the way.

Some days I was scared up there, but by pushing through that uncertainty I was gaining a special type of confidence that money can't buy: self-belief. You only have true self-belief when you know you've done something before and can do it again over and over. I jumped triples in good weather, in snow and in wind, and I was able to build my confidence and consistency by staying in one place and training.

By Christmas I was ready. I hadn't done a Lay-Double Full-Full yet, but I had done a lot of triples and I was starting to land them consistently. It was now just a matter of adding another twist, and with the rest of the World Cup season ahead there was still time.

> *Barbara: 'Lydia certainly learned to walk the talk. Staying back in Ruka was a huge step in itself. Sacrificing results for her was a considered strategy in preparing for Vancouver. She already had a World Cup title, but she didn't have any Olympic medals. In Ruka, she trained in the dark and the cold by herself, gutting it out in the wind. She knew when she had done enough and when it was time to call it for 2009. She knew when she needed rest. It was impressive.'*

******

In the World Cup openers in China, a young athlete called Xu Mengtao ('Tao Tao') had done a Lay-Double Full-Full. That made her the first woman on record to complete that triple-twisting triple on snow, and even though she beat me to it, we are still the only two women to have ever done the trick. It sparked a real fire in me, but at the same time I was confident that my plan was unfolding nicely and I didn't let it affect me. I was so focused on my own plate it didn't matter what anyone else did. I had a small break for Christmas and the New Year and stayed in Finland with Late and his family. I hadn't seen my husband for most of the year so I really enjoyed the time I had with him. Long distance relationships often do that—they make you appreciate every second you get to spend with each other and in some ways it adds an extra spark. The good news was that Late had accepted a coaching job with Finland and would be helping out with their mogul team, which meant he was back on tour and with me. He'd also be at the Olympics, and knowing he was going to be there was comforting.

Straight after the New Year we were on a plane to Calgary, Canada, for the next World Cup. I arrived safely in Calgary but my ski bag didn't show up. Normally it's not too much of a problem and your luggage shows up on the next flight, but when I went to track down my ski bag, Air Canada couldn't trace it. They had lost it.

I couldn't believe it. Everything was finally going to plan, and now this happened. I spent most of the week on the phone trying to trace the bag and obviously couldn't jump without my gear, so I had to miss some training sessions. One of my teammates, Bree, offered me her spare equipment to use, but I felt uncomfortable about jumping in someone else's gear. It felt wrong and would have been a mistake. I did go out one night with Ashley to ski around in Bree's gear, but it just felt way off. A couple of years earlier, I would have grabbed her equipment and jumped, but I didn't feel comfortable and I wasn't about to take any risks. *No mistakes, Lyd.*

Eventually Air Canada located my ski bag, which had somehow ended up going from Finland to Rome instead of Calgary. I got it back two days before the event and happily started training. There wasn't a lot of time but I did some doubles and got used to the site. Obviously missing the Chinese events meant I was not interested in winning the World Cup grand prix, so all my focus was geared to preparing for the Olympics. On the competition day we decided everything had been going fine and, as we weren't concerned about results, we decided to treat it as a training day and do some triples. I did Lay-Tuck-Full, a single-twisting triple, for the first round and landed it. Then we went in for lunch and a break while the men had their first round. By the time we came back for our second round, the weather had changed. It was so warm that the jumps had softened and become completely sticky and speeds were hard to read. I did one triple to warm up and as I skied up the jump, I felt like my skis got stuck on it. The jump sucked me in and my knees buckled under the force.

I did what we call a 'triple pumpkin'—three flips in a tucked position—which obviously wasn't what I intended, and ended up landing on my back with the wind knocked out of me. Alla Tsuper from Belarus did the same thing straight after me but she wasn't as fortunate and broke her shoulder. After that Mich and I decided to cut our losses and not take any risks, and dropped my second competition jump back to an easy double. I landed it, came fifth and was content, given the drama I'd had that week with my luggage.

> *Barbara: 'Although in Calgary the result probably wasn't what she wanted, I think there were two good takeaway points for me. Lydia played it smart during competition in those conditions and she handled the lost ski bag situation perfectly. The 'old' Lydia would have been tense and stressed and fretting about the missed time and losing ground on everyone else. In my opinion this was a big turning point from the previous competitive seasons. She was 'getting it'. She trusted herself and her team.'*

Deer Valley, USA, was the next stop on tour and if everything went well, we'd bust out my new trick. I got in some really good training early in the week and was landing my triples. The day before the competition, Mich said, 'Everything is looking really good—I think you're ready to do Lay-Double Full-Full now.' I couldn't have agreed more. Towards the end of training, we decided to go for it. By that stage, everyone else had finished jumping and I was alone at the top. Word spreads like wildfire when someone is doing a new trick and everyone was gathering on the knoll, waiting for me to go—talk about added pressure. Misra, our top guy, was with me at the top of the in-run, letting me know everything was okay. I was really nervous and I took time to visualise the trick in my head, just as I had done on water many times before. I just hoped I'd complete the jump and be safe and sound.

I did my first one and landed it to cheers and screaming from the crowd. Mich and Cord had their fists pumped and were high-fiving each other. I was so happy and so relieved and it really couldn't have gone better. Training was closed for the day and you couldn't wipe the smile from my face. I got back to the knoll and hugged Mich and Cord and my teammates. Mich was so happy and I had moved one step closer to that future self I wanted to be. It was like I was being drawn towards her.

The next day I competed my new trick in the competition and landed it, scoring 113.56 points, my highest score on a single jump. The finals were at night under lights and I performed a Lay-Full-Full and stomped it. My total score for the two jumps came up: 220.91, a new world record! I was elated and Mich and Cord were over the moon. Late was also there and it was great that he could share that moment with me. Everything felt perfect, and in my mind it was all coming together.

> *Cord: 'I was so proud. I knew that Lydia's goal was to be the greatest female aerialist of all time and I felt this day she put herself in that category. To see her accomplish that goal, something that she'd set her mind on 10 years earlier, was very inspiring. After that moment, I knew that win or lose at the Olympics nobody could ever argue how good she really was. I felt Australia had the best aerials team at the time—and by that I mean the whole team,*

> *not just the jumpers. It took some time for us to figure out how we would all work together, which is a little scary when you're less than a year away from the Olympics, but by the time the World Cup season started things were dialled in. Everyone knew their roles.*
>
> *'I learned so much from Mich throughout that season and still very much enjoy working with him.'*

That score of 220.91 would have placed me 10th in the men's competition. I still didn't feel that I had done my jumps perfectly, so there was room for me to do better. For the first time in my career I was finally doing what I had intended to do. It wasn't about the world record; it was about doing high-quality triples and jumping like a man. It was about pushing boundaries and living my potential.

I thought I was going to be doing it by Torino, but here nearly four years to the day and after so much turmoil, it was starting to come together. I was getting a certain respect, not only from the women but also from the male competitors, and that was great, a huge ego boost. Some even said, 'You do that trick better than I do,' which was pretty cool.

I was sponsored by Acer leading into the Olympics and that was a huge help financially. They also supplied me with some fun toys, and one of my favourites is my travel projector. I love movies and watch one every night before I go to bed—it's just part of my routine. I travel with surround sound speakers and have a great set-up. I'm all about gadgets and so is Late. The first thing I do when I get to a new hotel room is make sure I have a big white wall that I can project movies on to. Then I unpack the rest of my stuff! That night, Mich, Cord and I watched my record-breaking jumps in life size on my projector. It was really cool. Mich loved my set-up so much I ended up getting him his own Acer travel projector as a gift after the Olympics.

> *Barbara: 'The world record was just what Lydia needed to build confidence, and to serve notice to the other women on tour that she was ready. Not that we focused much (if*

at all) on what others thought, but it never hurts to plant that seed in the head of the competitors.

'She was really trusting in the team she had around her. Mich was there as the veteran calming influence, Cord as the technician and strategiser, Ashley as the glue that held it all together (sometimes literally). I felt like once 2009 ended and 2010 finally arrived, Lydia stopped searching and started believing.

'At that time, from the outside Lydia looked purposeful, deliberate, calm and appropriately selfish. She knew what worked for her and she stuck with it.'

Lake Placid was the next stop for the World Cup tour and it was the final event that athletes could use to qualify for a place at the Olympics. Our team didn't have the same issue as we'd had the previous Games because there were only four girls trying to qualify, which meant no one would be cut if they made the qualifying standard. David Morris, our only male competitor, had also qualified and Australia would be sending a team of five aerial skiers to Vancouver. After Deer Valley I felt tired—the week had taken a lot out of me. I talked to Mich about it and we decided to still do triples but perhaps back down on the difficulty and have an easier week. At that stage we weren't about to take any risks.

I competed with a Lay-Full-Full and a Lay-Tuck-Full and had made my jumps even cleaner than the week before. I wasn't just landing triples, I was doing them well, and the more I did the better they became. I won again and I was jumping better than ever. My confidence was high, and unlike the year before I had the confidence that came from numbers.

Two wins in a row leading into the Olympics was the perfect entry to my big stage. The jumps I wanted to do were ready and I had the world record. My pre-season was awesome and I was set to go.

CHAPTER 12

GAME ON

The week after Lake Placid we went to Mont Gabriel in Quebec for the final World Cup event. During that week we received information about our Olympic accommodation and where we would be staying for the duration of the Olympics, including arrival and departure times. Normally the Australian team organises sub-site accommodation away from the athlete village and away from all the hype and distraction of the Games.

But these Olympics were different, with special circumstances. We shared a coach with the Swiss Team, which always stayed in the athlete village, so I had requested to stay in the village as well. It was imperative that I was close to Mich, and Liz and Bree felt the same. But the accommodation advice said we would be staying in sub-site accommodation, one hour away from the athlete village but closer to our competition venue.

That would work for Jacqui and David because they were coached by Jerry Grossi and he would stay with them at the sub-site. But for Bree, Liz and me it was a huge stress. It was so important we had access to our coach whenever we needed it for video review or planning or even just a simple chat. Plus the athlete village had all the conveniences we would need such as 24/7 food, a fully equipped gym with ice baths and a polyclinic where you could book in for extra massages and physiotherapy. Late would also be staying there with the Finnish team and I definitely wanted him close by. It was an ideal set-up, with the only disadvantage the 45-minute travel time it would take to get to the competition venue at Cypress Mountain. The pros definitely outweighed the cons—we needed to be in the athlete village and not at the sub-site.

I emailed the Australian Olympic Committee on behalf of Bree, Liz and myself in an attempt to get the accommodation decision changed. After a few emails back and forth the directors of the AOC understood our predicament and, to our relief, arranged for us to stay in the athlete village.

I must say, I was a bit distracted that week and anxious to get it sorted out, and I didn't do well in the final World Cup. I crashed my first jump and didn't make the finals. I ended up fourth overall for the season, which wasn't too bad considering I had missed the two events in China.

In a way, it was good for me to carry the number four bib into the Olympics because there is so much more expectation placed on numbers one, two and three. The top three spots were occupied by Chinese competitors Nina Li, Guo Xinxin, and Xu Mengtao respectively. The Chinese team also had spots five and six, which just showed the pure dominance of their team at the time. They could only send four athletes to the Olympics, so their selectors faced a difficult choice considering they had five girls in the world's top six.

After the Mont Gabriel event, we had five days off before our Olympic training camp. I wanted to get away for a bit, as did most of the team, and we all went our separate ways for a few days. Bree and I found a good deal at an all-inclusive resort in nearby Cuba, so we booked it and off we went. It was good to get out of the snow and into the sun. We just lazed by the pool the whole time and although we were only there for three days, it was enough to relax and re-energise so that we could be ready for the final stretch of jumping.

We returned to Mont Gabriel and, to my delight, there were some packages waiting for me at the hotel reception desk. Cadbury, like Acer, had come on board as one of my sponsors before the Olympics and had asked me to request some yummy treats to be sent over. I compiled a list of my favourites and also asked my teammates what they wanted. I ordered a couple of blocks of Cadbury Dairy Milk, a packet of strawberry Freddo Frogs, Caramello Koalas and a lot more. But instead of a couple of blocks of each, Cadbury sent a couple of boxes of each! There was so much chocolate and other goodies that I filled up the bathtub in my room—there was no way I was going to get through it all! Needless to say, I was very popular that week and athletes and coaches from the Swiss and Belarusian teams dropped by to collect boxes of goodies.

The training camp ran for about 10 days. Because aerials are always in the second week of the Olympics, I chose to miss the opening ceremony to stay and train in Mont Gabriel. I watched the start of it on TV and saw Torah Bright, our flag bearer, lead the Australian team into the Olympic stadium, but I fell asleep shortly afterwards as we were in a different time zone there on the east coast of Canada and it was getting late. Staying behind to do the training camp was the right decision for me. Jacqui also stayed and trained while Liz, Bree and Dave went to march in the ceremony. The extra training gave me a chance to work on my triple-twisting doubles, but the main purpose was to polish up my triples. It was a very productive training camp and I ended up doing a new jump, a Full-Full-Full, another triple-twisting triple. My plan wasn't to compete it at the Olympics, but it was good to have it up my sleeve just in case I needed it. I was having a bit of inconsistency landing my triples during that training camp, which made me a little anxious, but the tricks themselves were excellent in the air and, having landed them consistently all season, I didn't read too much into it. Instead, I paid close attention to the Belarusian aerialists, the best 'landers' in the world, and even videoed some of their jumps. Jeffrey got me to visualise them landing and we did a role-play: I first visualised them landing and the techniques they used, then I visualised myself landing like them. Not only was I seeing myself mimicking them, I also tried to feel it, as if I was inside their bodies. It was a very effective and powerful technique, and as soon as I started jumping at Cypress Mountain, the venue for the Olympics, my landings were great and consistent again.

Everything was perfect in the athlete village. I shared an apartment with Liz and Bree, and by happy coincidence the Finnish team was in the same building so I was able to spend some time with Late. By the time I arrived his mogul skiers had already finished their event, so he had plenty of time to just spend with me. The Swiss team was in the apartment building next door so our set-up was ideal. I was in the village, I had my husband and coach close by, and most importantly, I was ready.

A couple of days before the qualifications, my manager at the time sent me a clip to approve for TV back in Australia. Up until that day I had never seen my crash in Torino, but when I opened up the clip to watch there it was! I was quite shaken up. I couldn't believe that I had spent four years avoiding that TV footage only to see it two days before the qualifications. The memory of me crashing and blowing my knee in the qualifying round four years earlier came flooding back. It created some anxiety in me and I struggled in training that day.

The weather in Vancouver was really warm all week, a nightmare for maintaining the jumps. They were soft and sticky to the point where the work crew and coaches used liquid nitrogen to keep them cold and hard enough for us to use. They also periodically sprayed the jumps with fire extinguishers throughout a session to try to keep them hard and free of ruts. The crew, led by Nicolas Fontaine, a former champion aerialist, worked around the clock carting snow from wherever they could find it just to maintain the site. Because of the snow shortage and the warm temperatures, they also used helicopters to fly in snow from higher altitudes. It was a massive job and amazing to see them pull it off.

At the Olympics, only the top 25-ranked aerial skiers in the world get to compete. There is also a maximum of four skiers per nation per gender, which worked out perfectly for our team since we only had four girls with the potential to qualify: Bree, Jacqui, Liz and me. From the 25 athletes who start the event, only the top 12 make it to the finals. My plan was to do doubles in the qualifications and then bring out my big tricks on the Triple for the finals. But first I had to make it into that top 12. Qualifying for the finals is actually more stressful than the final itself, because you can't afford to make any mistakes—if you do, you're out. I really wanted to compete my big tricks on the biggest stage but I had to get through first.

> *Mich: 'I knew that it was going to be hard deciding what jumps to do for the qualifications. It was very important to get through and I was happy with our decision to do doubles and happy that Lydia was comfortable with that decision too. I saw she was nervous, but my experience told me to stay calm because if I didn't, that wasn't going to help her. I had the feeling that our plan was working.'*

Months before, Mich, Cord and I had worked out that I would do one triple-twisting double, a Double Full-Full, and then a basic Full-Full, which should give me enough points to qualify. We aimed to qualify in the middle of the pack, around fifth or sixth, with a score between 170 and 180.

What it meant that week was that I had to get my doubles right and make sure I was prepared for the qualification round before I could move on to my triples. Because the majority of females do doubles, there is more traffic on the double jumps and when the weather is warm, the jumps take a beating. I was having a lot of trouble hitting my take-offs on the doubles—even Nina Li, the best doubles jumper in the world, was struggling—but I managed to get up to my tricks. Then I had to get started with triples. As soon as I moved over to the triples I felt at home and everything seemed normal. For a moment, I almost changed my plan of attack and thought about doing triples in qualifications because they were going better than my doubles, but in the end we decided to stick to the original plan. We weren't aiming to win qualifications, we just needed to be in the finals—just land two doubles and make the top 12.

On the morning of the qualifications we had to be up at 4am because the event was scheduled for an early start. I felt good and I was ready. I was definitely nervous but I concentrated on using the skills I had learned to keep me in control and relaxed. I just repeated to myself, *'Stay present Lyd. One jump at a time.'* I landed my first jump, but it wasn't my best Double Full-Full. I was still having trouble getting my take-off right on the jump and missed it a little. I managed to keep the trick together and had a solid landing. I scored 85.65 points, which seemed a little harsh, but there was nothing I could do about that. I have on many occasions scored in the 100s with that jump, so it was well below what I was aiming for and I really needed a solid second jump.

I rode back up the lift and stopped to talk with Mich and Cord to discuss our plan and whether it was going to change. In the end we decided to stick to it and do a Full-Full. I was feeling my nerves. I just wanted to make it through. I did a Full-Full and landed it, and as I skied away I felt instant relief that I had landed two jumps.

I don't know why I was so nervous. I had been jumping so well in training and all I needed to do was my normal nice jumps. But again, the jump wasn't my best ever and my nerves were choking me up. I received 81.90 points from the judges, another unusually low score, for a total of 167.55. It was painful to watch the other competitors do their jumps after me and I was desperate to know if I was in the top 12. Even if the judges were being harsh, it's okay as long as they are equally tough on everyone. But I noticed that the girls doing triples were not getting judged as harshly as those on the doubles. I started to panic as I was bumped further down the list.

We had predicted that the score to make the finals would range from low 160s to 190s, which is why we opted to do 'safe' jumps. However, a lot of girls that day came out swinging with their hardest tricks. Alla Tsuper from Belarus, who had made it back from her broken shoulder, pulled out her big guns and had two really nice jumps. She won the qualification round with 195.76 points. Nina Li did two triple-twisting doubles—stock standard for her—and qualified in second with 192.10. Guo Xinxin from China threw her biggest tricks on the Triple and crashed one, but still managed to qualify in third position with 189.16—a pretty good score considering she had crashed. Tao Tao (Xu Mengtao) also crashed one of her jumps but still made it through in eighth place. In ninth, 10th and 11th were me, Liz and Jac respectively. Unfortunately Bree missed out.

Cord: 'I always thought that if Lydia got through qualifications she would win, but I was worried going into qualifications that there was nothing to win and everything

> *to lose. She had some experiences in her past that haunted her—like blowing her knee in Torino—and I wasn't sure if they would surface and affect her. After she made it through I knew that all we had to do was get her speed right on the triples and she would take care of the rest. She was ready. The night before finals she had a great training session. Mich and I looked at each other and he said, 'That's it, we're done.' He was right—it was now up to Lydia.'*

The final 12 consisted of four Chinese, two Belarusians, three Americans, and three Australians. There had been inconsistency in the judging, but that's the nature of our sport. You hope they get it right for major events but you just never know. I was disappointed with my performance and especially for letting my nerves affect me. The good news, however, was that I'd made the finals and I would be doing triples—something the judges obviously wanted to see.

> *Jeffrey: 'Lydia was indeed ready. After the dubious scores in the qualifications she was justifiably frustrated and angry, so I wanted to do a good visualisation session with her to settle her emotions and refocus on the result she wanted in the final. After the session I felt we had achieved this and when we spoke the night before the finals she had retained that sense of focus and confidence we had worked towards.'*

We had one more training session the night before the finals. It was an unusual schedule, with the qualifications early in the morning and the finals to be held at night under lights. With one session left, it was my last chance to polish up my triples. I was glad to be rid of doubles. I wasn't nervous anymore and I wasn't scared. If anything, I was more pumped than ever before to go out there and show the world what I was made of.

At training that night it was snowing with poor visibility and the girls on the Triple were hesitant. No one was going. But I had jumped in worse and, drawing on my experience and the self-confidence gained from training alone in Ruka, was first off the jump. Once they saw I was all right and that the conditions were 'jumpable', the rest followed. I got through my tricks all the way to Lay-Double Full-Full with ease. I was landing everything, completely unfazed by the weather. I 'won' training that night, and more importantly I was focused, confident and ready for the final showdown the next day.

Late was watching training that night, and said, 'That was awesome, no one is jumping as well as you.' My ego was boosted and there was no trace of my nervous jitters from the qualification round. I felt like the only person who could stop me now was myself, and my plan was unfolding perfectly thanks to the help of my A-team and silent partner.

I had seen a few jumps from my competitors during training. Tao Tao was my biggest threat because she was performing the most difficult jumps: two triple-twisting triples. But she wasn't landing consistently and her form and her twisting mechanics were not as clean or as crisp as mine. I was confident I had one up on her. The Chinese hadn't placed all their expectation on Tao Tao, and being a very young competitor, she was a bit of a wildcard for them. They were getting her to jump the most difficult tricks now, so that in Sochi in 2014 she would be a force to be reckoned with.

Their real Chinese hope lay with Nina Li. She was their guarantee of a medal, the most reliable female aerialist on the start list. However, she was doing doubles and although she had Double-Full Double- Full, a very difficult quadruple-twisting double with a high degree of difficulty, it would not guarantee a gold if other athletes doing difficult triples nailed them. Guo Xinxin, who had experience on triples, was another important chance for China, but again, her jumps lacked form and crispness.

Alla Tsuper was jumping brilliantly and her teammate Assoli Slivets was looking good too. They were also doing triples, but they didn't have the degree of difficulty I had. Even though Jac was having a rough time in training, I would never underestimate her and she was in with a chance as well.

We arrived back in the village at about 11pm. I had dinner and went to the polyclinic for a massage and to give my legs a bit of a flush so they would feel fresh for the next day, then I watched videos of my jumps with Mich and Cord and we confirmed my plan of attack for the final. Back in my apartment, I packed a bag, waxed my skis and made sure my equipment was ready and that I had spares of everything. I talked to Barbara while I sat in the ice bath for 20 minutes, part of my routine to keep the swelling down in my knee and also to help flush out the lactic acid in my legs. It's all about routine and that was my routine. I got ready for bed, wrote in my diary and logged my jumps.

> *Diary entry: 'Great training even in terrible conditions. Really happy with the way I attacked training. Goals for tomorrow: stay focused on take-off and landing. One jump at a time. Go after it!'*

I sat on the end of my bed with a sense of peace knowing that I had left no stone unturned. There wasn't any more I could have done to prepare myself—whatever happened the next day I'd know I had given it everything. Before I went to sleep I called Jeffrey. I always liked to talk to him before I went to bed and, as I've said before, somehow just hearing his voice makes me relaxed and at ease. I told him about my great training session and that I felt like I was becoming 'her', my future self. She was just two jumps away.

****

I slept soundly and got up around 11am. I went to the big food tent and made myself a breakfast burrito—a tortilla with scrambled eggs and other goodies. Because the finals were at night we had all day to wait around, so I just tried to keep myself distracted by doing other things. I went to the gym for a spin on the bike and then had my daily ice bath. I always need something to distract me in the ice bath and divert my attention away from being freezing cold, so I took in my computer and sorted out some orders and invoices for Body Sphere—anything to keep busy.

I also read some inspirational quotes from a book Barbara had given me called *Whatever It Takes*, and then I had physio treatment with

Ashley and she strapped me up with tape. Someone delivered a package for me, which contained a massive Cadbury flag that said 'Go Lydia!' signed by all the staff, who had also written personal messages of best wishes and good luck. It was such a lovely gift and one I didn't expect.

Then I started to get ready. I played the movie *Gladiator* in my room while I went through some stretches and exercises. I didn't really watch it but it's one of my favourite movies and I just wanted to hear it playing in the background. Liz had also started to warm up and we were both going through our routines, focused and quiet. It was comforting to have her by my side.

When we arrived at the venue for the final, it was so foggy you couldn't see the jumps from the car park. It reminded me of our training camp at Mt Buller, where we had fog for most of the time, and I joked to the girls, 'Ha! This is just like Buller!' We all had a chuckle, which seemed to lighten the mood. The truth was that the fog wasn't an issue for me. It wasn't ideal because the visibility was poor, but it wasn't windy, it wasn't snowing and everything else was perfect.

We went to the athlete tent at the bottom of the landing hill. The coaches were already at the site because they'd been working to make sure the jumps were perfect and ready for us. Cord, Misra and Mich came into the tent to update us on the conditions and they confirmed that, yes, it was foggy, but it was good.

I put my on iPod, as most athletes do, and started warming up. There was a vacant physio room that I had been using for that purpose all week so I went in there and kept to myself. I felt really good. I had good energy and I was really calm.

In the past I've had a natural tendency to be in an incredible rush. I'm terribly impatient by nature and I think many of the mistakes I made earlier in my career were because I was always thinking too far ahead. When I first started working with Barbara she was quick to point out that my 'thinking ahead' was hurting my performances, and was one of my biggest weaknesses, so we worked hard on keeping my thoughts in the here and now, staying present and trying to focus on one task at a time. What really helped me with this was just slowing everything down. I slowed down my walking, my eating, even my driving and just really tried to stay in each moment. If my thoughts jumped too far ahead or if a negative thought popped up, I developed skills that would interrupt those thoughts, like a circuit breaker to bring me back to where I was. Here. Now. As I prepared myself for the Olympic final, there was no better time to use those skills, to keep me focused on one jump at a time.

I checked all of my equipment before I left the athlete tent and placed my spare parts in easy-to-reach areas. I took my iPod off and put it in my jacket pocket—I would need it later. I put on my glasses, my headband and my helmet. Next were my boots. Then I stuffed some lollies into my jacket pocket before putting on my gloves. I walked outside and looked up at the jump site. I couldn't see the jumps because the fog was so thick but it seemed eerily calm. I put my backpack down near the lift as well as some apple juice and a banana. Barbara was there, but she didn't need to say much.

I rode the lift up to the top of the jump site and slid down to talk with Mich and Cord. They seemed really calm and I could feel them wondering if I had started to get nervous. The fog was very thick, and from the top of the in-run you couldn't see the jumps at all, so I got the coaches to make sure they painted extra red lines on the in-run and transition to emphasise where to ski into the jump. We would need to rely on the radios tonight. Speed checks started in five minutes, so we went through the final plan and I went back up the lift to prepare for them.

After 15 minutes of speed checks the jumps were opened. I did a couple of jumps on the Double, as I always do, and then moved across to the Triple. The fog was very thick, but as you skied through and got further down the in-run, the jumps came into view. You just had to trust that you would see them eventually and try not to panic. Misra was at the top relaying messages to Mich and Cord, and they were radioing messages back to him, in particular about the speeds. I always like to know my speeds.

The crowd was building up but I couldn't see them from the top. I couldn't see anything really—not Mich or the windsock. But he assured me through the radio that there was no wind. I progressed through my jumps, starting with the easiest and building to the most difficult. I was jumping great and finished on a couple of Lay-Double Full-Fulls, which carries the highest degree of difficulty in the women's competition. The last one I did in training was the most perfect I had ever done, perfect in the air and on landing. At that time I was hoping I hadn't just wasted all my great jumps in training, but reassured myself that I could pull off two more. Because Lay-Double Full-Full was the last jump I had done in practice, it was going to be my first jump for the final, and because I qualified in ninth and the start order is reversed, I would jump fourth.

Jac and Liz both jumped before me, but I couldn't tell how they went. The fog had cleared slightly and I was able to make out the rough shapes of the jumps. The judges cleared me to go. *Just hit your take-off, Lyd,*' I thought. And then I went.

The jump felt great in the air but I landed a touch on my heels and did a bit of a wheelie on landing. It wasn't quite the landing I had hoped for and not like the one I had done in practice, but I was happy to be on my feet. It was a great jump in the air, so the only thing the judges could deduct points for was the landing. It was a small error, but because the jump has the highest degree of difficulty in the competition the score was still going to be good. I scored 106.25 points—still on target.

Tao Tao from China competed a Full-Full-Full and landed it. I didn't see it, but she scored 108.74 points and was sitting in first place. I was in second place with one round to go. Two points wasn't a big margin and I was confident with my plan. I had no idea how the rest of the competitors had jumped.

> *Barbara:* '*The biggest test of all of our work came after she landed that first jump in finals, elated and relieved and so satisfied to have done her best ... but it wasn't over. They don't award the medals after the first round, thankfully, because it would have been silver. She took a few seconds to celebrate and then forgot the jump ever happened. The best athletes have the worst memories. By the time she was on the lift to the top that jump was over. Randall (my husband) has a picture of me holding*

Lauri and I on our wedding day; a magical day that I will never forget. Our wedding party consisted of (from left): Olivia Leontiades our flower girl, Courtney Purcell, Taryn Saxionis and Erica Whitfield, then Sami Mustonen, Jussi Kinnunen ('Legs') and Janne Lahtela. PHOTO: LUCAS DAWSON PHOTOGRAPHY

Dad was so proud to walk me down the aisle. Our wedding ceremony was held at a castle overlooking a picturesque lake in Finland, on 6 July 2007.
PHOTOS: LUCAS DAWSON PHOTOGRAPHY

Having finished second on four different occasions, I was so glad to finally shed the 'bridesmaid' tag by winning my first crystal globe after the 2009 World Cup season. PHOTO: GETTY IMAGES

Bree Munro has been with me the whole way and she was so happy for me after my win at Lake Placid in 2010.
PHOTO: LAURI LASSILA

Mid-flight during qualifications at the Vancouver Olympics in 2010.
PHOTO: GETTY IMAGES

After winning the Gold at Vancouver, an Aussie fan threw me their flag to take onto the podium after making my way through the media maze.
PHOTO: GETTY IMAGES

It's not every day you get your face on a stamp. Thanks Australia Post!
PHOTO: GETTY IMAGES

It's hard to describe that moment when you stand on the podium after receiving a gold medal and they then play the Australian National Anthem. By the look on my face, it was pure joy (with a touch of relief as well!).
PHOTO: EPA VIA AAP/VALDRIN XHEMAJ

After I flew home, I went straight to Diggers Rest Primary School to share my medal with all the kids. They were so excited and had made posters and banners to welcome me home.
PHOTO: AAP IMAGE/LUIS ENRIQUE ASCUI

Well, here I am carrying the flag at the closing ceremony. I was exhausted after a few days straight of barely any sleep and lots of media but proud to be waving the Aussie flag after a picture perfect Olympic campaign.
PHOTO: AAP IMAGE/JULIAN SMITH

Capping off a remarkable year in 2010, I was awarded the most prestigious annual award in Australian sport, 'The Don', named after the great Sir Donald Bradman. What an honour! PHOTO: LUCAS DAWSON PHOTOGRAPHY

My biggest rivals in recent years have been the Chinese girls. Pictured with me inside the Birds Nest Stadium in Beijing at the 2013 World Cup are: Zhang Xin, Xu Mengtao ("Tao Tao") and Li Nina.
PHOTO: LEO BAKER

My two biggest supporters, Lauri and Kai. It was such an amazing moment when we became parents for the first time in 2011.
PHOTO: LEO BAKER

Kai attended all my gym sessions when I was returning from childbirth. Here he's helping mummy to regain her core strength and balance. PHOTO: LEO BAKER

We would train at the VIS during everybody's lunch break so that I could bring Kai along. I loved having him there with me, and he enjoyed hanging out with Harry Brennan, my trainer. PHOTO: LEO BAKER

The colour was bronze, not gold, but it meant just as much to me because I had finally performed the quad. This was right after I picked up my Bronze Medal at the medal ceremony in downtown Sochi. PHOTO: LAURI LASSILA

Lydia's shoulders, my feet between her skis so she couldn't move, looking her in the eye and reminding her— same routine, same process. Now go do it.'

There was a bit of a wait until my second jump because the order was re-set based on the results from the first round. I would now be jumping second last. So I went for a toilet break. As I sat there, I thought, 'Gee, if I land my next jump, I might win this.' Even though that was a positive thought, it was one focused on outcome, so I immediately interrupted that thought by saying aloud 'STOP!' I'm not sure if anyone heard me, but it was a trick I had learned from Jeffrey, a circuit breaker to snap out of that thought, to remind myself to, 'Stay present—one jump at a time.' And that's really what kept me calm and got me through the Olympic finals.

I spoke to Barbara for a little while down at the bottom and she said the same, 'Be where you are Lyd, just focus on one last jump.' Late was also there. I was too focused to talk but I gave him a wink to let him know I was okay.

I rode up the lift and stopped to talk to Mich and Cord and we confirmed what we were doing. 'The plan's the same, right? We're going to do a Lay-Full-Full?'

'The plan is the same,' said Mich. 'You're sitting in a good position— just jump the way you can jump.'

I was a very different person to the one I was in the qualifications. This time I was confident and meant business. It was now just a matter of waiting.

CHAPTER 13

IN THE MOMENT

Not long after I rode the lift back to the top of the in-run for my last and final jump, I put on my iPod to drown out the noise of the crowd. My choice of music was pretty mellow, Imogen Heap. I've never used music to pump me up; rather, I need it to calm me down and get me into an optimal zone. My zone.

My first jump had been a Lay-Double Full-Full, which, as I said, has only been done by two women in the world—Tao Tao, who was now sitting in first place, and me, close behind in second. I would be the second last to jump. My final jump was planned as a Lay-Full-Full, a double-twisting triple, and if done well it would give me a solid score. It needed to be perfect and I wasn't going to let this opportunity slip away. Tao Tao was going for another triple-twisting triple, but she had been having trouble landing her jumps in practice before the competition and on the night before the final, so this gave me confidence that she might struggle to land two big jumps under pressure. I knew when I landed my first jump that I was going to take some beating and my odds were looking better than hers.

There was a long wait for my second jump. I scanned the field waiting up there. It was game time and I had my game face on. When the final round of jumps started, the crowd noise was deafening so I cranked the volume on my iPod. I didn't want to know what was happening or who was or wasn't landing their jumps. I kept reminding myself that this jump was about me and what I could do, and I was going to give it everything that I had and that is all that mattered. While it's important to be in the zone, it's equally important to be able to zone out, to switch off and let your brain rest. To maintain a high level of intensity for the duration of the competition would be very draining, so it's important to be able to switch on and off when you need to. During the wait, that's what I did. I took a seat and enjoyed the music blaring in my ears. I didn't want to over-think things.

With about five jumpers to go before me, I started to zone back in again and began visualising my jump from start to finish. I didn't need to do anything special; after all, 'It's just another event.' All I had to do was what I knew I could do, and keep it as simple as possible. I got up off my chair and stretched out my quads and did a bit of a run on the spot to make sure my body was still warm. I practised some landing drills to wake up my legs and knees. Then I clicked on my skis and double-checked my bindings. I went through my arm movements—right from the take-off position to the movements I needed to do to create the twist.

Other than the fog that night there were no complicated variables to deal with. The wind was calm and, unlike the previous night in training, there was no snow falling. I had a plan and I was going to stick to it. My first jump had been solid and placed me closely in second. '*This is where I want to be. Stick to the plan.*' If I had missed my first jump or if I hadn't landed it, I would have probably done another triple-twisting triple to try to redeem the situation. But because my first jump had been strong and I was sitting in second place, I didn't need to take that risk.

I still didn't know anything about how the competition was going, it wasn't important. The only thing I could control now was my jump. Before I slid into the start gate I took off my iPod—I don't like to have it on when I'm ready to go, that's just never been part of my routine. Some athletes have their headphones on right up until their names are announced, then get rid of them and jump, but I like to know what's going on around me and I like to feel the wind on my ears. I want to hear the sounds around me and be aware of my surroundings. I want to be in the moment.

Nothing prepares you, however, for the cheers of the crowd in an Olympic final and I remember thinking as I slid down into position, 'Wow, that's loud!' With two competitors to go, there was no backing out now. I asked Misra if there had been any changes with the speed and he said, 'No, everything is perfect.' I continued my warm-up routine and visualised myself doing a perfect Lay-Full-Full. *'Be where you are, Lyd'.* I was in my zone. I stared down at the jump and could just see it through the fog. Everything else seemed blurry and faded into the background.

Nina Li jumped before me. Although I couldn't see from the top of the in-run, I knew she had landed it because the crowd erupted and her coaches celebrated. I expected no less of her. But I reminded myself that it didn't matter. *'Game on.'* It was all about me now.

'Next coming up, Lydia Lassila from Australia.'

After your name is announced, the judges indicate they are ready by flashing a green light and from then you have 10 seconds to start your jump. I was ready. I was confident that my speed would be right; I had no doubts and no second thoughts. I was completely committed. The cue I focused on was, 'Take-off.'

I accelerated and hit the transition leading into the jump. I kept my body position strong up the jump and committed to the take-off. *Whoosh!* It felt like I was in slow motion. I could feel every part of what I was doing and was in complete control the whole time. The take-off was strong and powerful, which is what set the height and rotation of the jump. I remember thinking in the air, *'This is feeling really good.'*

I could hear my coach Mich screaming instructions to me, 'Stretch, stretch, stretch!' But I didn't stretch—I didn't think I needed to. I was flipping slowly and I was in complete control of my rotation and I could see the landing the whole time, so in the end I just made my own decision. I landed perfectly and let out an almighty scream as my fists pumped to the sky. The landing felt so light and it was probably one of the best landings I've ever done on a triple. It felt so easy and I knew that it was the best jump I could have done at that point. The crowd went wild, but I was still in my moment—I was floating. I was so relieved that it was all over. I was relieved that I performed under pressure. The rest was now out of my hands.

I looked over to Late. He was crying and mimed, 'You've done it!'

My score came up: 108.49. I was leading with a total score of 214.74. But Tao Tao was still to come. It was my best performance at an Olympic Games so far and I felt that I had done my job. If Tao Tao was going to beat me she was going to deserve it. I congratulated Nina Li and Guo Xinxin but still had no idea of their scores. They seemed very happy with their performances, too. I quickly ran over to Late and gave him a hug. He said again, 'You have it,' and was so proud. It was so special to have him there and see me perform like that.

I ran back to take my position on the big white couch where Nina Li and Guo Xinxin were sitting. As I sat down, I felt the weight lift off my shoulders as I breathed out the air in my lungs. It was a great feeling, a satisfying feeling knowing that I had withstood the pressure. What happened four years ago at Torino didn't matter now—I'd overcome it. I'd overcome all the injuries. Everything I had been through to that point in my career was all worth it, just for that moment.

With Tao Tao still to come I couldn't celebrate. I had visualised that final so many times in my head, including me jumping up and down screaming, crying and celebrating if I'd won. So many different scenarios except for the one I was in. I hadn't visualised myself in the gold medal position with one jumper to go, so I kept a lid on myself.

Tao Tao was doing a Lay-Double Full-Full on her second jump, the triple-twisting triple I'd done on my first jump. She was swinging pretty hard for a young competitor with not a lot of experience, although she has been jumping since she was a kid. But this was her first Olympics.

As she left the jump I knew it was going wrong for her. I saw her legs start to come apart in the twist, which caused her to rotate slowly. She was behind in the twist and it finished late, meaning she wasn't able to get a good visual on the landing before her skis touched the ground. She didn't pick up the landing until it was too late, landed a bit stiff-legged and crashed.

I sat there in shock, realising of course that I had won. Tao Tao was covered in snow and she, too, looked shocked. Her scores came up and put her in sixth place. Her English isn't very good and she didn't understand what was happening until Nina told her where she had finished. She was confused about what had happened and I looked confused looking at her. But I wasn't—I just didn't feel it was right to jump up and down in her face while she was still dusting off the snow.

It would have been good to see her on the podium—not at the top, obviously, but she deserved a medal. Had she done a Lay-Full-Full and stuck it like I did, she might have won. But she was young and I was sure she wouldn't make the same mistake again. In terms of tricks of the trade, she would continue to be the one to challenge me post-Vancouver, and I always looked forward to it.

For a while, I was internalising all my excitement, which is quite unusual for me and not the way I'd envisioned my reaction if I won. In the midst of the thousands of people there, I managed to have a quiet moment with myself where I kept repeating to myself, *'I did it! I did it!'* A wave of satisfaction spread through my body, knowing that I had finally done what I had set out to do. And I did it my way.

I finally snapped out of it and just wanted to find Late. I spotted Liz in the crowd first and ran over to her and gave her a big hug. 'Oh my God, you did it!' she squealed in my ear. I said the same thing. 'I know, I can't believe it. I did it! I did it!' and we were crying and squeezing each other so hard. Liz has been there for the whole journey and she is very special to me; we were gymnasts together and now we were aerial skiers competing in the Olympic final. I knew she'd had a rough final, but at the time I think she was pretty happy for me. Jacqui also had a sensational performance, finishing fifth in courageous form given her shaky preparation. She, too, had fought hard to come back from injury and managed to put down two great jumps on the world's biggest sporting stage.

At that time, Mich slid down the landing hill and came to congratulate me. I thanked him and he thanked me. We had developed such a strong relationship and bond and he'd been great to work with. He is an amazing coach and he had believed in me every step of the way. I'm so glad he took us on board when he did—it was the best thing that could have happened for me.

> *Mich: 'To be a coach of an Olympic champion is the best thing about my job. I was happy to help Lydia get there.*

IN THE MOMENT

> *I've coached many Olympic champions before and it's always a great experience. I think Lydia and I have a special relationship—we always work well together and that's what I liked about it the most. We proved we could do big tricks and they were going to work. That's just super. That is something you will never forget and something we shared together.'*

I couldn't spot Late before I was dragged off by the Games officials to get ready for the podium ceremony. Cord was by my side to congratulate me and he had an elated look on his face, even more elated than when I broke the world record. He had been a great addition to my A-team and he never doubted my ability to win.

> *Cord: 'It was an amazing experience and an amazing ride and I was proud and grateful to be a part of it. Lydia was so calm through the final, like it was just another event. She was right where she needed to be mentally and that made me realise even more so that Mich was right, we were done. The event was close after the first round but the numbers were breaking down as we expected and it really seemed like everything was working. We'd looked into every scenario and we had planned our way through all of them—nothing was left to chance. After the first round, things where shaping up nicely. With Lydia in second we knew that would put pressure on the Chinese to land the biggest tricks they had, which was not the best position for them to be in—even the Chinese feel pressure. When Tao Tao came off the jump and I saw her twist timing was off I could see it was going to be hard to land. She missed, Lydia won. The rest was just a blur. I don't think I could have been happier than I was at that moment. After it was all over it was more a sense of relief that the right girl won.'*

In the end, it was up to me to land two jumps. No one else was going to be able to do it. But I wasn't a one-woman show and I have my A-team to thank for that. There is no way I could have prepared myself as well as I did without them. Late had been by my side through thick and thin and has always encouraged me to chase the dream. Mich was vital and it was he who made me feel important and helped me believe. Cord couldn't have come at a better time and he worked so well with me and Mich. Barbara, among many things, taught me how to get out of my own way and Ashley kept me functioning physically. Without them, I would be lost. And if it weren't for my silent partner, Jeffrey Hodges, I doubt I would have developed the self-awareness that I have today.

It was strange to stand on the podium at the venue for the flower ceremony but not be presented with my medal. It was special to sing our national anthem, but it would have meant more to me if I had been awarded the medal right then and there in my ski boots, rather than a day later wearing my runners in a massive production in the city. Even though the medal ceremony is great and they put a lot of effort into it, I would have preferred to have received the medal at the jump site where I had won it.

There were so many Australians in the crowd at the jump site because Canada is full of Aussie skiers. I remember looking into the noisy, cheering mob and spotting people I knew. The Grollo family were there and I saw them wildly waving the Aussie flag. Not only have they been huge supporters of winter sport in Australia, but they have been great supporters of me and the aerial skiing program for a long time now, too. Mt Buller, their mountain, was where it all started for me, so it was wonderful to see Rino and his wife Diana and the rest of the family in the crowd.

After the flower ceremony I was ushered into a maze of media and delivered interview after interview. At one point someone handed me a phone and on the other end of the line was the Australian Prime Minister, Kevin Rudd, who had called to congratulate me. It was nice for him to do so and I thanked him for the call, but then said, 'Does this mean we can build a water ramp facility in Australia now?' I completely surprised him and he said, 'Pardon?' so I repeated myself. 'Well,' he said, 'I'm sure can we work out a way to help you.' It was pretty funny. I'd just won an Olympic gold medal and there I was trying to lobby the Prime Minister for funds. I figured I should strike while the iron was hot. Mum called after that and she nearly flipped when I said I'd just got off the phone with the Prime Minister. She was at home with family and friends, celebrating, crying and hugging. I missed them and I know they would have loved to have been there to see me win.

The next 24 hours were a chaotic blur—a mixture of partying non-stop with my teammates, AOC officials and friends, constant media interviews and photo shoots. I didn't get more than a few hours sleep. By the time I arrived for the medal ceremony the next day I was exhausted. But when I first felt the medal placed around my neck I was elated. I was an Olympic gold medallist and it was the most beautiful medal I had ever seen. I looked into it while I was on the podium and I saw my whole life in that medal—22 years of dreams and burning desire. It was proof that what I thought and believed I could do was finally done. Satisfaction spread through my entire body as I sang the national anthem, knowing I had achieved something I'd been chasing for a very long time.

Late was with me the whole time and his face spelled pride. We had to pinch ourselves constantly because we just couldn't believe it was all real. He was passing messages to me from his parents, family and friends in Finland who were also very happy for me. Finland didn't win any gold medals in Vancouver, so they adopted me as half-Finnish, claiming part of the medal as their own. And that's okay with me.

The thing that amazed me afterwards, when I had a moment to myself, was that I asked myself, 'What's next?' I thought I would get the feeling that Olympic gold was enough and that I would want to hang up my boots, but the feeling was the opposite—I felt as though I was finally doing the tricks I had always wanted to do in this sport. I was finally starting to live out my potential and I decided very quickly that I wasn't finished yet. That's human nature, I suppose. We always want more. If I look back to my goal map, 'Olympic gold' was just one piece of the puzzle in achieving my purpose—to be the best female aerialist who has ever lived.

Diary entry: 'Wow! I'm Olympic champion! My dreams have come true. I have come a long way since Torino and it's nice to finally be the aerialist I thought I could be. Mission accomplished. Now it's on to the next challenge!'

Granted, I would need some time off jumping to let my body rest and recover, and to spend time at home with Late and my family and friends, but I knew I wanted to defend my title at Sochi 2014, and I knew that, next, I wanted to achieve the goal I had set for myself at the start of this adventure—to jump like a man.

CHAPTER 14

FAMILY AND FRUSTRATION

It was a great buzz after winning the gold medal. When I arrived home, I received the warmest of welcomes and was treated as a hero. People wanted to hear my story and requested me at their events. Winning gold allowed me the opportunity to share my story with a wider audience, and people could know who I really was; I wasn't hidden behind a ski mask any more on some remote mountain top. I shared not only what I had gone through to reach the pinnacle in my sport but also the *why* and *how*. I never set out to inspire other people, but, it's a nice bonus to have done so. To have complete strangers come up to me and say how much my win inspired them has filled me with pride. I always tell them I am an ordinary person just trying to do extraordinary things while believing that if you want something enough, you'll find a way to make it happen.

When I got home I also began lobbying for the water ramp that I had briefly discussed with Australia's Prime Minister, Kevin Rudd, over the phone in the immediate aftermath of my gold medal jump. But more on that shortly.

After a well earned break traveling the world, I fell pregnant in August 2010. Late and I had already decided in Vancouver that I would have a break from aerials to start a family and then go back to defend my title at the 2014 Sochi Winter Olympics in Russia. As usual, it wasn't difficult to decide what I wanted, but coming up with a plan as to *how* was going to be more challenging. As I had done with my aerials program in the lead-up to Vancouver, I needed to formulate a similarly structured program around giving birth and recovering in a way that would allow me to get back into training as soon as possible.

We met with my obstetrician, Dr Peter England, in Melbourne, to discuss our plan. Fortunately, Peter understood exactly what I was trying to do and was very supportive. He knew I wanted to get back to elite sport, so we took a measured approach on how we would be able to achieve that. Our aim was to have a natural birth as it would most likely mean a quicker recovery time; we worked hard on having that outcome.

Other than me being pregnant, it was business as usual. No jumping of course, but I trained at the VIS through my pregnancy to keep as fit as possible with the mindset that I was just on maternity leave and that I would be returning stronger and better than ever towards my campaign to Sochi. I ran up the steepest hills of Lorne, I swam, I lifted weights. I also met, on a number of occasions, with coaches and support staff from other sports where athletes had returned as mums, in order to gain an insight into what to expect when returning to elite sport as a mother. It was great at the time (to have so much support) but in hindsight, it didn't matter how many people I had sitting and advising around a boardroom table—nothing could prepare me for motherhood or the journey that was about to begin.

I can't say I enjoyed being pregnant. I'd put it down to the 'selfish athlete' in me. A lot of women have said to me (including my own mother) that being pregnant was the best they've ever felt, but I'm not sure I share that view. Hell, I'm an elite athlete! Of course I've felt better! I wasn't sick or anything like that, but I didn't particularly like being pregnant. I didn't like feeling heavy or the fact that I couldn't see my toes…for a very long time! I was so used to seeing this cut, fit, elite athlete in the prime condition of her life. When I'd catch a side profile of myself in the mirror I'd just about fall over in shock. But that aside, I knew it was a means to what would be a great outcome and a necessary but temporary process. On the plus side, I had luscious hair and big boobs—the latter definitely a novelty.

FAMILY AND FRUSTRATION

I had a really easy pregnancy. I trained within my comfort zone and everything was going as planned. I guess being my first pregnancy, I was oblivious to how many things can actually go wrong with both the mother and baby. I was naïve as to how vulnerable we are and to how fraught the actual process is of growing a baby. But there was one major incident in the final two months of my pregnancy that really highlighted that fact: That was the tragedy surrounding Alisa Camplin's baby boy, Finnan. Alisa was 32 weeks into her pregnancy—just four weeks ahead of me—when she began to feel unwell, and after a number of tests it was determined that the right side of Finnan's heart looked too big, but he was still too underdeveloped to be delivered early in order to have surgery. He was born by caesarean two weeks later and was immediately given open-heart surgery. In all, he endured six operations in 10 days, but, sadly, the doctors at the Royal Children's Hospital were unable to save his life. It was a terrible shock.

Like me, Alisa had taken every precaution throughout her pregnancy, and as I was approaching a similar stage in my own pregnancy, it made me sit back and realise that I had this person inside me—it wasn't just a bump on the outside—and there were a lot of things that could go wrong. It shook me up and I backed off on my training. I just didn't want to overdo it or jeopardise my baby's health in any way, so I tried to take it easy and enjoy the last few weeks of my pregnancy.

The birth itself was fairly measured and clinical. I was right on time, which was great. We couldn't have picked a better day, either: May 8, 2011, Mother's Day! But all planning aside, I don't think any mother is ever fully prepared for childbirth and what your body is going to experience during that process. In all my years as an athlete, there hasn't been an experience I could compare it to. I have never felt anything quite like it and as one of my friends delicately put it 'it's kind of like an exorcism'. I wanted to escape my body and at many moments I didn't think I could actually do it. The female body is an amazing vessel. Truly. I placed all my trust in the hands of Peter and he guided us through the experience safely, however, after 22 hours of labour, he was no longer there for the delivery, as his shift had ended! He left us in good hands though and our baby boy finally arrived to catch the final hours of Mother's Day. All in all it was very successful: perfect baby, healthy mum, no tearing, good to go.

Following the birth we were able to then go and spend four days in the Park Hyatt where they have a whole floor dedicated as a maternity ward. If you're lucky enough to have a trauma-free birth like mine was, you have the option of going and staying there instead of the usual hospital ward. I know Mum was very envious—when she had me she was in the Footscray Hospital sharing a ward with 10 other new mothers, amidst hospital renovations, and here I was spending my first few days as a mum in five-star accommodation at the Park Hyatt!

****

While it was all new for me, it was also new for Late and I'm sure he didn't know what to expect. In fact, he did not have that natural paternal instinct. He wasn't the kind of guy who would naturally goof around and play with kids, let alone babies, as my brothers would, so it was such a beautiful moment to see him become a dad for the first time and to see him fall in love with our son the moment he was born—as did I. We were now three with this new life that we had brought into the world, it was just incredible. We enjoyed the moment. It was so precious, so intimate to finally meet our surprisingly blond little boy. Sure, going from two to three meant that life was going to get crazier than it already was, but we were really happy and ready for the next phase of life: parenthood.

We quickly found that deciding baby names was not an easy task, particularly in our family with two different cultures coming together. Many of the Finnish letters are pronounced differently. For instance, if you are using the word 'J' in Finnish, it is pronounced as a 'Y'. So for a name like Kyle in Australia, it would sound like 'Kuu - leh' in Finland. Conversely, in Finnish a common name is 'Janne', (pronounced Yan-neh) which is John in English. So Late had his list and I had mine, and it was quite a challenge to meet in the middle and find this happy medium of a name which would work across both cultures and not get mispronounced. Growing up with a name like 'Ierodiaconou', which nobody could pronounce, I had a bit of a phobia of my child having a name that nobody could say correctly.

We chose Kai—Kai's great-grandmother was Kaija (pronounced Kay-ya), so we chose his name because of that connection. His second name is Erik, after his grandfather Erkki in Finland. From day dot Late spoke Finnish to Kai, and he has only ever spoken Finnish to him, so Kai has grown up fluent in Finnish. My mum, on the other hand, has spoken only Italian to him, so he is now tri-lingual and can switch in and out of each language, English included. But if I start speaking Italian or Finnish to him he gets really angry and he tells me 'you only speak English, don't speak Italian' or 'don't speak speak Finnish to me!' Although I understand a lot of both Finnish and Italian, my speaking of them is behind because, unlike a child I'm embarrassed to make mistakes. Kai's development teaches me that we can always learn and we are always learning.

****

As I mentioned earlier, immediately after winning my gold medal I received a phone call from then Prime Minister, Kevin Rudd, who congratulated me on my achievement. Still riding the high from my medal-winning jump, I asked the Prime Minister: 'Does this mean we can build a water ramp facility in Australia now?' Once I returned home, and all throughout my pregnancy, I threw myself into lobbying for a water ramp. I knew that, with a baby on the way, the challenges of continuing to train overseas the way I had previously were going to be greater. So, having a world-class water ramp on home soil was going to make life a whole lot easier, not only for me, but for all Australian freestyle skiers now and in the future. It's a competitive market for sponsorship dollars in sport, so to be able to train in Australia will encourage more athletes to take up aerial skiing, which will ensure continued success in the future. Lobbying for a training facility is a lot of work. I basically became a full-time consultant for the project. I went around the world gathering specifics on ramps and talking to coaches, as well as people who had built similar ramps before. Spearheading the project with me was Geoff Henke – a former Australian ice hockey player and chairman of the OWIA. At 89, he is well qualified to speak on winter sport in this country, having seen it grow from very humble beginnings into the large organisation it is today. He is certainly aware we still have a long way to go, which is why he is so driven in his pursuit of establishing a year-round water ramp here at home. We certainly had support from others like Geoff Lipshut, Jacqui Cooper and Alisa Camplin for example, but Geoff and I were the real drivers behind it. I was focused on fine-tuning the jump and pool specifications and determining what we wanted to build. We really put our heart and souls into the project and it consumed the very little spare time I had. But I really wanted it to happen. I needed it to happen. We presented our pitch to the Federal and Queensland Governments which soon enough granted us support for the facility. We then worked closely with the architectural and engineering firms, fine-tuning all the specifications and details which meant many trips to and from Queensland to discuss, advise and oversee their progress. At the end of 2010, it looked like we had the project over the line. It was reported at the time:

> *Sportstar.com, 12 December 2010: 'Olympic gold medallist Lydia Lassila's dream of a purpose-built high performance aerial ski water ramp facility based on home soil will become a reality after a $4 million joint funding agreement between the Australian and Queensland Governments. The investment will fund the construction of a water ramp training facility at Sleeman Sports Complex in Brisbane to benefit the training and preparation of Australia's aerial skiers in the lead up to Winter Olympic Games and world championships. Sleeman Sports Complex will house six ski ramps up to 24 metres in height at the end of a 4-metre deep Olympic pool as part of a series of upgrades to the facility ... "This facility will help our younger athletes and have them just pouring into a facility and training all year round. We will be unstoppable in Sochi," Lassila said. Queensland Sports Minister Phil Reeves said this will be the first aerial ski facility constructed in the Southern*

FAMILY AND FRUSTRATION

> *Hemisphere, which can be used throughout the year. "Currently there is no high performance training centres [for aerial skiing] in the southern hemisphere. This will be the only aerial ski water ramp training facility in the southern hemisphere accessible for 12 months of the year," Mr Reeves said. "The success of Australian athletes in these sports has seen other nations restrict access to our champions. This investment ensures they have an all season location to train."'* [1]

We were dealing with Government though, and as we all know, things don't ever happen very quickly when Government is involved. The pool was built, with a $250,000 bubble system installed, so it was beginning to move ahead. But then, in March 2012, just as things looked on track, the Liberal National Government, led by Campbell Newman, got into power and by June they had axed the funding we had been promised under Anna Bligh's Labor Government. Out of nowhere they simply squashed the whole project. They decided that they didn't want to support winter sport in Queensland, which was crazy when you consider that the first ever Winter Olympic gold medal for Australia was won by a Queenslander in Steven Bradbury!

I found that decision, or non-decision, quite disheartening because Queensland was the perfect place to have the ramp due to the warmer climate that would have allowed us to train there all year round. It was also going to be based in the Sleeman Sports Complex, which was an existing facility that housed all the supporting facilities that we would need as part of our training and recovery. I found out that the project had been canned through a newspaper article in Brisbane's *The Sunday Mail*, where we were likened to the Jamaican bobsled team:

> *Darrell Giles, The Sunday Mail (QLD), 17 June 2012:*
> 'Forget the Jamaican bobsled team, Queensland was on track to star in its own version of the movie Cool Runnings

---

[1] Read the full article at: http://sportstar.com/gazette/funding-for-aerial-ski-water-ramp.

... Although Queensland is renowned for its tropical rainforests and golden beaches washed by warm ocean waves, the Bligh government had wanted the state to be a centre of excellence for snow ski-jumping ... Cool Runnings was a hit film based on the true story of the first bobsled team from Jamaica to compete in the Winter Olympics, even though members of the team had never seen snow before. This set the scene for a sequel. The new State Government - grappling with an avalanche of debt inherited from its predecessors - will today scrap the project, which was on track to be built for 2013 ... "It's snow joke," said Sports Minister Steve Dickson yesterday, describing the plan as a waste of taxpayer money. Mr Dickson said Labor had approved the development of the 36m high, 10m wide behemoth - complete with hydraulics and purpose-built lift - at the Sleeman Sports Complex, using the centre's new 50m swimming pool as a landing area. "Day by day, week by week the people of Queensland are discovering just how reckless the former government was with taxpayers' money," Mr Dickson said. "The fact that a Winter Olympic training venue was considered a priority at a time when 96 per cent of the Labor government's capital spending programs were being sourced through debt is simply beyond belief. I've no hesitation in cancelling this project, which was approved and progressed using some of the most financially unsound reasoning I've seen ... According to what little information there is available, potential usage indicates that fewer than 10 elite athletes would have used it for training purposes ... With no credible business case to speak of, and no tangible usage agreements, all this scheme would have achieved was to put a brand new pool off limits for actual swimmers ... This is a luxury item the people of Queensland can neither afford nor need when the state is facing such dire economic circumstances.

FAMILY AND FRUSTRATION

> *It's hard to imagine how this ill-conceived, inappropriate project was ever progressed, let alone paid for with Queenslanders' taxes, however the waste stops today.'* [2]

We were made to look like a joke. I was very hurt by that outcome and the way we were portrayed. They did not even have the courtesy to contact me, or any of my fellow lobbyists directly, to explain the decision. They just pulled out and moved on. After all the hard work we had dedicated to the project we were left with nothing. Taxpayer money went down the drain and so did my dreams of back-to-back gold. I was in Utah at the time, with baby Kai, and it was devastating to learn of the decision second-hand. That was as shattering as any of my major injuries that I had suffered to that point. I was so hurt and so insulted by the article, particularly that we were seen in that light. I can certainly understand Government cut-backs and of not wanting to waste public money, but this was going to be a multi-purpose facility that winter and summer athletes were going to be able to use. It was very disheartening; the competitive edge we were hoping for was now gone.

> Dad: 'The politicians, they're a funny lot. They made it look like an absolutely stupid idea. They likened it to the Jamaican bobsled team: they ridiculed the whole thing. To Lydia it was devastating, because she'd put a lot of effort into trying to get that facility. But, you put your faith in politicians and that's what happens; you get a lot of disappointment.'

The Newman Government just shut the door on it and threw away the key. They wanted nothing to do with us. While we had support from the Federal Government as well as the AOC, who understood the importance of the facility, we were now without a location and the support of a State Government. I learned a lot from the whole process. I learned that I certainly would never go into politics. I learned that a 'yes'

---

2 Read the full article at: http://tinyurl.com/jg7yadj.

can quickly become a 'no' when dealing with government and I learned that a purpose-built pool, 13 lanes wide, with a bubble system, worth a quarter of a million dollars, sitting at the bottom of it, could sit barely used. Money well spent?

In fact, looking back on it now, I am 100 per cent confident that the decision not to go ahead with the facility made all the difference between the gold that was in reach in Sochi and the bronze that was the result. The non-decision completely derailed my comeback. It hurt, and I was disappointed, but I still had an Olympics to prepare for and I tried to make it work for me the best that I could. Geoff Henke remains as our number one lobbyist. He remains as determined as I am to get the final 'okay'—whenever that may be—to see a world-class water ramp *finally* be built in Australia.

CHAPTER 15

PATH TO SOCHI

Two weeks after Kai was born I was back in the gym. I had a new trainer in Harry Brennan from the VIS. It was obvious straight away that Harry, a native of Scotland, was a master in his field: well respected, measured and sensible. What I loved most about him straight away was that he had no ego – a rarity in the field of physical trainers. Harry and I mapped out a program to bring me back to peak physical fitness. Our approach was 'slow and steady' as my body gradually healed from childbirth. I needed my body to be able to handle massive loads when I would jump again, which meant that there was a real risk in going too hard, too quickly. I didn't ask Harry whether he had worked with athlete-mums before but I didn't need to. I could tell he had done his research; he was the perfect person to guide me through my comeback.

Fortunately for me, my body sucked straight back into shape. In fact, in a lot of ways, my body was in much better shape than it had been leading into Vancouver; I was recovering from childbirth, I wasn't recovering from a knee reconstruction, which made returning to peak shape that little bit easier.

When I told my family I wanted to go on again after Vancouver, they were all very supportive of the idea. But, as I later found out, they weren't sure whether it was the right thing to do.

Dad: 'Even after winning the gold, it only took a few weeks and she'd made up her mind: "That's not enough, I can do better. Back-to-back gold would be fantastic." And you sort of say "Oh, you're joking, aren't ya?"'

George: 'We thought it wasn't really realistic. We didn't think she could do it. We have children and we know what it's like to have kids and the work that goes into them. We didn't think it was possible. We thought, you know, having a kid her priorities would have changed and she would have lost that desire to compete and succeed in aerials, and that she would re-focus towards being a mum. But that wasn't the case.'

I could understand their concern but you can't tame that feeling of wanting to achieve more; the feeling of having unfinished business and the search for wanting to push boundaries. For me it wasn't about just winning another gold medal, it was about leaving my mark: going where no woman had gone before. Fortunately for me, Late understood that. He respected that too. I never got any resistance from him, and I still don't. From early on he was like, 'if you want to go back, then we'll make it happen,' and he's always been amazing like that. He has sacrificed a lot so that I can chase my dreams and he has patience of the likes I've never seen before. He's seen me go through some really hard times. He's seen me lose confidence and self-belief and he's seen me get injured and seriously hurt. He's also seen me come through all that and succeed. Either way, he's been there every step of the way. So, me winning in Vancouver was a huge victory for him too. His career as an athlete had its own series of highs and lows and he knew the risks involved but he supported my decisions and on many occasions encouraged me to continue.

Late: 'After Vancouver it was never a quitting position. We knew pretty much straight away she wanted to keep on going for another Olympiad, which was obviously a decision that I fully supported, and I think that's the right move that she's done. If I was in the same position as an athlete I'd want to do the same thing myself, and that's why it was natural for me to quite easily and quite comfortably support it. But we both obviously wanted to get started with a family, so we thought that, "okay, we've got a couple of years to make it happen." I know what it takes. I know the sacrifices and the training that you've got to put in to make it happen. In Lyd's case it's six seconds every four years, so it's brutal. There's only one winner. For every gold medallist, there are a couple of hundred people who didn't make it, and we never hear about them. That's what makes it so special.'

We knew though, that this time around, things were going to be very different. It's not as simple as hitting the repeat button and doing it all over again. This campaign was going to be tough and with its own set of challenges.

****

I had the 2011 season off from competition, and started jumping on the water ramps in November of that year. A month earlier I had re-joined the team for a fitness camp at the Australian Institute of Sport in Canberra; I was still building my way back up towards full fitness. My mum came with me to help look after Kai when I was training. Even then, I knew I was in for a challenge, which is why it was so important to have the support and help wherever I went.

As I did in 2010, I surrounded myself with an A-team, only now the A-team had expanded. I had Harry, my mum *and* Late's mum to look after Kai. Kai himself became our team mascot! I needed people around me who I could not only trust, but who I knew would completely, 100 per cent, look after Kai and ensure that he never felt in any way neglected. I knew that so long as I had that peace of mind, I could focus completely on my training. If I didn't have all that, it wouldn't have worked.

Geoff Lipshut and the staff at the OWIA were really supportive; they understood my plans to come back, so I had buy-in from them. They organised a lot of my meetings with staff and coaches from other sports which had had mothers return to elite sport. While I was still pregnant, I was attending meetings to learn all about the dynamics that went on with these other mums, and it was really good for me to get my head around what to expect after having Kai.

During my pregnancy they asked how I felt towards coming back as a mum and typically I had no hesitation or any doubt that it wouldn't be possible. They cautioned me that this might change *after* the birth and sure, that was the big unknown. So after having Kai, I was relieved that the same hunger I had before was still there. What had changed though, was that I was now more aware of the risks associated with aerial skiing. It's not that I wasn't aware before I became a mother, it comes naturally with age and experience. It was just that now I was responsible for this tiny being, and whatever happened to me would have a greater impact on him, so those risks were of a greater concern to me than they had been previously.

Aerial skiing is not like swimming or running or basketball, where you don't experience that sense of danger or being on the edge each time you go out to compete. When you're doing a sport like mine, things can go wrong on *any* jump. You experience fear and sometimes you get that bad feeling in your gut or your mind can conjure up bad images of things you don't want to happen. We all know the risks, but as soon as you think too much about them you're a goner in this sport.

Fortunately for me, after having Kai, not once did Late bring that up and use the risks as an excuse to call it quits. Other people certainly did, but it never came up in conversations between Late and myself. Neither motherhood, nor the risks of the sport would keep me away. If Late truly felt I needed to retire and focus on new and safer things then he would certainly have said so. He says what he means, so he wouldn't have encouraged me to go for it if he didn't truly believe in me or if he believed I was past it. I knew I had his buy-in, whereas there were other people— family and friends included—who couldn't understand the point of going back to do it all again.

I'm very lucky to have had Late on my side. In his case, he'd been there himself and he understood what it was like to have dreams and desires that don't quite fit into the norm. He understood that these opportunities don't last forever, and that I would regret it if I didn't continue to try and reach my full potential. I'm sure at times he's felt neglected as I charged on in full focus, but I could never have done what I've done if he wasn't on board 100 per cent.

Harry was also a huge asset to me as my return progressed. Being a dad, he understood the day-to-day challenges of what I was going through: broken sleep, feeding and sleep times for Kai, running my business Body Ice; not to mention the logistics of bringing Kai with me to training and in and out of car seats. To say the least, Harry was incredibly patient. To make it easier on myself, I'd scheduled most of my training sessions in the VIS during lunchtime when it was supposed to be closed. That way I had it to myself and could bring Kai along without feeling like I was imposing on other athletes by having a baby in the gym. By taking him with me, it also meant I didn't have to rush my workouts to be back home to feed him and Late could get a few hours of peace and uninterrupted work! I'm fairly certain babies weren't really allowed in the gym but I guess it was a first for the VIS too, and they supported me and let me roll with it. In the beginning it was fairly easy. Kai slept most of the time and if he was awake I just put him on his playmat and I worked out beside him. It got a little more complicated though as he grew and started to crawl and then walk. We then had to get creative on how we could entertain him. I'm not going to lie, there were times where we'd just have to let him play on a few iPhone apps for a few minutes, or Harry would take him for a walk or throw him a ball, so that I could finish the set I was working on. I would often have to pause my workouts to change or feed him, and I had to be flexible and be okay with the fact that my workouts took longer than they had previously. Throughout it all Harry was there and helped me in so many ways beyond exercises and reps. He was as committed and as focused as I was, which was fantastic.

****

I started jumping on snow again in November 2011. I made my way to Ruka with Late and six-month-old Kai and Leena joined us too. Honestly, I don't know how we could have managed without supportive grandparents. I was so excited to be back on snow and that's when the journey felt like it was really beginning. I remember being so happy even just shovelling snow and helping get the jump site ready, let alone jumping. I had missed even the most mundane of tasks. It was great to be reunited with Mich as well. We had kept in contact over Skype but it was nice to be around him again. Mich has a son of his own, so he totally understood my limitations and the other challenges I was facing in coming back as a mum. We needed to be efficient with training so that I could get back to Kai and recover properly for the next day. In terms of coaching, there really isn't anyone better suited to me than Mich. He just gets it.

I felt like myself again once immersed into a training routine. My body felt great as I started jumping and doing basic single somersaults to ease back into things. For that season, the aim was to do basic jumps, keep building up on my physical fitness and just ski. Then, the plan would be to return to competition the following year. It was just about getting back into the swing of things with Mich, seeing how the body felt, and also seeing whether I still, truly, wanted to do it all again. Deep down, I knew I did but we had to make sure. I did a lot of skiing that season all over the world and that really reinforced how much I had missed the mountains, the snow, the people and the environment. It confirmed that I did want to be there.

Late certainly had a lot on his plate while I was out jumping, but it would only be for a couple of hours at a time before I was back as 'mummy'.

For me, it was just like riding a bike and pretty soon I was back into the monotonous groove of training, which I love! I had done some water ramping in Lilydale before getting back on snow, and I was only doing single somersaults, which are as easy as it gets for an aerial skier. So it was a stress-free return and a good opportunity to test life on the road as an athlete mum without the intensity of competition or difficult jumps. I knew the next year would not be as easy.

****

The real planning for Sochi, however, really started in May 2012. A lot of that strategic planning was done with Cord, Mich and Barbara. I decided I wanted to split my summer water ramp season between Utah and Switzerland. In Park City, I'd train with Cord who, since Vancouver, had become the Australian team head coach. I'd also be re-united with the Aussie team, a new generation of young girls as well as David Morris—still our only male team member. I felt it was important to be training back with the team. I'd then head off to Switzerland for the second half of the summer to train with Mich, who remained my head coach. Cord would assist him, which was basically the same set up as we had before Vancouver. I figured if it 'ain't broke, don't fix it'. Everyone was on board with that plan. As for physical training, that was led by Harry and he had a big part to play in knowing how my body was going, and how I was progressing; he really had his finger on the pulse. I also had a new physio, Diane Alvis, with whom I had started working with in Melbourne. She was really switched on treating me whenever I was home. Then there was Ashley and the medical staff at the VIS who were all informed on how I was doing. I felt like I was in good hands and it was nice to have such great people working with me and who really cared about what I was trying to do.

I made my way over to Park City in June with Kai and my mum. A lot had changed in the team since Vancouver. All of my old teammates, besides Dave, had retired. During my time away, the junior team had progressed in leaps and bounds and were now on the World Cup circuit. I was now the veteran of the group and the 'new' team had a different vibe from what I was used to. They were a lot younger and I was obviously in a different stage of my life too, being a mum now, which meant I had different priorities and responsibilities. I stayed in separate accommodation with my mum and Kai, which meant we had our own space and weren't going to be a nuisance or distraction to other team members. We all trained together though and I tried to integrate as best as I could.

It didn't take long before I noticed that aside from being a lot younger than me, they were also very competitive against each other and, I guess, against me. I had come from a team that was also very competitive, but the difference was that we were still very supportive of each other. If someone did a good jump or had a great day, we would high-five and acknowledge that, even if you didn't get along or even like the person. If someone was having a hard time or was in the midst of a meltdown, we would, likewise, offer support. I certainly didn't get that feeling with these girls initially. They were different and had already established their own culture and team morale (or lack there of). On the other hand, Dave was great and I was happy to be training alongside him again. We supported and pushed each other. I really needed his encouragement, especially as I progressed from double flips to triples after not having done them for two years. I made sure I was there for him, too.

When I first started out, we all used to watch video analysis together as a group, which is confronting because you don't really want everyone nit-picking your jump in slow motion. But what I liked about it was that you could learn something from your teammates and they could learn something from you. And if you had a bad day you had to suck it up and watch it anyway, in front of everyone. There might be tears, frustration and the works but in a sense it was team building, which is really important when you spend so much time travelling around the world together each year. It also creates healthy competition because you can see everyone's strengths and weaknesses and their analysis would give you ideas on how to improve your own jumping. But with our new team, everyone's program was very individualised and video was secretive, which is okay when you're a more mature athlete, but I think the younger athletes were missing out on a learning experience. To this day I ask Dave all the time if I can sit in on his video sessions because I feel I can learn something from him, and I always do.

Things didn't start smoothly for me in the summer of 2012. I had made some adjustments to my stance as I skied into the jump because, for most of my career, I skied into the jump with wide skis, which burned off a lot of my speed. Changing my stance to become narrower meant I would carry my speed more consistently into the jump but, in turn, it had an effect on my take-off, which had been always very consistent. I started making mistakes on my take-offs and I started catching edges coming into the jump and I was lucky to escape injury a number of times. Those close calls rattled me a lot, and I started to lose confidence—never a good thing. I felt as though I was racing the clock to try and get my tricks up to speed, figuring out my take-off and all those little things that I needed to feel comfortable with in order to progress.

At about the same time, we found out that our water ramp project in Queensland got cancelled. It was definitely a rough patch and I felt as though forces were completely against me in my quest for back-to-back Gold. It was good to have Mum and Kai there but, at the same time, there were days when I was so frustrated I just wanted to come home and bury my head into a pillow and cry. I couldn't do that though and had to put on a brave face and accept the challenges I was going through and believe that, day by day, jump-by-jump, if I just kept at it, things would eventually turn around. Kai always managed to pick up my mood and was a great distraction from the issues and stress I was dealing with. He brought perspective to the situation and reminded me to be grateful for what I did have.

While I was in Park City a good friend and old teammate of mine, Katie Bender, came out from Los Angeles for a visit. She had been working in the film industry for a few years since giving away aerial skiing and wanted to ask me if she could produce a feature documentary on me. Her timing wasn't great to be honest. My confidence in myself was low. I wasn't really on track with my jumping. The axing of the water ramp project had crushed my timeline even more. I was stressed and worried and the only person holding me together was Jeffrey Hodges, who I Skyped with on a weekly basis. A feature documentary was the last thing on my priority list. I certainly didn't think my story was worthy of a documentary but Katie was so enthused and committed that I couldn't turn her down. She started straight away on her storyboard and had crews come out to commence filming. At the time I wasn't sure if it would actually happen, but Katie had a vision and was determined to see it through.

****

With the way things were going, I needed a change of scenery so I decided to finish off the rest of the summer with Mich in Switzerland. I did that for a few reasons. One, I didn't like the environment in which I was training, in terms of team morale, or lack of team morale. It felt suffocating; this feeling was probably compounded by the many other issues I was dealing with personally. Two, I missed Mich and his team. Three, and maybe most importantly, I chose to leave so that I could be around more male jumpers, particularly the Belarusians, based in Switzerland, who were my idols. I needed to be in a positive environment.

The training facility in Mettmenstetten, Switzerland is nowhere near as glamorous as the facility in Park City but I knew I'd be happier there so I packed myself up with Kai and we headed over. Mum went back to Australia and Leena was called in for duty in Switzerland! I had planned on going to Switzerland anyway, but perhaps not so soon. I felt I had an obligation to train with my Aussie teammates, and to re-immerse myself in the team—that's why we went to Park City in the first place—but I realised I needed to do what was right for my own progression and that was to go to Switzerland right away. I would miss Dave, but I also knew he'd be fine without me and we'd be training together in the winter anyway.

****

It was great to be back in Switzerland. Like Park City, it felt like a home away from home and everything was familiar. The last time I had trained there was before Vancouver so it was nice to be back—this time with a little passenger in Kai. We stayed in my usual abode in the small town of Mettmenstetten, south of Zurich. It was a very basic set-up in the 'Kinderheim', which is an orphanage. We had our own small apartment on the top floor and all the children lived with their carers on the floors below. It was nothing like the beautiful spacious condos in Park City, but it was fine by my standards and it would allow me to get the job done. It was a great set-up for Kai with loads of children to play with and great playground facilities and animals, all backing on to a lush forest.

The training facility we trained on was also equipped with trampolines so Kai had plenty to do, especially for someone that had just started walking for the first time a couple of months earlier in Park City.

I loved being back with Mich and his team and I brought him up to speed on how my summer was going and on some of the issues I had been dealing with. Day by day we worked through them and I started to make some great progress and got back to doing high-quality triples. As I mentioned, I began working with Jeffrey again in 2012, when things started to get a bit more serious. When I first contacted him about getting back together he said, 'I've taught you everything I know, so what else can I possibly do for you?' And I said, 'I don't know. Make something up!' He told me he didn't want to create situations where his athletes were dependant on him, and that after having done his program, he wanted them to be able to continue working on his material independently. I wasn't having any of that and I said, 'I need you and I want you on my team,' and so I pushed him to develop the next phase of our mental training. We re-visited some of his earlier concepts, which was important because *I* was different now. I was a mum with different responsibilities and pressures. Together, we crafted a new program, which was more centred around hypnosis. We delved into an even deeper level than we had before by working at more of an unconscious level. It was really interesting. I pushed him for more and, by doing that, it helped him to develop his programs even further. While he was pushing me to go beyond *my* comfort zone, I was also pushing him to go beyond *his*.

Jeffrey knew my ambitions and desires, my fears, my strengths and weaknesses. He knew what I wanted because it was the first question he would ask every time we spoke. 'What do you want Lydia?' My answer was always, 'I want to be the best female aerial skier ever'. He was on board with my vision and never doubted my intentions. He knew what I was dealing with, and he knew the challenges of juggling a family because he was a dad himself. He gave me ways to get rid of any negative thoughts I had about my own ability to achieve my goals. Those sorts of things were really important for the times when I had to leave Kai and spend time away from my family. He helped me handle all the moving parts of our bigger family. We weren't the little A-team that we were before Vancouver: it was a much bigger unit this time around, and Jeffrey just got that.

No matter where I was in the world, we spoke weekly and we would even go through the hypnosis training over Skype because we couldn't do it in person. While it might not have been quite as effective as doing it face-to-face in the same room, it allowed us to keep working through the program no matter where I was in the world. I was so used to working with him that just hearing his voice was an instant trigger of calm for me. I needed his reassurance in order to go around again.

It helped to be around more male jumpers and particularly the Belarusians, so it was a good move to relocate to Switzerland and into a more relaxed environment. I made some great gains in a short space of time and finished off the summer feeling like myself again. I was ready to have a great winter. I wanted to dominate the season and show I was just as good as when I won Olympic gold a couple of years earlier.

The first couple of years after an Olympics are always interesting because many people tend to retire or have time off. I was off having Kai, and Li Nina was having a break and not competing either, Jacqui Cooper had retired, while Tao Tao was having a bit of a breather by not doing triples. So it gave the younger up-and-coming athletes some great opportunities to place on the podium with easy tricks; tricks that would normally struggle to make the top 10 let alone the podium. In a sense, it gave them a false confidence. So the standard had dropped significantly while I was off having Kai. But that's part of the continual evolution of the sport. Those same girls now, who are four years older, are doing the harder tricks. We all had to start from somewhere.

My plan for the season was to focus on a slow and steady build-up and get back to where I had left off. Back to jumping triples even if there were no other women doing them. I knew Tao Tao would start doing them again, especially leading into a major event—the 2013 World Championships in Norway.

****

My winter started off on the glaciers of Saas-Fee in Switzerland with

Mich and his team. It was great to be back in the Alps surrounded by snow-capped mountains. It was so exciting to start skiing and jumping again especially after sitting out a couple of seasons of competition. It's amazing how your muscles remember exactly what to do and everything went really smoothly. I had a productive 10 days there, first on the Single and then up to double flips. I had left Kai in Melbourne with Late so I could return to jumping with full focus until they joined me in Ruka, Finland, a couple of weeks later. There had been a few instances during the year where I had been separated from Kai—it was sometimes a couple of days or a couple of weeks. The longest amount of time I would allow myself to be away from him was a maximum of one month. Leaving him behind was gut-wrenching and difficult. I would be a complete mess saying goodbye to him, always wracked with feelings of extreme guilt, and I'd always walk away from him with a heavy heart. I questioned whether my quest for personal excellence and fulfillment was worth it? How would it affect Kai? I never doubted he was in good hands with either Late or his grandparents, but it was always painful to leave him. It was like an invisible umbilical cord was still attached and stretched over great distances. I never got used to it.

From Saas-Fee, Mich, the team and I went to Ruka determined to keep everything moving forward on snow. Kai, Late and Leena joined me there and it was great to have our family back together again. The first week was rock solid and I progressed quickly through more difficult doubles. I was jumping and landing great but at the same time, I started to feel really stiff in my lower back, which was a sensation I had never felt before. I'd get really stiff after jumping and I even felt it putting Kai in and out of his cot. Ashley had been treating it, but didn't think it was anything serious. Nine times out of 10, if I say something, isn't right, it most certainly isn't. I continued to jump and I was jumping really well but my back was getting stiffer and stiffer and the pain was becoming more intense. You would think I'd be an expert in 'red flag' signals by now.

Then, one day, the day Mich and I decided I was ready for triples, I landed a jump and I felt this twinge in my back, and I knew straight away that I had done something really bad. I skied away hunched over and frozen. I couldn't breathe; the pain was so intense, and my back was in spasm. Mich was concerned and so was I. I got back to my apartment and Late helped me get my ski gear off. I was trying to play down the pain so Leena and Kai wouldn't get worried. Ashley examined me but it wasn't clear what was wrong so she booked me in for an MRI scan the next day and we drove a couple of uncomfortable hours to Oulu. Needless to say, I was really upset. Here we go again. What now? Why did this happen? I didn't deserve this, not after all the work I had put in. I felt I had done everything right in my preparation since having Kai, but this was just another one of those familiar moments from my past. I felt I was drifting back into that old pattern of getting injured at crucial moments, something that had seemed to follow me all through my career. The scan showed I'd prolapsed two of the discs in my lower back and I was not going to be able to jump for at least a couple of weeks. I spent the first couple of days just lying on my tummy and then I started light rehab in the pool and gym.

I was so frustrated. It really threw a spanner in my works, and it threatened to derail my entire season because the pre-season training sets you up for the whole winter. It's that important.

That setback meant I couldn't do triples as early as I had intended to. Instead, I had to rehab my back on the eve of the season, which is never fun, all the while not knowing exactly what had caused it. I took about two weeks off, then went back and tried to start jumping again. I was limited to only a few jumps with the intention of building up numbers slowly until we got my back under control. We had a small break over Christmas before the season kicked off with the first World Cup in China, and, my return to the professional circuit. I took a conservative approach by not doing triples and very few numbers. I managed to come second to Tao Tao, which was a fair effort, all things considered.

Next stop was Val Saint-Côme in Canada. On my final training jump the day before the World Cup event, my back went again. Not as bad as the first time in Ruka but bad enough to take my breath away and double me over. I hadn't crashed. I was being careful. Why was this happening? Ashley said, 'Look, we're going to have to pull you from this competition', and I said, 'Can we just see how I pull up in the morning? If I can't get through the warm-up then we'll pull the pin.' Ashley had set up a specific set of warm-up drills and tests when we were in Ruka. If I could do these tests without pain then I was good to go.

I woke up and my back still felt a bit tight and I honestly didn't think I'd be jumping that day. But I decided to go out and do the warm-up to see how it felt. I got through it, and surprisingly my back felt okay. By that stage, everyone else had started jumping, and so we made the call to go out and do one warm-up jump to get my speed and, if that was okay, I'd go straight into the competition qualifier. Again, I got through it and everything was fine; stiffness but no pain in my back. All I had to do now was one qualifier jump. I nailed it and was now through to the finals. The men then came out and jumped their qualifying jumps, which meant the women went inside for a break. Half of me was relieved that I could rest my back, but the other half of me was annoyed because I'd have to warm up all over again. For the competition, it was the same deal. I could do one warm-up jump and if everything was okay, I'd go straight into competition. And that's what I did.

I went out and did my warm-up jump, which was basically just so that I knew my speed, and then the next jump was competition. I stuck my landing and was straight into the Super Final, where I thankfully landed, which meant that I somehow ended up on the podium again behind Tao Tao—she was back doing triples and she was nailing them. I had done a total of five jumps for the whole day, three of them being competition jumps. This was not even half of what the other competitors had done and, even though I was happy with another podium finish, I certainly didn't want to have to go through this process at every event for the season, particularly when all I really wanted to do was begin doing regular triples. But that was how things were for the rest of that World Cup season. Every week, at some point, I would tweak my back again, and we would have to change my training around to accommodate that.

We decided to start doing triples at the Lake Placid World Cups – a double event.. It was great to be doing them again, I hadn't performed them since Vancouver, but by the time we reached Lake Placid my confidence was diminishing. Understandably, I crashed out on the first day and didn't make finals as I was still getting used to being back on the triple jump. But the next day I started to do a bit better and was able to finish on the podium again, this time behind Yang Yu from China. It was such a frustrating period—I was only allowed to do a handful of jumps. I didn't feel as though I was progressing and was certainly far from dominating—it was more like surviving. At the same time my back was getting worse, which was wearing away at my confidence. I found it scary to jump, because I had no idea which jump would be the one that would tip my back over the edge and put me out of action again.

After the Lake Placid World Cups, we stayed on to do a mini-training camp before the next event. I was hoping to be able to get a few more triples under my belt, but it was extremely cold the entire time we were there. I managed to do a few triples before my back went again. This time it was really bad. My pelvis had also shifted out of position and it was obvious my body wasn't anywhere near as stable as we thought it was going into the season. In the gym you can't really replicate the forces of jumping and landing. Sure, you can jump off boxes, but you're not going to get the same feeling and the same impact that you get from actually jumping and landing on snow. I thought I was strong but what we learned later was that I was unstable in my pelvis, most likely from childbirth, and that, in turn, had overloaded my spine causing my discs to prolapse.

With the amount of constant pain and impact, the muscles supporting my spine basically shut down and became weaker and weaker as the season progressed. I should have just called it quits for the season, as it was clear my back wasn't going to improve and there was really no point trying to force my way through it. Instead, I wanted to push on and try and compete at the World Championships.

It was probably a good thing that Kai and Late didn't come to China or most of North America with me because I was having a pretty tough time of it, mentally. I was able to do some triples in Deer Valley, but not enough to find my form let alone consistency and confidence. I became quite tentative on my landings in anticipation of pain, which is never a good thing. Committing to triples is hard enough when you're healthy but doing them with a tentative or negative mindset is a recipe for disaster.

I went to Sochi for the next World Cup as I really felt it was important to jump at the site of the 2014 Olympics. The night before the event,

I was doing triples when, on the very last jump, I threw my back out again. Again, the pain took my breath away. It felt as though I had been stabbed in the back and this time I struggled to walk, sit or do anything. I was a mess. That night Ashley pulled me from the World Cup as it wasn't worth the risk and more importantly she was concerned I would do further damage. I've had some low points in my career, but I remember that season as being the most difficult. It had everything: fear, frustration, pain, and moments of hope, which turned to moments of despair.

Mich wanted me to fly home and miss the World Championships in Norway. He told me, 'You can't go on like this because I don't want you to get really hurt.' We were both discouraged because it was not at all how we thought the season would play out. I had had such a good summer, so this was something that neither of us could see happening: it really came out of nowhere. It didn't seem fair.

After the Sochi test event our team went back to Ruka for a mini training camp before the World Championships. Mich and I had reached a compromise that if I were to compete at the Worlds, then triples were out of the question. We decided it wasn't worth the risk.

For most of the camp, my back felt okay. I did very few numbers and just stuck to doubles. I tweaked it a couple of times, but nothing really bad. Our team flew to Norway for the Worlds. By that stage, I just really wanted to finish on a positive and go home. I'm fairly certain I wasn't the best teammate to be around. I was fragile and not in a great place mentally. I was worn down and on numerous occasions I wondered if any of it was worth it. Was it worth missing my family and especially Kai? Was it worth the pain I was going through?

The actual event, like all of my World Championship campaigns was a flop. I took a massive stack in training just before the competition and I landed on my stomach facing the jumps because I didn't know where I was. I had blood coming from my nose and a torn lip: I had done a real job on myself! I managed to make it through to the finals but was knocked out of the tournament one round short of the Super Final. I ended up fifth at the Worlds, which was not what I had wanted when I first sat down and planned out my season with Cord back in the summer. Tao Tao, who had dominated all season, won by a mile.

The gap between her and the rest of us was embarrassing, but, on a positive note, my teammate Danielle Scott took the bronze—her first career podium. My suit and competition bib was covered in blood and torn from the crash and my pride was shattered. I threw it in a pile outside and set it on fire; it wasn't coming back to Australia with me. I cried for a few hours in my apartment that night. What worried me and scared me most was that I thought my career was over. I definitely knew I wouldn't survive another season like that and I didn't want to just survive, I wanted to dominate. At that point I couldn't see the wood from the trees. I really thought it was all over.

Despite all the drama and the disappointment, I still finished the World Cup season as number three in the world, which didn't say much for the rest of the field. Ashley still didn't really know exactly what the issue was with my back, so she booked me in to see a guru in the field, physiotherapist Trish Wisbey-Roth in Sydney. We flew to see her once I got home to Melbourne, desperate for answers and hoping there was a way we could fix it. You could tell Trish knew her stuff straight away and assured me everything was going to be okay and that she and her team would figure out what was going on. Needless to say I was fragile and I broke down which seemed to happen fairly often during that period. As Trish examined me she looked at me and said, 'How in the hell did you jump? In fact, how the hell could you do anything with this type of injury?' Again, I was very emotional and she fully understood what I had been dealing with. I had come to thinking that this injury was one I would never fully recover from but Trish assured me they would get to the bottom of it. I liked her straight away.

Trish and her team examined me for a couple of hours. On top of physical tests, they also performed an ultrasound where they examined the stabilising muscles in my pelvis and back. From the three months of pain and trauma I had endured, those muscles were so thin and whittled away that they couldn't even see them on the ultrasound! I tried to activate certain muscles when they asked me to, but there was no response. It was like the circuit had been shut down. They told me that in all their history of treating people with bad backs, they had never seen a patient this bad before.

It wasn't great news but from Trish's thorough examination she was able to identify what the issue was. My pelvis was the culprit. It was unstable and not strong enough to take the load of jumping, which then overloaded my spine. Trish gave me hope by telling me she had no doubts at all that I would get better and make a full recovery. She said it would take a lot of work, but I would get better as a result, and that was all I needed to hear. I was so relieved. She put me on a program where I was to do very subtle and specific exercises to get my deep stabilising muscles firing again. No lifting weights, no impact activities and from there we would gradually begin to build up my stability and my strength. I was prescribed a range of exercises that Harry monitored. He was so committed to seeing me recover, and I just wanted to start feeling like me again. Day by day I made small improvements and, with time, my back started feeling like it was on the mend. Perhaps I *wasn't* done with yet.

****

Jeffrey Hodges also suggested that I go and see his yoga guru, Duncan Ewing, at Yoga Arts Academy in Melbourne. I had enjoyed Yoga in the past but it was never part of my daily routine. I called Duncan and explained my situation and I arranged to start going to his private tuition classes. I had nothing to lose and trusted Jeffrey's judgment, so committed to going to his tuition for five days a week from 6.00am to 8.00am, until I was better and ready to start water ramping again. I'm no morning person, so it was hard getting up at 5:30am but at least we lived close to the city centre and there was no traffic at that time of day. I arrived at 6.00am and entered this dimly lit room. There were already people on their mats either meditating or doing weird moves and breathing exercises I hadn't seen before. It was fairly intimidating and I felt completely out of place. In this type of tuition everyone goes through their own specific yoga sequence for two hours while Duncan would circle the room correcting and overseeing each person as they went through their practice. The only problem was that when I showed up, I didn't know what to do. This was hardcore. And Duncan was hardcore and a true master of his craft. This was no hip-hop yoga, bikram or another spin-off. This was the real deal. I liked Duncan straight away.

Eventually Duncan came over to me and gave me some positions and sequences to start on, manoeuvring my body and showing me how to breathe properly. By day two I had already noticed an improvement—it was like magic. So I found a new routine, which began with a two-hour yoga session in the morning, followed by another hour or so in the gym with Harry, and then I'd be back home just after Kai had woken up. My training was done by 10 o'clock and I did that for four months until it was time to start the water ramp season again. I kept progressing through Trish's exercises and flew up to Sydney to see her a number of times. Each time she was not surprised by my progress—she knew her program worked and it was obvious to her that I had been doing her exercises relentlessly. Harry and I also made massive improvements in the gym. I was getting stronger, and my back didn't seem to be an issue anymore. Sure, it would need constant maintenance and the true test would be when I would start to jump again, but I felt great. I had made some changes with my diet too, which was influenced by Duncan. I had green smoothies everyday, I cut down on dairy and meat and totally gave away alcohol. I was committed to being 100 per cent healthy and did everything I could to give myself the best chance to heal. I also felt a shift in my focus and mood. I was calm and I was back in control and I attribute that to my yoga practice. It was an amazing transformation. In four months I went from being a complete beginner to being able to practice two hours of yoga by myself, and my back was symptom-free. I was hooked and my body craved it, so I continued to practice every day right through to Sochi.

There is no doubt that Duncan and Trish were the game-changers for me and the new members of my A-Team. I had also been seeing a new physio in Diane Alvis, who was incredibly switched on so I ended up taking her to Switzerland with me for the water ramp season. I didn't go to Park City at all that summer; I just went straight on to Switzerland with Mich and spent the whole summer there.

※※※※※※

When I met back up with Mich we had a plan to build up really slowly to make sure my back was okay. Neither of us wanted to experience the disappointment and frustration we had the season before. We would start with singles, then doubles and build up to triples from there, but he was still quite concerned about my back and whether it would stand up. So, to begin with, we took it very cautiously, with very small numbers, and it coped fine. We just kept moving along like that through the summer and soon enough I was up to doing double sessions in the morning and afternoon. I progressed through double somersaults and once we knew my back was okay and I was ready, we began triples. Even though we had a long way to go, Mich and I were fixated on doing the quad triple-twisting somersault: The Full-Double Full-Full—a trick only the men had mastered, and a trick I had always dreamed of doing on snow. Harry flew over too, making sure I was doing the right load in the gym. And I had Diane with me to look after and treat my body. Ashley was with the rest of the Aussie team in Park City but we kept communicating on my progress.

As I've said before, when we're learning new tricks we try them on water before attempting them on snow; particularly for a big trick like a quad triple-twisting somersault—you need to do it repeatedly so it's clear in your head. That way when you do it on snow, you have enough feeling to react in all kinds of situations.

I had planned to go back to Australia mid-August to train some jumps on snow—just as I had before Vancouver. Unfortunately the snowfall hadn't been great and my camp was looking pretty grim so, in a desperate attempt to pull it off, I called up my dad and asked him if he'd be able to build me an artificial jump so that we wouldn't need to use as much snow. He is semi-retired and didn't mind the challenge of building something he had never built before…and in such a short deadline—two weeks! I got the dimensions of the jump off Mich and sent them to my dad; the only problem was that the plans were in German! So Dad called up his mate Martin, a retired engineer, who also happened to be German to come and help. In two weeks, the two of them had delivered a beautiful artificial jump for me to transport and use at Mt Buller. I arrived home and still the snow conditions hadn't improved. Unfortunately, we had to cancel the camp and so Dad's jump never made it to the snow and is still sitting in his paddock in Diggers Rest. I felt so bad, but I didn't have time to waste and headed back to Switzerland to finish off the summer.

Although my back was under control, I was still having issues with my take-off and it lacked consistency. Time was running out. It was now or never, we needed to start building up to the quad.

I started hammering them out towards the end of the summer and by the end I had done about 20. Normally I would like to do at least 40 to 50 attempts at a trick to get it really ingrained in my head, especially a big trick like that, but there just wasn't enough time. I just tried to focus on making each one count. They were consistent, they were safe and that was enough for me to at least feel comfortable to try it on snow. Was it polished? Probably not, but we had no time to get picky!

It took a lot of mental energy, every single time I performed the quad. And that is the case whenever you are trying a new trick: it takes a lot to concentrate, to analyse and to set yourself up with the right cues. Then, as you repeat the trick over and over the movements become more automatic and you need to think less and less about them because they begin to happen like autopilot.

It was late October and so it was starting to get pretty cold in Switzerland jumping into water, so we had to really knuckle down. I couldn't help but wonder how different my lead-up and preparation would have been if we hadn't have lost the water ramp. I would have had so much more time to perform the amount of jumps I needed to perfect it, and I wouldn't have had to cram it all into such a short time frame. Plus, if we had the ramp up and running I may well have chosen to come home early from the previous horror season and spend time on the water ramp. They are all hypotheticals, but those little things along the way can make all the difference for an elite athlete, no matter their sport. Mich was happy and I was confident it was good enough. Surprisingly, after all these years obsessing over it, I realised that the quad wasn't *actually* that hard.

I flew home for a short break to see my family and give my mind and body a mini rest before the winter season. I caught up with Harry and Duncan and each was happy with how my body was holding up.

PATH TO SOCHI

****

We headed over to Ruka as a family for pre-season training. That would be our base until the Sochi Olympics in February. Katie Bender also made her way to Ruka along with co-director and partner Leo Baker to commence filming their documentary, which they had now titled *The Will To Fly*. I needed to get a lot done in the pre-season to set myself up for the winter—there was a lot on my plate and I needed to keep distractions to a minimum. Katie and Leo did a great job and gave me the space I needed and, without being intrusive, they captured what they needed to.

I jumped really well on the doubles but when it came to triples, I struggled with landings and it took a while to find my feet. I didn't get up to the quad in that camp as we felt it was best to get the basic triples consistent and to use the other opportunities during the season to go for the quad.

Our first World Cup events were in China. The first in a place called Beida Lake and the second was going to be a stadium event in Beijing's Bird's Nest stadium, the venue that had hosted the 2008 Beijing Summer Olympics. It had taken me some time to get used to the site at Beida Lake—it was very different to Ruka and I was really struggling to make my landings. The night before the contest Mich and I decided we would play it safe and qualify with doubles, then I'd do triples once we were in the finals. Unfortunately, that plan backfired and on my qualification jump I went over the handle bars and broke my ski on a double! I felt like a real idiot, just completely hopeless to crash out of the finals that way.

I remember going back to my hotel room fuming. Soon after came a knock from Katie and Leo wanting a post-comp interview. It wasn't the time and I didn't want to talk to anyone. I was just so angry at myself for playing it safe and wasting a good opportunity to do more triples. I let them get their interview after I calmed down a bit.

Diary entry, 15 December 2013: 'Landing percentage this week was shocking. You should be ashamed of yourself. No wonder you crashed something as basic as a Full-Full. Is something wrong with you? Is this not important to you? How can you mess up so bad? I need answers. I want to know if this really matters to you?'

I needed to get my head right so I busted out my Anthony Robbins' tracks that I had worked on previously as part of Jeffrey's course. I did a mini-workshop on my own for the next few days to figure out what was happening in my head. I needed to remind myself of all the positive reasons for why I was back competing in the first place. When you're in a slump it's easy to only see negatives so I worked really hard to turn things around and get myself back on track for the Beijing event.

By the time we got to Beijing, I was fired up and ready to redeem myself. The event was going to be amazing. I had competed on similar scaffold set-ups like that before, but this was the first time in China and it was going to be an incredible experience. Our hotel was by far the best we'd ever stayed in in China, which was funny, because all the rookie athletes that hadn't been to World Cups in China before had been told all these horror stories about how bad the food and accommodation was. This time it was the opposite. The food was amazing, the rooms were super clean and they were all like, 'what are you guys talking about? This is awesome!' And it was, particularly compared to some of my earlier trips to China.

I had turned myself around that week and was on a mission. My triples were looking good and my landings were back on track, which boosted my confidence. It was an important week. The Chinese organising committee decided they would run with the Olympic format—a replica of what we would have in Sochi in less than two months' time. I really wanted to see whether I could make it all the way to the Super Final. First though, I had to make it through the qualifications, then three stages of elimination rounds. All up the event would go for at least five hours. Mich and I were on the same page. Our plan was to qualify with triples and if I made it through to the Super Final, I would try and do a Full-Full-Full, a triple twisting triple, which is the trick you do in preparation for the quad. I hadn't done any by that stage so it was important to use the opportunity that presented itself. We kept with that game plan for the remainder of the season—win or lose, it was important to just keep progressing my triples.

I was completely focused and I was hungry for redemption. I made it through every round right to the Super Final. The format was exhausting and to keep up the intensity and concentration I really had to dig deep and fire myself up. Pre-Vancouver I was so calm and I wouldn't say much out loud before a jump. But coming into Sochi, I got very vocal with my cues and self-talk to help psyche myself up for almost every jump.

I jumped great that night and made it through to the Super Final, which would decide who was going to take home the medals. Mich and I saw our opportunity to do the Full-Full-Full, which I had only ever done once on snow before, way back before the Vancouver Olympics. It was basically a new trick since it had been that long since I'd tried it and a part of me didn't want to go for it but I knew the time was right. It was a beautiful jump in the air and I all but landed it, just coming unstuck, and I ended up skiing down the landing hill backwards. It was so close and I would have won by miles if I had skied it out cleanly. I still managed to come away with a second placing so I was happy with that. In fact, I felt buzzed that I had made it through that format, plus my jumps were awesome. The progression plan was on track, and that was a big step in the right direction.

So, in seven days I had turned my campaign around 180 degrees... with a little help from Anthony Robbins!

> *Diary entry, 21 December 2013: 'Wow—a massive day and I am so proud of myself. I finished second but it felt like a win today. I jumped great when I needed to and [it] feels good to be skiing all triples again. I am most happy with my FFF. It was tough to compete the Olympic format but I made it to the end. I did great.'*

****

At Deer Valley, Utah, some three weeks later, after a Christmas break, I ended up coming in too short and stomach-dropping on a jump. I totally got my speed wrong and I crashed, which put me out of the event. I was really hoping to get some good training in while we were at Deer Valley, but we got snowed out all week. That meant that not only was I not going to get to do the quad there, I wasn't even going to have enough time to get any triples off other than in competition. We had planned to do the quad there for the first time but we could not control the weather. It was another opportunity lost.

We moved on to Val Saint-Côme and half the team sat the event out because they wanted to rest up before the Lake Placid World Cup, which would take place just a couple of days later. I had intended to miss the Canadian event, too, but I was upset at my result in Deer Valley, so I packed up with Mich and half our team and we made our way to Val Saint-Côme; but our ski bags didn't! We only had three days before the event and for the first two days, thanks to lost luggage, we had no gear to train with and were forced to sit around and wait for our bags to turn up while it rained heavily. We weren't the only team inconvenienced, as the Chinese too, had lost their bags. We were frantically ringing the airline and trying to track down our gear, and finally, the day before our competition, our bags turned up, giving us only one day to train before we needed to compete. There was no more time to lose so I hustled and got to triples that day and jumped really well.

On competition day we decided that if we made it to the Super Final we'd do another Full-Full-Full. We made it through as planned. I did the Full-Full-Full and landed it this time. I was so close to landing it in China, so I was really determined to ski this one out cleanly. I nailed it and I won the event: my first World Cup victory since coming back after having Kai. I'd had my fair share of silver and had been so close on many occasions so it was nice to be back on the top of the podium— finally! Harry had also flown over for a couple of weeks so it was great he was there to see me have a win. I didn't go into that World Cup season aiming to win every event; I went to progress, while peaking at the Olympics, so to have a win was great for my confidence and really rewarding. Plus, it was exactly a month out from my event in Sochi, so it felt like everything was coming together at the right time.

Diary entry, 14 January 2014: 'What an amazing win today. I jumped superbly and am so proud of myself. I went the distance, stayed hungry and focussed and nailed my FFF!!

Good work. Well done. Rest. BUT stay hungry. Conserve your energy and keep imagining great things.'

I entered the final event of the World Cup season at Lake Placid three days later really confident, but I didn't even make it through to the finals and wasted yet another opportunity for more triples. I finished the season in fourth place, with the other four places in the top-five taken up by the Chinese girls. I wasn't too concerned about the Chinese winning four of the five World Cup events, because a lot of the time they were doing doubles. Tao Tao wasn't having the best season, and I felt that she was going to be my real threat leading into Sochi. So, too, were Ashley Caldwell and Alla Tsuper who, like Tao Tao, were yet to find their consistency on the Triple. I felt like a yo-yo. Up and down results. Missed opportunities. Bad weather days. It certainly wasn't smooth sailing.

Cord: 'I would say that the season was up and down, given the results. There was one good, one bad, one good, one bad. The nature of what we were trying to do and build towards was trying to put her in a good spot at the Olympics. There was almost no other goal as far as the World Cup goes, or anything like that, besides being ready for the Olympics. So you'd have a good week and then you'd have to push a little bit. Behind the scenes, Mich and I would talk: "What do you think about this week?" We'd know we'd have to push, with the result at the end of the week not being exactly what we wanted, but we were trying to taper for the year to get things right. She definitely had some tough days there when she was disappointed. Seeing her in Lake Placid after she crashed, it was pretty tough to go up to an athlete after they have crashed and pat them on the back. As a coach you do truly believe it's okay and we'll come back but, Lydia being who she is and being ultra-competitive, she's not going to accept that answer. She's not going to accept that failure today, and you just have to kind of ride out that storm with her and let her battle her inner demons. Because, that's what makes her good: the fact that that's not acceptable on that day: that that's not okay. She'll rip herself apart, but you just weather the storm and keep supporting her through that. Let her go through it. Then, the next day, two days later, when we get ready for the next week she re-focuses and comes back.'

It was a short World Cup season in the lead up to Sochi. We had scheduled one more mini training camp in Ruka before we would head to Russia and time was closing in on us. I really needed to have a productive camp and do everything I could if I was going to do the one jump I had come back to do.

CHAPTER 16

LEAVING MY MARK

Time feels very precious as the days count down to an Olympics. Every day is important. Every opportunity is important. I could feel time slipping away and I still had much to do. My triples lacked consistency and I was still nervous doing them. The heaviness of my goal was weighing down on me and I was desperate for a productive camp before we made our way to Sochi. At that point, I had a choice to make, I had two flights on hold: a flight getting me to Sochi before the opening ceremony and a flight getting me to Sochi after the opening ceremony. Stay in Ruka, train and miss the opening ceremony or go to Sochi and have a few days off. I had so much to do. I had not even performed the quad yet, which seemed insane so close to the Games. The quad *was* my reason for competing at these Games. The quad kept me hungry and motivated, it kept me going during the days, weeks, months of pain and frustration!

There had been talk and speculation in the media about who would be given the honour of carrying the Australian flag in the opening ceremony at Sochi, and my name was being thrown forward as a likely candidate. To be honest, my gut told me to stay in Ruka, miss the hype and continue training, just as I had done in Vancouver. Yes, it's a great honour to be flag bearer, but by that stage of my preparation I was so desperate to get more jumps under my belt. What added to my desperation was the fact that we'd had a real cold snap of weather in Ruka of temperatures below minus 20C. It was hard to jump let alone do triples and, as a result, my back was starting to play up. The forecast predicted warmer weather and I had to make a decision. Stay and take advantage of the warmer weather and try and do the quad before heading to Sochi. Or go to Sochi and let my body have a rest.

We really wanted to know if I was flag bearer or not—a decision our *Chef De Mission* Ian Chesterman would announce a couple of days before the Opening Ceremony. Obviously the decision had already been made; however, we weren't able to get any information. Geoff Lipshut, our CEO, ended up saying 'she should go,' and so I assumed that I was going to be the flag bearer. I figured that Sochi could very well be my last Olympics and I would regret it if I didn't take up the honour. We cancelled my later flight and went on the earlier one. It meant that I had to push myself hard and try and get as many jumps as I could in Ruka, but the weather was too cold and I wasn't very productive. I left Ruka and made my way to Sochi to give my body a chance to recover and get some valuable rest time. But the heaviness of not having done the quad still weighed down on me and I questioned weather it was going to happen at all.

The morning I woke up in Sochi, Ian called me up to his office in the Olympic Village. 'I just wanted to let you know that I've chosen Chumpy (Alex Pullin) to be the flag bearer'. My heart sank and I sat there in silence waiting for him to continue. Inside I was angry. I wasn't angry that I wasn't flag bearer. I was angry because I had made the wrong decision and should have stayed in Ruka. He continued: 'I've chosen Alex to be the flag bearer because he's been the most successful winter athlete over the last four years.'[3] I couldn't speak so I internalised my thoughts: 'Umm … yes, well, I had a couple of years off to have a baby.' Still I didn't say anything. I was gutted. We had wanted to know this sooner rather than later, given it would, quite significantly, affect my preparation.

---

3 Snowboarder, Alex 'Chumpy' Pullin, won gold at the 2011 Snowboarding World Championships in Molina, Spain, and he won Gold again at the 2013 World's in Quebec, Canada. He also won Gold at the 2011 New Zealand Winter Games.

It seemed to me that more importance was placed on the announcement, than on my needs as an elite athlete heading into Olympic competition. While I respect the processes involved, I felt like my preparation had been compromised. Had I known the outcome I would have stayed in Ruka as planned.

Ian continued his reasoning. 'I've chosen Chumpy because he represents the generation and spirit of our team.' Still, I remained silent and thought, 'In other words you're saying I'm too old to lead this team? Is it because I'm a mum?' I felt I'd been stitched up. I certainly held no grudges against Chumpy – he's a great guy and an amazing athlete – but in that moment I felt ripped off. After everything I had ever done, everything I had come back from and achieved, with the Olympics always in the forefront of my mind, I felt like I represented the spirit of the Olympic team more than anyone in that squad.

It got worse. The next thing he said was, 'So because you carried the flag in the closing ceremony at Vancouver, we want you to pass it on to Alex at the flag bearer's announcement.' It was clear then that this had been planned all along. I was just a pawn in a 'grand' announcement. Then he said: 'And, I want you to walk in line with me behind Alex, in the opening ceremony.' It took immense control at that point to not lose it. When I'm in the final stages of an Olympic campaign, I work hard at deflecting information that isn't useful to me so that I can remain focused on my jumping. By this stage, I was ready to get out of the room.

> *Diary entry, 6 February 2014: 'Today I found out I will not be flag bearer at the opening ceremony. It was a shock to me and others, but I know Chumpy is a worthy flag bearer. However, I am angry. I am angry that I "don't represent this generation". I was made to feel small today. If I had known, I would have stayed in Ruka and changed my plan to jump when the weather was right. But I can't change that now. I will show them that they were wrong. I am going to fight every ounce for this gold medal and they will then see what I am capable of. They will see my spirit. I WANT THIS SO MUCH and today's events have made me*

> *even more hungry. Stay calm and in the present. The only competition is me. No one else exists. Your confidence will not be shaken. I LOVE YOU. I am grateful for all that I have in my life. LET'S DO THIS BIG, LYD.'*

I ended up doing what I was told and walked alongside Ian during the opening ceremony out of respect for Chumpy and the team. I remained silent. I don't think anybody in power realised how much a decision of that nature could have affected me and my ability to perform at my best. But being angry or getting worked up was not an option at that point. I would have only been wasting the precious energy reserved for one purpose: to make it to the Super Final and to do the quad. I had to keep focused and I had to conserve my energy—whether it was emotional, mental or physical, I needed it all. I did my best to stay positive but it was hard not to think about it, especially given most of my team was still in Ruka, training, which is where I should have been. Not only did I need that extra training time, my back had flared up and I was away from Ashley, which stressed me out even further.

> *Late: 'I was pretty certain that she would have been the flag bearer in Sochi. All credit to Chumpy, he's a champion and all that, but still, we're talking about the Olympics. Chumpy's got no Olympic medals. Lydia is the defending Olympic champion for her fourth Games. So I think they should have given it to Lyd.'*

An extra day of rest, or an extra jump in training all add up and mean everything in the final stages. When you're talking inches in the end, every choice makes all the difference between performing at our optimum level or not. Messing around with an athlete's head so close to competition, can be the difference between gaining that edge over an opponent or losing it. Elite athletes are like Formula One cars. Fine-tuning can make or break them.

I could tell Mich and Barbara were concerned and we spoke openly about it. They knew the effort I had put in and the sacrifices I had made.

I didn't leave my son behind countless times throughout the campaign to be treated like a pawn at the most important time. But I had a choice and there were two roads here: the road that I can go down where I dig myself into a hole and have a really good excuse for why I stuffed up at Sochi; or, I could get on with it and prove them wrong. I chose to prove them wrong.

****

The competition day was scheduled for 14 February—Valentine's Day—and usually Late gets me a Victoria's Secret voucher, but I don't for the life of me remember what he got me that day. It was the day I had been working towards, ever since I took up the invitation to learn the sport back in Year 12 at High School.

After the flag-raising debacle I put up my shield: everything from that point on was about focusing and training, and we were fortunate to get a lot of training days in Sochi. The weather was warm—a little too warm—but it meant that I could actually do some jumps and get a lot of triples done, and that's what we did. We were three days out from competition when I started to find a groove. My landings were still inconsistent but my take-offs and airs were starting to look really good. I had already done nine triples that day and most of them were Full-Full-Fulls—a triple-twisting-triple, the one that precedes the quad. It was the most I'd done all season in just one session. The weather was stable, my jumps were good and I felt energetic and focused so we took advantage of the opportunity to get a lot of jumps in.

After my ninth jump, I looked up at Mich from where the radio was at the bottom of the landing hill, and he was standing up on the knoll. What we've always done was this thing with our fingers whenever we were trying to tell each other that we were ready to move on to the next thing. We hold up a finger and spin it like a spinning top, to signify that we are good to move on to the next jump. We didn't say anything over the radio. I just looked up at him and I did the spin thing, and he just nodded, and we both knew what that meant. It was time.

> Mich: 'I could see that she was ready. On that day, in the morning when we went and she did all the Full-Full-Fulls, I knew we had to go for it there. I knew she should go. I didn't say anything to anyone, and when she went all the cameras were on her, already waiting. I thought "how is that possible?"'

We were finally going to do it. Then he told me over the radio, 'Yah, just focus on your take-off.' That was about it. It was getting late in the day, and it was going to be pretty much the last jump anybody did for the day. I got to the top and I started doing my arm movements in preparation for the quad. Visualising and going through the motions. Anyone in aerials can tell what trick you're doing by the way you do your arm preparations. It wasn't long before people started to crowd around the base of the jump, video cameras pointed at me. They knew. I was nervous enough as it was and now the whole competition field was standing there gawking at me. I felt sick I was so nervous. But it was now or never, we had to do it. So I went for it. I hit a good take-off and as soon as I was in the air, I knew I was okay and I did the trick easily and skied away from it.

> Mich: 'It was difficult to get there, there were always challenges. But she stayed patient and took the right moment. We only got one day when we could go, and we went there and then; and she was ready. And I think that was great, that was super. Everything we did, we did because we wanted to do this jump.'

Everyone was cheering, including my competitors: they were all really happy for me. It was high-fives all around, because I had just become the first woman ever to ever do it, the Full-Double Full-Full. I could hear the tune from the *Rocky* movie playing in my ear: 'Da-da-da, da-da-da, da-da-da, da-da-da; Da-da-da, da-da-da, da-da-da, da-da-da....' It was a victorious moment and one that will stay vivid in my memory quite for some time.

> *Diary entry, 11 February 2014: 'What a monumental day! I have finally done FDFF and it felt great. I did it with ease. So cool to be the first female to do it. So relieved.'*

That incredible weight I felt on my shoulders had been lifted, it was almost instantaneous. It wasn't as hard as everyone made it out to be. It was a massive rush, because I was pretty nervous beforehand. I was hoping first of all that I'd make it the whole way around and not do anything stupid. I knew the risks involved and there's always that feeling of unknown when you attempt something for the first time. I had spent the entire season fretting and wondering when I would get a chance to do the trick. I had begun to worry that the chance would slip by so it was nice to finally have it out of the way. I felt relieved and I could breathe freely again. We called it a day after that and Mich, Cord and I were buzzing. It was the confidence boost I needed and it had been the most productive day all season. Word spread quickly that night that I had done it, sending subliminal messages to my competitors. If anything, they knew I wouldn't play it safe. I was going all in with nothing to lose.

> *Late: 'One of the reasons she agreed to go on for another four years was the trick that no woman had done in the history of the sport: the Full-Double Full-Full, which means four twists and a triple back-flip. It's a jump that only the guys do and compete with, and that was something that was basically a dream of Lydia's: to jump like a guy. That was one of the tricks she had her mind set on for a long time, and now knowing that she's actually done it is obviously great; it's a massive relief for her and the pressure is off. It's not about the gold, it's not about winning, it's to actually put a mark on the sport and to do something no one's done before. She's basically done what she set out to do in the sport, and it's great.'*

The next day my mum sent me a text message saying, 'Are you okay? What's happened?' Apparently the media back home had been showing footage of me crashing out on some of my training jumps. Sure, my landings hadn't been solid all season, but I was really working on getting my take-off consistent more so than my landings. For me, if I get my take-off and air consistent, the landings generally take care of themselves. But the Australian media got a hold of me crashing my jumps and blew it out of proportion. And guess what? They missed the important detail that I'd just done the quad!

****

Coming into an Olympics as the defending Olympic champion always means more media attention in the immediate lead up. They wanted interviews. I was reluctant at first because I wanted to stay in my bubble, but I eventually agreed to do one before the event. It was a live cross to Australia, and to my old teammate, Alisa Camplin. She commented on how I was having a difficult time with my landings and that the snow conditions were tough due to the warm weather. I was quick to brush that aside and said: 'You know what? I actually made history yesterday! I became the first woman ever to do a quad-twisting triple somersault.' That gave them something else to comment on. They had no idea sitting in a recording studio in Melbourne that I had been steadily building and I had just gained a bucket load of confidence right before the big day.

I was fired up but I knew I still had so much work to do. It was a step in the right direction though, and it gave me that extra lift that I needed to keep going. It was confirmation that things were on track. It wasn't perfect, and sure I could have used more time. But I had that feeling that everything was finally coming together. Mich and I debriefed, looked over video, and discussed my game plan.

We had a day off after doing the quad for the first time so I could recover from the massive training session. We still had one more training day before the competition and we went out and I did one more quad. I skied out of it but it wasn't a clean landing.

I had really been having a hard time on my landings. I was feeling huge amounts of pressure because I could see Alla Tsuper, from Belarus, landing a bunch of jumps, and I could see America's Ashley Caldwell doing the same, not to mention a few Chinese competitors who were looking really strong. They were definitely not struggling as much as I was, so I was really starting to question myself. The landing hill was steeper than I was used to, and it was taking me longer to adjust to it. I was *close*, but close is not good enough. I spent a lot of my down time visualising landings. I just tried to make up some ground through mental rehearsal. I knew I had them in me. I just had to figure out how to make it all come together. Late was at the final training session, which would be the last time I would see him before the competition. He gave me the space I needed yet was there to support me every step of the way. He had his own battle, travelling six hours a day on Russian public transport!

The evening before the competition, I had my final session with Jeffrey Hodges. We worked on landings and prepared for the big day ahead. As always, it was just good to hear his voice and that in itself was comforting for me. I sat down with Mich and we went over our plan. He assured me everything was on track. I was going to make it all the way to the Super Final and I was going to do the quad.

Before I went to sleep, I sat on my bed, as I had four years earlier in Vancouver. I reflected on my preparation and all the things that had gone right and wrong. It certainly was not like pre-Vancouver where everything had gone perfectly. I thought about the water ramp and how my situation could have been different had we had that facility in Australia. I thought about the back injury that had nearly ruined me the year before and how I had worked to come back from that. But I had to tell myself that what was done was done, and that I could only control what was in front of me. The rest was water under the bridge. I looked around my room at all the messages of support from my friends, fans and family. I had positive affirmations plastered everywhere in my room, and so I read and re-read over them.

> Jen Schaeffer: 'Lyd, you are the definition of inspirational. Your unwavering self-belief and effortless ability to support and encourage all those around you is truly special. Thank you and good luck. You are already a superstar, but I know you have more to show the world!'

Denita Preston: '*Lyd, you have paved the way for women in sport with your incredible athleticism and determination. You are an inspiration to us all! Keep flying high and conquering your goals. Eye of the tiger, Lyd. Eye of the tiger.*'

Lainie Cole: '*Know that we will all be with you on Valentine's Day sending our love, so after you watch Rocky on repeat, give that jump the death stare, go out there and enjoy every second because whatever happens nothing can take away the fact that you are a true inspiration, and what you have already achieved is beyond amazing.*'

Bree Munro: '*Do it for all the mums out there who have big dreams but don't realise they have the power to make them happen.*'

I sat there drawing on every single positive message I could. I sat there feeling grateful—for my friends, my family, for Late, for Kai, for Mich and my team. I wrote in my journal and did some yoga. I reassured myself I was capable. I knew I was going to need to dig deep and that I was going to need to find another level in myself to get through the gruelling competition ahead. There were five jumps to do, over five rounds of competition: two qualification rounds and three finals, of which the third was the deciding Super Final. I was grateful for the opportunity I had at the Bird's Nest Stadium a few weeks earlier in Beijing, which had given me the confidence I could make it through the gruelling format.

This Olympics wasn't necessarily going to be about who was the best, but I knew it was certainly going to be a battle of the toughest and the most resilient because these were the competitors who would be the ones to get through each round. According to the program, it was going to take six hours and for a sport like ours, it was like turning a sprint into a marathon. It was going to be about energy conservation, about maintaining focus and about being in each individual moment. You had to be strong. It was around 2.00am when I fell asleep. I had been trying to get my body clock on the late schedule seeing that ours was going to be a night competition.

I slept soundly that night and woke around midday feeling ready for whatever the day was going to throw at me. I went through my preparation as per normal: breakfast, yoga, packed my bag, visualisation, then warm-ups, followed by taping my knee. At some point Dave must have slipped a beautiful note under my door which I read before I was about to head to the venue. It was time. Time to give everything I had.

One of the best parts about the Sochi Olympics was that we could ski directly to our venue from the athletes' village located in the mountains, normally not the case at an Olympics. We would usually have to take shuttle buses, this time I *skied* to the venue and despite Sochi's lack of snow and warm weather, our jump site was in good shape. We had learned a lot from Vancouver about how to keep the jumps hard in warm weather by using dry ice, so the work crew and coaches were busy preparing the jumps, packing on the dry ice so the jumps could withstand the six hours of competition in warm weather.

****

My biggest fear leading into the competition was not making it through to the Super Final. If I didn't make it, then I wasn't going to get the chance to do the quad. I've always been most nervous for the qualifying rounds and this was no exception. First, I had to qualify in the top 12 to make the finals. We would get two jumps. If you were in the top six after the first round, then you wouldn't need to do another qualifying jump. If you were out of the top six, you needed to jump again. I crashed out on my first jump; my nerves had got the better of me so I had to go into another round. I thought to myself, 'Ah typical, Lyd! Making it difficult for yourself! If you'd just landed that jump you could go inside and put your feet up and get an extra 30 minutes of rest. Instead, you're still out here and you still have to qualify.' My teammate, Danielle Scott was through; Li Nina was also through, and Ashley Caldwell nailed a Full-Full-Full and was in the top spot. Tao Tao, who had struggled all week, was in the same predicament as me. The pressure was enormous. I really needed to find my feet and land the next one otherwise I'd be out.

It took a lot of focus to deflect negative thoughts and fear of *not* making it. I had to keep calm. I hit a good take-off, spotted the landing and nailed a Lay-Tuck-Full. Relief. I finished first in that round, which meant that I was the seventh best qualifier. Being in the middle of the field is a good position to sit, as there isn't the same pressure as there is on the person jumping first or jumping last.

After qualifying, there was a scheduled break, which was frustrating. It would have been much easier on us athletes to just keep the competition rolling, instead we had to go back into the athletes' tent for an hour. One hour is not enough time to have a real rest, but, in that time, your body cools down completely; so the break was nothing but an inconvenience, dragging out the already long night. It was bad for the spectators, too, as they had to stand around and wait for the event to start again. A lot of people ended up leaving before the finals actually started, which was horrible, but totally understandable.

After warming up again, we had a 45-minute period of training before the first of the finals jumps started. I did a speed check in case the conditions had changed during the break, but everything seemed the same so I started to jump. On my first training jump, my speed was way off—around two kilometres per hour too slow, which resulted in me landing on the flat part of the knoll, just before the landing hill. Upon impact I felt my right knee hyper-extend and I toppled over the handlebars, crashing down the landing hill. Immediately I felt a sharp pain in the knee. 'Oh no! That did not feel good,' I thought to myself. I then tried to put weight on the leg and I had this shooting pain right down my leg. I thought 'No, you've got to be kidding me? This is not happening.' I stood there stunned for a bit and Mich was screaming down to me, 'Are you all right?' I waved to signal I was okay, trying to stay composed while not giving too much away. I skied away on one leg down the landing hill and found a spot away from the media to take a breather.

We called Doc Braun over and then Ashley came rushing down as well, both trying to make an assessment of what I'd done. The pain was sharp and on the side of my knee. Meanwhile, the other finalists were getting their training jumps in. 'Typical', I thought, 'As if tonight wasn't going to be hard enough as it is!' After a while of rubbing and digging my fingers into my knee I started to get some movement again and I could put some weight on it. I told Ashley to meet me back on the knoll with painkillers and tape. I then skied up to the lift. As I rode up, I couldn't help but think things were going pear-shaped. 'What the hell just happened? I'm losing time? Can I even jump?' I slid down to where Mich and Ashley were waiting. We then had to lift my ski suit up so that she could tape my knee. It was a disaster and way too much drama for my liking.

I did a few practice rides up the jump to test how it felt and I got the same sharp pain when I straightened my knee up the jump. I felt helpless and desperate. Mich asked me, 'Can you jump?' and I said 'Yeah, I think so, we can only try.' I took some painkillers and went back up to the top of the in-run to prepare myself. I tried to regain my composure but I was so nervous because I had no idea whether my knee would hold as I rode up the jump; let alone survive the impact on landing.

I very tentatively attempted a jump and pulled through the landing to my back so as to limit the impact on my knee. I just wanted to know for starters that I could get off the jump. I'd have to figure out the landings after that. It was tolerable and my guess was that the painkillers had started to work. I found out quickly that I had to keep rubbing and moving it or else my knee would lock up on me. Everyone else had finished their warm-up and I had about 10 minutes to go before the competition started. I limped my way through the last few minutes of training, getting off another three more jumps. They weren't good jumps at all, but at least I was able to jump, in a way. The media was having a field day with the drama that had unfolded, questioning whether I could make it through to the next round. I later learned that my poor mum was now freaking out during the wee hours of the morning back home.

I was now in a sticky predicament and it was definitely a fight or flight moment. Part of me felt it was useless and it could all be over if I crashed out on the next jump. Everyone would understand and it would be a valid excuse. The other part of me wasn't ready to give in.

If I was going to have any chance of turning the night around I knew I had to find a different level within myself. I had to draw on every experience I had ever had. I had to dig deep and find reserves within that I didn't even know existed. I prayed. I tried to breathe in strength and energy. I remember looking up to the full moon, which was so beautiful that night, and I asked it for help. *'Please get me through tonight.'* All that time I was rubbing the knee: I did not let it stop and cool down. *'One jump at a time, Lyd.'* There was a lot of self-talk that night.

Even with all the drama of the night, my game plan hadn't changed. My next jump was a Lay-Full-Full. I hit my take-off and didn't take my eyes off the landing. I landed and felt relief spread through my body. At that point I didn't know who else was through. After each jump you had to ski past the media pit to get onto the lift. I skied through, not making eye contact with anyone. They knew now was not the time for questions and I went straight up the lift to prepare for my next jump, a Full-Full-Full. I had done one in training earlier, but it was rubbish because I missed my take-off. *'Hit your take-off, Lyd,'* was all I thought about.

As I left the jump I knew my take-off was good. Again I spotted the landing and got my body in the position to land. I was a little heavy on my right knee but I held on and skied away. I knew at that point that I was through. I had made it through! After nearly six hours of jumping, the knee drama, the missed jumps and shaky preparation, I was right where I wanted to be: in the Super Final. I now had the chance to do what I came here to do. To defend my Olympic gold and do something I had been dreaming of for 15 years. There was no question, we were going for the quad twisting triple somersault. The Full-Double Full-Full. Mich and I had already decided that we wouldn't back down if I made it to the Super Final and in that moment we still felt the same. My moment had arrived.

****

There were only four of us left, and I looked around at the final four and smiled. Li Nina, Tao Tao, Alla Tsuper and myself. *'This is going to be a great final.'* In that moment I felt grateful. I felt exhausted yet charged and ready. I knew I wasn't jumping perfectly but it didn't matter now. All of that was behind me. *'Just hit this take-off,'* was playing on repeat. There were a few jumps in training where I'd been too tentative, and I knew that I could not be tentative for this jump. I had to be strong. I watched on as Alla, then Li Nina took their jumps: Alla landed a Full-Full-Full and Li crashed out attempting a Double-Full Double-Full. It was my turn. My heart was beating out of my chest and I worked hard to keep my cool. Mich and the coaches placed me in the right position for speed. The judges signalled they were ready and I turned down the course. *'Strong take-off, Lyd.'*

I came in a bit faster than I had wanted. I must have gotten a small tail wind. I was aggressive on take-off and I knew straight away that I needed to stretch my body in the air to try and slow down my rotation. It was a great stretch—four twists and three flips with my arms stretched way above my head—a reaction many men aren't capable of. I saw the landing but I could feel it passing by. I tried my hardest to save it, but I couldn't and my back hit the snow. I felt stunned. It was so close, only inches off. In the moment it was hard to believe it was all over. I felt disappointment at first and my heart sank as I looked back up the landing at Mich and Cord. We had all come so far and Gold was within reach. My score came through and I sat in second place behind Alla. It was at that point that I realised what I had endured that night and I shook my head in disbelief. I hugged Alla and congratulated her. She had also had a shaky start to the competition, crashing in both qualification jumps and miraculously qualifying in twelfth position; right on the bubble. But that didn't matter now because in her fifth Olympics, she was now sitting in the gold medal position.

Tao Tao was the last competitor to jump—the identical position as in Vancouver. The pressure on her was enormous and the Chinese team only had eyes for Gold. Anything else would mean failure. She too crashed her jump, a Lay-Double Full-Full, skiing out a little cleaner than me, but certainly not enough to take the gold from Alla. The final scores came in – Tao Tao in silver, Alla in gold and I took the bronze medal; Li Nina was in fourth. All four of us hugged and cried. It had been a long and strenuous night and we were so exhausted. The emotions we had all contained for the last six hours came flooding out. I was so happy for Alla who sat in amazement—she too was a mum and in her fifth Olympics!

Diary entry, 14 February 2014: 'What an emotional day! Bronze is not Gold and I wish I landed that FDFF. I stretched for my life but couldn't hold on. It was a beautiful stretch and a beautiful effort. I am proud to have made it to the Super Final. I did not crumble under pressure. I am the greatest ever!'

It was bittersweet. Obviously I wanted to land the quad and if I landed it I would have won. But by that point I was glad that the event was over. I was completely drained of my mental capacity and my emotional capacity, because of what I'd had to fight through that night. I had nothing left which was a comforting feeling because I knew, without a doubt, that I had given it my all. It was so close. I was right there. Even half a kilometre per hour slower would have made all the difference. But I did everything in my power to save it. In fact, a lot of guys came up to me afterwards and said that they couldn't even stretch a jump like that, which was nice to hear.

Mich: 'The Full-Double Full-Full she will keep, always. To have that jump is special. She always said she wanted to jump like a man, and if you watch that jump and you see how she stretched that jump, then you have to say that she definitely got there.'

As we waited for the podium ceremony the adrenalin started to wear off and my knee cooled down. It stiffened up straight away and it was painful to walk on and I realised I had done some serious damage. I got back to the hotel that the AOC had booked outside the village where media was waiting for interviews. I still had all of my ski gear on—I was too exhausted to even care about removing it. Late and a 'celebration crew' were also there and it was the early hours of the morning before I finally took my ski suit off. I remember lying on the floor of the shower, I was so completely exhausted. I lay there crying for hours as I reflected not only on the night but the whole journey. I cried especially for Kai who watched the Olympics with Leena and Erkki in Finland. I cried for all the times I had left him behind.

I didn't sleep a wink that night. That final jump replayed in my mind over and over. I couldn't stop it. What if I had a little less speed? What if I didn't hurt that knee? What if the competition had been three hours in length instead of six? There were so many what-ifs. What if I had been able to stay and train longer in Ruka? Would I have been better prepared? In hindsight I would have made different decisions in regards to preparation but there was never a feeling of regret for doing the quad.

The next day I struggled to walk so I had an MRI on my knee in the Olympic Village. I had cracked the joint cartilage on the outer side of my knee, which explained why it hurt so much when I straightened it. It wouldn't need surgery, which was great, but it would take several months of rehab before it started feeling better again.

I still wonder how I made it through that night, and I marvel about how our bodies can do amazing things when we will them to. That's all it was that night: sheer will. When you're in the moment, and you can almost reach out and touch your dream, touch that thing you've spent your whole life chasing, you find a way to make it happen. You have to, because you might only get one chance. To do the quad was a win. It paved a new way for women and it meant more to me than another gold medal.

A lot of people have asked, 'Would you have done it differently? If you had your time over, would you have gone for a safer option to secure the win?' And the answer is no. It's simple. I know anything different would have nagged at me forever. Doing the Full-Double Full-Full was part of me reaching my potential, which is what I always wanted as an athlete. I wanted to milk every ounce of effort and to bring the best out of myself. Playing it safe is just not my style, and I would have regretted it. Even if another jump put another gold medal around my neck.

******

I'm not sure exactly what keeps me going and persisting beyond levels that are comfortable. I've endured so many setbacks and have been through the real highs and lows of sport and everything in between. But what I do know is that somehow I've always had a clear vision for myself. I've always had the ambition of being the best female aerial skier who ever lived; not the most consistent, but the *best*. The one who could shatter glass ceilings and make a difference in the sport. One who could close the gap between males and females—proving we are just as capable. That's what I have always been chasing, and that's what I felt was my purpose, and why I was doing this sport. I believed in my vision and that's what got me through the times where I didn't think I could go on. When the risks outweighed the rewards. That same vision propelled me when my confidence was high, and reinforced that mission, *"Yes, I can do this. I can be the person I want to be. I will never give up.'*

AFTERWORD

WHAT NEXT?

The time after an Olympic campaign is always bittersweet. Bitter, because the thrill of the day-to-day life of an athlete comes to a standstill; and sweet, because the stress is over, and you get to sleep soundly and go home to family and a normal life.

Post Sochi was a bit of a blur. I was exhausted and although I was lucky to avoid surgery, my knee was sore for a good three months before it started feeling better.

Lauri and I shifted our focus to extending our family and Kai was presented with a baby brother, Alek, in February 2015. We also shifted our focus to running our two businesses, which had been neglected while our joint focus was on my Olympic campaign. I was able to throw myself into growing *BodyICE*, which saw the introduction of new product ranges and expansions into Europe.

With the support of the OWIA, in particular Geoff Henke, we continued to lobby for an Australian-based water ramp facility—still to come to fruition. That outcome will help me answer the most common question I'm asked: whether I will continue on for another Olympics. I certainly have the heart for another campaign and, boy, would I like to ski that quad away, but I know that without a water ramp in Australia, my chances are slim.

Travelling for 10 months a year with two children is just not feasible this time around and the challenges involved would prove counter-productive. So at this stage, my continuation in my sport is in the hands of politicians: which is never a good predicament to find oneself! I'd like to be able to retire on my own terms, when I'm ready, not because I don't have the opportunity to train on home soil.

Selfishly I'd like to see the facility built so that I can have the opportunity to go to a fifth Olympics, but I know time is running out. Whatever the case, I'd like to see it through so that we can keep producing champions of winter sport in Australia. With the proper facilities at home we can develop our own home-grown talent, and our own coaches, and retain our athletes for longer.

Retirement from sport will always be a difficult transition and not something I feel ready for at the moment. Even though my life is full and I have so much to look forward to, I don't think I'll ever be ready to call it quits. The advice I've received from retired athletes is 'if you still have the desire, don't deny it' and 'once you're retired, you're a long time retired'. I miss jumping and I certainly miss the snow and my snow family. Do I have enough fuel in the tank for one more round? I believe so, but only time will tell whether I still have the *will to fly*.

MY SIX STEPS TO GOAL-SETTING

As an elite athlete and mother of two young boys, I certainly know a thing or two about goal-setting. It's something I've done my whole life and something I've become quite good at.

Firstly, goal-setting isn't about wishing something to come true. And, it's not about a resolution on the first day of every year (which rarely ever lasts into February!). Goal-setting is making a commitment. It takes work. It takes thought. It takes discipline. It takes guts to follow through and have a go. It takes patience and it takes constant adjustment and revision. But, if you maintain focus on each and every goal, I'm living proof that the rewards can be life-changing.

The way I go about goal-setting is comprehensive. It's very detailed and, in essence, it's a map that describes where you are now and where you want to go. It can be applied to any aspect of your life: your business, your sport, your family, your relationships.

I love this process because it breaks down large goals—those goals that, at times, can be overwhelming—into small bite-size pieces. That way, each and every day you can progress by focusing on your daily priorities. Your goals won't seem so overwhelming any more because you now have a detailed plan as to how you're going to achieve them in the time that you set for yourself.

This is my plan to set goals, and achieve what you set out to do:

1. SET YOUR VISION

This is where you need to ask yourself the most important question of all. What do you want? Above any medal, financial gain or result, *who* are you trying to become and *what* are you trying to achieve?

(Eg: To be the best female aerial skier who has ever lived)

2. SET YOUR MILESTONE GOALS

In order to become your vision, what are the milestones you will want to achieve?

(Eg. To win at the Olympics)

TIP: *It's not realistic to try to achieve **all** of your milestone goals at once: you may have several. These are big goals; some may be once in a lifetime achievements. Just pick one (and certainly no more than two) to focus on at any time.*

3. SET YOUR CHALLENGE GOALS

In order to achieve each of your milestone goals, what are some of the challenges you will face?

(Eg. Staying healthy and injury free)

TIP: *You may have several challenge goals—I know I did. Don't see them as a negative though, just as a challenge along the way.*

4. SET YOUR FOCUS GOALS

Now break each challenge goal down further into focus goals. In order to meet these challenges, what do you need to focus on?

(Eg. Make sure I recover between sessions by doing rehab, gym, yoga and physio daily)

5. SET YOUR GOAL ACHIEVEMENT STRATEGIES (GAS)

What are your daily reminders that will keep you focused on your goals? Did you achieve them? YES or NO?

(Eg. Be smart. Listen to my body and don't take unnecessary risks)

6. SET YOUR TIMELINE

Now place a time reference to these goals so that you know by when you need to achieve them. It's no use having goals if you don't set yourself deadlines.

TIP: *Once you have your timeline in place, a powerful exercise is to visualise yourself achieving each milestone goal. You can even 'walk the timeline' and 'stop' at each point along the way to really experience those moments and to imagine how you would like each to happen.*

Good Luck!

Lyd.

THANKS

There are so many I must thank for this wonderful journey, but most of all my husband Lauri who has stuck by my side through every moment of my story; and my sons Kai and Alek—my greatest achievements. My family and friends have been there throughout, providing unconditional love and support, but in particular my parents, and Lauri's who have done everything in their power to help me and to support my dreams.

My current and past sponsors have been so supportive and without their help I am sure I would have fallen short of achieving my goals.

Thank you to the publishing team at The Slattery Media Group—Geoff Slattery, Courtney Nicholls and Chris Downey, and my co-writers, Dan Eddy and Andrew Clarke for drawing this story out of me and to the many people who assisted with the writing, design and production of this book. Thank you to Katie Bender and Leo Baker for turning my story into a feature documentary.

Thank you to all my teammates and coaches of past and present—you have been my family away from home, and I have a lifetime of memories and great times thanks to you. Thank you to the Olympic Winter Institute of Australia, the Australian Olympic Committee, the Victorian Institute of Sport and the Australian Sports Commission for supporting my journey, my training and my competition.

THANKS

And finally, my day to day support, my A-team—Michel Roth, Cord Spero, Ashley Merkur, Barbara Meyer and Jeffrey Hodges. Thank you for having such faith in me, for pushing me, for pulling me back, for keeping me together, for being a shoulder to cry on, for celebrating my victories, for encouraging me in defeat. It's been a pleasure working with you.

A story like mine can only be told because I have had these amazing people around me and who supported me and believed in me.

I will forever be grateful.

Lydia Lassila

LYDIA LASSILA,
January 2016